Ethics, Money and Sport

There has always been money in sport, but in recent decades commodification has transformed elite sport. Access to sport has a high price tag as broadcast rights are sold to the highest bidder, and marketing turns athletes and their clubs into brands. Sports administrators are business managers, under pressure above all to meet financial targets.

Commodification in itself is neither virtuous nor vicious but many are concerned about the changes that are taking place in the world of sport. The central thesis of this book is that such concerns have considerable substance.

Combining sociological evidence with the analytical tools of philosophy, *Ethics, Money and Sport* articulates and explores the main concerns about the way money has changed our experience of sports.

Clearly written and illustrated by examples from major sports around the world, *Ethics, Money and Sport* enables students, researchers and policymakers – as well as anyone with an interest in the future of sport – to engage with this crucial debate.

Adrian Walsh is a Senior Lecturer in Philosophy at the University of New England in Australia.

Richard Giulianotti is a Senior Lecturer in Sociology at the University of Aberdeen.

Ethics and Sport
Series editors
Mike McNamee
University of Wales Swansea
Jim Parry
University of Leeds

The Ethics and Sport series aims to encourage critical reflection on the practice of sport, and to stimulate professional evaluation and development. Each volume explores new work relating to philosophical ethics and the social and cultural study of ethical issues. Each is different in scope, appeal, focus and treatment but a balance is sought between local and international focus, perennial and contemporary issues, level of audience, teaching and research application, and variety of practical concerns.

Also available in this series:

Ethics and Sport
Edited by Mike McNamee and Jim Parry

Values in Sport
Elitism, nationalism, gender equality and the scientific manufacture of winners
Edited by Torbjörn Tännsjö and Claudio Tamburrini

Spoilsports
Understanding and preventing sexual exploitation in sport
Celia Brackenridge

Fair Play in Sport
A moral norm system
Sigmund Loland

Sport, Rules and Values
Philosophical investigations into the nature of sport
Graham McFee

Sport, Professionalism and Pain
Ethnographies of injury and risk
David Howe

Genetically Modified Athletes
Biomedical ethics, gene doping and sport
Andy Miah

Human Rights in Youth Sport
A critical review of children's rights in competitive sports
Paulo David

Genetic Technology and Sport
Ethical questions
Edited by Claudio Tamburrini and Torbjörn Tännsjö

Pain and Injury in Sport
Social and ethical analysis
Edited by Sigmund Loland, Berit Skirstad and Ivan Waddington

Ethics, Money and Sport
This sporting Mammon
Adrian Walsh and Richard Giulianotti

Ethics, Money and Sport
This sporting Mammon

Adrian Walsh and Richard Giulianotti

 Routledge
Taylor & Francis Group

LONDON AND NEW YORK

First published 2007
by Routledge
2 Park Square, Milton Park, Abingdon, Oxon OX14 4RN

Simultaneously published in the USA and Canada
by Routledge
270 Madison Ave, New York, NY 10016

Routledge is an imprint of the Taylor & Francis Group, an informa business

© 2007 Adrian Walsh and Richard Giulianotti

Typeset in Goudy by
Book Now Ltd
Printed and bound in Great Britain by
TJ International Ltd, Padstow, Cornwall

British Library Cataloguing in Publication Data
A catalogue record for this book is available from the British Library

Library of Congress Cataloging in Publication Data
A catalog record has been requested for this book

ISBN10: 0–415–33338–5 (hbk)
ISBN10: 0–415–33339–3 (pbk)
ISBN10: 0–203–41300–8 (ebk)

ISBN13: 978–0–415–33338–2 (hbk)
ISBN13: 978–0–415–33339–9 (pbk)
ISBN13: 978–0–203–41300–5 (ebk)

'Verily, Mammon-worship is a melancholy creed'

Thomas Carlyle, *Past and Present*, III, ii

Contents

Series editors' preface   ix
Preface and acknowledgements   xi
List of abbreviations   xiii

1   This sporting Mammon?   1

2   Moral philosophy, sport and commodification critique   12

3   Financial motives, venality and the ideals of sport   32

4   Commodification and objectification: treating athletes and
    sport itself as *mere* means   65

5   Sport, commodification and distributive justice   82

6   Scoring an own goal: when markets undermine what they sell   107

7   Moral philosophy out on the track: what might be done?   120

Notes   132
Bibliography   145
Index   152

Series editors' preface

The *Ethics and Sport* series aims to support and contribute to the development of the study of ethical issues in sport, and indeed to the establishing of Sports Ethics as a legitimate discipline in its own right. It does this by identifying issues of practical concern and exploring them systematically in extended discussion.

Given the logical basis of ethics at the heart of sport as a practical activity, every important and topical issue in sport necessarily has an ethical dimension – and often the ethical dimension is of overwhelming significance. The series addresses a variety of both perennial and contemporary issues in this rapidly expanding field, aiming to engage the community of teachers, researchers and professionals, as well as the general reader.

Philosophical ethics may be seen both as a theoretical academic discipline and as an ordinary everyday activity contributing to conversation, journalism, and practical decision-making. The series aims to bridge that gap. Academic disciplines will be brought to bear on the practical issues of the day, illuminating them and exploring strategies for problem-solving. A philosophical interest in ethical issues may also be complemented and broadened by research within related disciplines, such as sociology and psychology.

The series aims to encourage critical reflection on the practice of sport, and to stimulate professional evaluation and development. Each volume explores new work relating to philosophical ethics and the social and cultural study of ethical issues. Each is different in scope, appeal, focus and treatment, but a balance is sought within the series between local and international focus, perennial and contemporary issues, level of audience, teaching and research application, and variety of practical concern. Each volume is complete in itself, but also complements others in the series.

In sport, as elsewhere, philosophers often hear the complaint from social scientists that their theories are not empirically grounded, while they (with equal frequency and intensity) make the counter complaint that social scientists' work is not always conceptually coherent. This new contribution to the Series is, then, a most welcome collaboration between social science and philosophy. Adrian Walsh and Richard Giulianotti offer here a sophisticated account of the malaise of *hypercommodified* sport. Their systematic approach is not based on some nostalgic yearning for a time when sport was somehow pure. They reject this picture as mythical. Yet they do present a forceful critique of what they characterise as the *hypercommodification* of sport. Their aim is to identify the moral pathologies of what they perceive as a contemporary malaise.

Their theoretical critique is influenced by sources as diverse as Aristotle's and Immanuel Kant's moral philosophies, as well as the political philosophy of Michael Walzer and Elizabeth Anderson's work in the philosophy of economics. These sources are supplemented by a deep knowledge of sports themselves, suitably framed in cultural and historical contexts.

In sports talk, much is made of ethereal notions such as the 'integrity of sport' or the 'spirit of sport' which it is alleged that (hyper)commodification corrupts. In this volume, theoretically informed answers give weight to this thesis with ample exemplification from a range of sports across the globe. We hope that the volume invites critical dialogue from scholars in the social sciences of sport as much as from the philosophies of economics, politics and sports.

Mike McNamee, *University of Wales Swansea*
Jim Parry, *University of Leeds*

Preface and acknowledgements

This project came about when, as a visiting sociologist to Australia, Richard Giulianotti found himself housed in a corridor of philosophers, including Adrian Walsh. It was a fortunate happenstance since we soon found that we had a mutual love of sports of many varieties. Amongst other things, both of us were concerned with the commodification of elite sport. Our early conversations centred on the question of how exactly one might explicate the harm involved in such commodification and led to the publication of the article 'This Sporting Mammon: A Normative Critique of the Commodification of Sport' (*Journal of the Philosophy of Sport*, vol. XXVII, no. 1, 2001, pp. 53–77). This book is a development of the ideas initially formulated in that essay. The article and book are united by a common question: What exactly might be wrong with transforming sport into a commodity? We hope to provide an answer to that ethical question in this book.

As the reader will soon realise, although our central question is ethical we do not rely solely on philosophical resources to solve it. In addition to the writings of moral philosophers we also make extensive use of sociological and historical materials. This is not only to 'set the scene' – to provide a clear picture of the nature of the social phenomenon with which we are concerned – but we believe it is necessary in thinking through our ethical principles and ideals regarding sport. As will become especially clear in our discussion of Amateurism, all too often our thinking on the ethical status of certain sporting practices is influenced by false historical and sociological pictures of the nature of these practices. If we are to deal with the ethical status of sport in an adequate manner, then we need to begin with an accurate picture of the origins of modern sport and to understand the ways in which our ethical ideals might be influenced by false histories. We hope that our use of material from a number of disciplines provides a better basis for answering the question of what might be wrong with the incursion of the market into elite sport.

In the writing of this book we have incurred a number of debts and we would like to thank all of those who discussed these ideas with us over the past few years at our respective universities. We are grateful to The University of Aberdeen, the University of New England and the Centre for Applied Philosophy and Public Ethics at the University of Melbourne for providing us with congenial research environments. We would like to thank the editors of this series, Jim Parry and

Mike MacNamee, for their advice and for having faith in the project to begin with and the editors at Routledge, Samantha Grant and Kate Manson for their help in assisting with the passage of this book. Rutger Claassen who read and made extensive comments on the manuscript provided invaluable assistance. We are also very grateful to the *Journal of the Philosophy of Sport* for allowing us to use material from the article published in 2001 in this book. Finally, we would like to thank our partners and families for their patience and forbearance whilst we have been immersed in this project.

Adrian Walsh and Richard Giulianotti
February, 2006

Abbreviations

AFL	Australian Football League
ARL	Australian Rugby League
ECB	England and Wales Cricket Board
FA	Football Association (UK)
FIFA	Fédération Internationale de Football Association
IOC	International Olympic Committee
MLB	Major League Baseball (USA)
NBA	National Basketball Association (USA)
NCAA	National Collegiate Athletic Association
NFL	National Football League (USA)
NI IL	National Hockey League
NRL	National Rugby League (Australia)

1 This sporting Mammon?

Sport as commodity

Elite sport is now, more clearly than ever before, a commodity – a commercial enterprise governed by the laws of supply and demand. Its aims, ethos, institutional organisation and very ludic structures are increasingly determined by market forces. One need only consider various commercial phenomena to see the radical transformation that has occurred over the past thirty years all over the world. We might begin by walking into any major sporting arena and counting the number of sponsor signs. But that is minimal compared to the advertising that occurs on our television screens. Televised coverage of American football's Superbowl features approximately 60 advertisements during each 15-minute quarter; advertisers paid on average $2.3 million for each 30-second advertisement at the 2004 fixture.[1]

The revenues generated by the major sports are staggering. The annual turnover of world soccer was reckoned at some £250 billion, a figure equivalent to the gross national income of the Netherlands.[2] In American football, the 32 teams that made up the NFL in 2003 were estimated to be worth a total of over US$20 billion. In baseball and basketball, the MLB and the NBA each had total annual revenues of US$3–3.5 billion in the early 2000s. At college level, American football generates around US$5 billion annually.

Consider too the increasing professionalisation of athletes, many of whom are industries unto themselves. The commercial 'bankability' of elite sportspeople is such that many generate seemingly unfathomable sums from their sporting identities. In its annual assessment of athlete wealth, *Fortune* magazine found that for 2004, the top five sport stars in terms of earnings were Tiger Woods ($80.3 million), Michael Schumacher ($80 million), Peyton Manning ($42 million), Michael Jordan ($35 million) and Shaquille O'Neal ($31.9 million). In the United States, by mid-1998, Michael Jordan was reported to have had a $10 billion impact on the national economy in terms of generating revenues from his stature as a leading basketball player and endorser of products (notably Nike merchandise).[3] In English soccer, it was recently estimated that David Beckham was worth £65 million, heading a list of major players such as Dennis Bergkamp (£37 million) and Michael Owen (£30 million), although the report noted he was only 41st overall in the list of soccer's money men.[4] Such money-making is facilitated by the rise of markets in players that also permits sports people to move regularly and routinely between clubs whenever it is deemed suitable to their financial interest. The old sporting language of club loyalty, camaraderie and 'playing for the jersey' appears antediluvian amidst the free flow of player movements between teams, notwithstanding these athletes' penchant for 'kissing the badge' when celebrating after victorious performances.

The commodification of sport appears to bring with it a radical overthrow of prior social, economic, political and cultural arrangements, in the service of maximizing profit. Here one is reminded of Marx's prophetic comment that under capitalism 'all that is solid melts into air, all that is holy is profaned'.[5] We have seen radical changes in the very structure of sports. United States sporting competitions are peppered with artificial advertisement breaks that change the rhythm of games. The injection of vast new volumes of capital by media corporations has led to the wholesale reinvention of particular sports as 'entertainment'. Consider, for example, the 'World Series Cricket' circus that was bankrolled by Australian mogul Kerry Packer in the late 1970s, or the Packer–Murdoch media combination that effectively bought control over rugby league in Australia and England.

We have also seen radical changes associated with the very names of sporting competitions and sporting venues. The hundred-year-old Sheffield Shield cricket competition in Australia becomes the Pura Milk Cup. Sporting theatres forsake their identities to acquire the names of commercial sponsors. In Melbourne, Prince's Park is now the Optus Oval and sits alongside the Telstra Dome, the Vodaphone Arena and the Teac Oval. Here we have a revolutionary attitude towards nomenclature almost as radical as the Bolshevik renaming of the ancient city of St Petersburg, or the Khmer Rouge's re-titling of city streets in Cambodia.

Perhaps the most shocking of these naming rights involves individual persons. The occasional practice of parents in naming children after teams or athletes – sometimes with curious results – has long been a humorous part of sport's fanatical culture.[6] However, a categorically different form of naming arose in the case of Gary Hocking, an Australian Rules football player. With the aim of raising funds for his heavily indebted Geelong side, Hocking changed his name temporarily by deed-pole to that of a cat-food brand as part of a sponsorship deal. The name 'Whiskas' looked exceedingly odd on the team sheet. Similarly, the snooker player Jimmy White engaged in a similar name-changing exercise for commercial ends. White agreed to a request from HP Sauce to change his name by deed-poll to Jimmy Brown, after the company announced that it would sponsor the brown ball at one snooker tournament in February 2005.

Concomitant with all of these changes has been a shift in the self-understanding of players and administrators. When Michael Jordan said after the first loss by his new team, the Washington Wizards, that he was going to 'teach this franchise how to win', his language betrayed the established US thinking that sport is primarily commercial in nature. It is a form of language that Margaret Jane Radin labels 'market rhetoric', in which all human interactions are understood fundamentally as forms of commerce.[7]

We have thus far only considered the legal influence of money. To make matters worse there is also a great deal of dirty dealing. The enormous sums of money involved in sport provide players in particular with tremendous temptations for individual corruption. Take, for example, the enormous sums bet on cricket in India and the opportunities for vice that follow. While cricket is seen as a game solely of the old Commonwealth, and thus of less global relevance, its popularity in the Indian sub-continent, particularly at one-day level, means that it generates considerable betting revenues. The *Times of India* estimates that punters in India bet nearly one thousand crore rupees (approx. US$227 million) on each one-day game.[8] Little wonder then that more money-oriented individuals are tempted. The most stunning case of such corruption in recent years involved the late Hansie Cronje, the captain of South Africa's cricket team from 1994 to 2000. As a practicing Christian and intensely proud South African, Cronje had been lauded by his compatriots as the personification of moral fortitude and national loyalty. Yet, after investigations into corruption, he was found to have accepted at least £82,000 to rig matches and, following his death in June 2002, further allegations emerged that he had held over 70 illegal bank accounts to stash his illicit gains.

Moreover, sport is replete with opportunities for institutional corruption. The growing commercialism of sport has generated new kinds of entrepreneurs – notably athlete agents and political lobbyists – who will strike deals for their paymasters, often in highly unscrupulous or illegal circumstances. The Olympic movement has been struck by strong evidence of vote buying in the battles between cities to win support from IOC members, and thereby secure the rights to host tournaments. The Toronto bid for the 1996 Olympic games involved the alleged expenditure of at least CA$800,000 to buy votes.[9] Two officials representing Salt Lake City paid more than $1 million to 24 IOC members in a successful bid to win the rights to host the 2002 Winter Olympics. Moreover, the IOC and the civic authorities that bid to host the games have effectively bought off many journalists by providing endless personal perks and benefits in return for uncritical media reports.[10]

If we concentrate on the legal aspects of sport's structural transformation, then the sheer volume of these changes is sufficient to generate considerable disquiet among fans, athletes and commentators. In the early 1990s, the reinvigoration of English professional soccer was driven by an initial £304 million in television money, to produce the 'Barclays Premiership', soon dubbed the 'Greed is Good League' by the leading soccer journalist Brian Glanville. Television money too was behind the reorganisation of Rugby League and 'Australian Rules' football in Australia as old clubs were forced to close or merge to make way for the founding of new franchises in large 'target markets' where these sports were barely known. In North America, sports club owners constantly employ political blackmail by threatening to move from their 'home' city to a new location.[11] The local authorities must build new stadiums and provide lucrative tax concessions to prevent exits. In its pursuit of the largest markets, the IOC has also placed profits and political influence ahead of the integrity and excellence of sporting competition.

Certainly, the incursion of business-thinking within sports is reflected in myriad 'sport management' degree programmes at universities, and in the proliferation of supporting texts that allude to the triumph of money over play, with titles such as *Football INC*, *The Name of the Game: The Business of Sport*, or *The Sport Business*. Yet, on the other hand, consider too the rage of investigative journalists and other sports analysts in regard to the corruption of sport. For example, Andrew Jennings writes in *The New Lords of the Rings* in a chapter headed 'Roll Up, Roll Up, Ideals for Sale':

> Tune in, slump back and welcome to the Olympic Global Bazaar! Candy bars blessed by Coubertin! Junk food with a moral message! Roll up, roll up, whatever you need, the Olympic bazaar has got it! And you can buy it all! Wander through the virtual reality aisles, pick up some five-ringed plastic at the money-lenders and fill those wire baskets. . . . Try and get away – you can't. Tune into American TV? They're screening Olympic *Wheel of Fortune* and Olympic *Jeopardy*. Want to blot it all out? You can do with a five-ringed product. Slip on the sanctified sunglasses, sip a preferred beer, swallow the approved painkiller.[12]

We also get a sense of this when people talk about the 'subversion' of sport, such as through the entry of corporate backing to the extent that athletes become advertisement sandwich boards or competitive fixtures are staged according to the dictates of television broadcasters.

What is going on here? On its own, the commentary provided above does not amount to moral critique. It is not enough, for our purposes at least, merely to satirise modern sports. Rather, we need to tell a story about what exactly is the ethical case against such commodification.

Cursory examination of these criticisms shows considerable revulsion at the very idea of Sports-as-Business. In one sense such criticisms might be thought naïve for sport clearly is a business – at least under one level of description. Elite sport generates too much wealth for anyone to refute realistically the idea of it as a business. Moreover, in the minds of many pivotal figures – players, administrators and promoters – sport is nothing but a business. Yet there is another significant and truthful level of description of sport as it presents itself to the enthusiast and spectator. This involves viewing sport as an arena distinct from the everyday mundane world in which athletes pursue non-commercial goals, whether they be the good of their side (such as club or national team), individual excellence and so on. This is what we might call the 'Manifest Image' of sport – that is how sport presents itself to the fan. This is a crucial aspect of sport which fans find compelling.[13] For the dedicated fan, sport raises the kinds of passion that as Tim Park notes 'once attached themselves more readily to religious fundamentalism and political idealism'.[14]

What is especially clear is that the idea of Sports-as-Business is at odds with this Manifest Image.[15] Indeed, it is this conflict which motivates the juxtaposition of Sport and Business that we see in such book titles as *Sport Inc*. Such titles are intended to be provocative, but they can only be so if one has a vision of sport as something other than business. If, and only if, one thinks of the Olympics as being primarily about, for instance, the pursuit of individual excellence along relevant dimensions of athletic achievement, or of Premiership soccer being genuine battles between sporting rivals who represent distinct constituencies, could one find such juxtapositions striking, let alone disturbing.

Further, in many ways, part of the allure of sport, at least for its fans, is that it is a refuge from the world of economic imperatives and business that must be dealt with outside the sporting arena.[16] At the same time, this is not to deny that sport is also a sphere in which social conflicts and identities might be symbolically played out or ritualised by the various participants.

In partial support of the Manifest Image, it must also be said that as a business sport is decidedly odd. Historically, compared to other domains of potential 'investment', modern sport has tended to offer more attractions in terms of status-promotion rather than large and quick financial gain for those owning and controlling institutions.[17] As Mike Marqusee notes of soccer and cricket:

> Conventional economic models rarely apply to commercial sport. Even soccer club owners are frequently guided by considerations (vanity, politics, loyalty) other than the maximisation of profit which is the ruling principle in their other activities. If this is true in soccer, how much more so in cricket, with its pre-industrial baggage? Despite cricket's recent embrace of the market, what might be called its political economy continues to function in a kind of parallel universe, not quite conforming to the norms that govern other commercial ventures.[18]

Sports are also exempted from some crucial legislation regarding the regulation of business affairs. For example, 'antitrust' or 'competition' legislation in North America and Europe functions to ensure that monopolies or oligopolies are not established in any commercial sphere to the market detriment of competing businesses or consumers. However, the 'special case' status of sport allows team owners exemption from this legislation, by enabling them to establish league systems that involve 'restraints on trade' (such as preventing new clubs from being established and competing) which would be prohibited in other realms of 'business'. In effect, the AFL, the English Premiership, MLB, NCAA and NHL are examples of sporting monopolies since each of these league systems does not have to compete against similar groups of clubs in the same nation in the same sport.

At club level in the United States local teams often have monopoly supply positions since they are the only club in the neighbourhood that competes in a specific league.[19] Yet we might consider the paradox of competitive monopoly peculiar to sport, in that it is counter-productive to defeat and eliminate all of one's rivals. Whereas Microsoft or News Corp would benefit immensely from the demise of IT or media competitors, Manchester United and Chelsea would enjoy truly Pyrrhic victories if their domination of soccer were to force all other clubs into bankruptcy.

Evidently, the relationship of sport to commodification is a complex and, in our view, highly unusual one. In this book, we attempt to answer specific ethical questions on this issue. What exactly is wrong with the commodification of sport? How could money make a moral difference to sport? If we think about both structural changes to sport and individual corruption in sport, why might they be morally significant?

Equally, we need to acknowledge that the commodification of sport has brought many benefits to spectators and players. One need only think of the countless athletes who have died in penury after a lifetime of service to a club or to a sport to see the contrast. Some of the most tragic cases involved world champion boxers from the past who were reduced to destitution by varying combinations of criminal exploitation and disastrous financial guidance. Joe Louis retired penniless and was reduced to taking a 'meet and greet' job at Las Vegas casinos. Sonny Liston died at the age of 38 from a highly suspicious drug overdose, following a career that was manipulated by organised crime. Elite players in the pre-eminent sports now receive considerable recompense – indeed some might say over-compensation – for their efforts and, profligacy notwithstanding, they should have little danger of spending their later years in penury. Despite the continuing involvement of parasitical promoters such as Don King, the sheer volume of money earned by contemporary fighters like Lennox Lewis, Evander Holyfield and Mike Tyson means that a far more secure retirement is now attainable by fight champions.

Alternatively, the commodification of sport has made some contribution to the improvement in stadia conditions. We might contrast the Dickensian ground conditions endured by some sports fans through most of the twentieth century with the comfortable facilities enjoyed by spectators in new stadiums built over the past two decades. Yet we should recall that all too often such improvements must be forced by state legislation or directed by the public purse, rather than by naked market forces. In the United States, stadium-building is largely paid for by the civic authorities. Across France and Italy, superb sporting theatres were erected, largely through public investment, to host soccer's World Cup finals. In the United Kingdom, it required the 1989 Hillsborough disaster (at which 96 soccer fans perished) and government legislation to force many sports clubs to bring their stadium conditions out of the Victorian era.[20] Thus, part of our challenge is to identify the undesirable, irrelevant or beneficial aspects of commodification in regard to the modern aspects of sport.

Commodification critique and the spectre of market abolitionism

One spectre that haunts all commodification critiques is that of 'market abolitionism'. Criticism of markets and commodification, be it in sport or elsewhere, has traditionally been made, in the main, by those who would abolish markets in their entirety. Thus, Marxists, for instance, have criticised the commodification of sport as part of a more general and thoroughgoing critique of market society. The aim of the Marxist is to institute entirely different social relations to those currently in place. In many ways, its critical economic focus ensures that Marxism provides a useful theoretical framework for understanding the forces that shape modern sport and for understanding in part what might be undesirable about at least some of those changes. Market abolitionism may appear to follow naturally from a repudiation of the commodification of sport. If one objects, for instance, to the market rhetoric involved in regarding a team as a franchise or in transforming sport's rules to accommodate the needs of capital, then such criticisms would seem to lead one naturally towards an attack upon the market *per se*.

However, the commodification critique need not be interpreted in abolitionist terms. As a matter of logic, one may be opposed to many features of modern commercial sport but this does not necessarily lead one to advocate the overthrow of all market relations. One might, for instance, simply be in favour of state regulation to halt the excesses of the market in sport. On this line of reasoning, commercial relations are morally admissible so long as they are adequately constrained by state legislation. Alternatively, one might think that there are some aspects or spheres of sport that should not be subject to market influence. Thus, while the commercialisation of sport is in general morally permissible, there might be some areas of activity, perhaps the naming of grounds, that would receive sanctuary from market interference.

Further, there are in fact good reasons for wanting to dissociate our commodification critique from the radical views of market abolitionists. First, markets can be the occasion of significant social benefit and this is as true in sport as it is elsewhere in society. The commodification of sport has – along with many of the problems to which we alluded at the outset – brought considerable benefits for players and fans alike. With the money and freedom from material necessity that professional sport brings, elite players have opportunities to develop their skills to far higher levels than would be possible if they were restricted to part-time play due to other working commitments. Players enjoy better training facilities, opportunities for travel, and a host of other benefits that derive, at least in part, from the commercialisation of sport. Fans gain the benefit of seeing higher standards of play than would otherwise be possible. Moreover, when a sports 'market' goes into decline, the sporting authorities must rethink their game to attract fans back into stadia, otherwise clubs will fall into bankruptcy. The results can be beneficial for the aesthetic development of sport. For example, one-day cricket was invented to increase crowds and revenues, in order to help the English county sides to survive financially. In the long-run, it could be argued, the skills developed by players in the one-day game have been transferred into other forms of cricket, making these more competitive and aesthetically pleasing.[21] Commodification also suits particular groups of fans who are able and willing to pay to enjoy further benefits from sport's commercialisation. The plethora of sport on subscription television means that the paying 'armchair fan' is far better catered for than was previously the case. At least some of these aspects of the commodification of sport must be counted as benefits. To wish to follow the market abolitionist would be, we contend, to throw the baby out with the bathwater.

A second point, and this is simply just a matter of *realpolitik*, is that market abolitionism is not currently a viable political alternative and perhaps will never be so. If our commodification critique were to seek to eliminate markets entirely, then it would be pursuing an aspiration that is frankly unrealisable within the foreseeable future.

Part of our challenge then will be to show how we might provide the grounds of commodification critique without recourse to market abolitionism. From another direction it might be argued that if we concede the necessity of markets, then why should we believe that sport ought to be more cosseted from commercial effects than other social forms. Why should we think that sport ought somehow to be different from the society in which it is embedded? The sports historian Martin Polley, writing in opposition to commercial sponsorship, notes that more simplistic criticisms of commercialism have been generally ineffective and arguably misguided since he sees no reason why sport should somehow operate in ways distinct from the rest of society. 'To deny links between sport and the society in which it exists is ahistorical, and sport would not exist in its present form were it not for commercial involvement.'[22] Again, this is a challenge that we must meet.

Commodification critique and the socio-historical challenge

A second spectre that haunts commodification critique is the suspicion that it is based upon, or grounded in, an unrealistic and ultimately naïve conception of the intrinsic nature and actual practice of sport prior to its incorporation into the modern market. The idea is that commodification critique objects to modern sport on the basis of an entirely specious socio-historical picture of the pre-commodity world of sport – if such a pre-commodity realm ever existed. This we might label the 'socio-historical challenge'. It is important for an ethical project that focuses on a particular form of social change to meet this challenge.

There are many different ethical grounds upon which one might object to commodification, but one of the most common in regard to the 'socio-historical challenge' is amateurism. Proponents of amateurism differ from Marxists and other supporters of market abolitionism in that their aim is the maintenance of sport as an entirely non-commercial sphere within an otherwise undisturbed, capitalist society. Instead of advocating a societal revolution, amateurists argue that sport is a special sphere of society; sport should be undertaken entirely for its own sake, rather than for extrinsic rewards, be they monetary or otherwise. Amateurists are critical of commodification because they believe it represents a corruption of the ideals and goals that should properly animate athletes. Athletes should be motivated by goals specific to sport, such as the pursuit of excellence, rather than financial ends. The ideal here would be based on *Tom Brown's Schooldays*, following the British 'Games Ethic' which inspired amateur sports such as rugby union, cricket (when played by 'gentlemen'), and track and field athletics. A more recent illustration of pure amateurism might be a figure such as Roger Bannister, an Oxford medical student, who ran the first official sub-four-minute mile in 1954.[23] What distinguishes these exemplars of amateurism is the commercially disinterested pursuit of sporting virtues such as excellence and 'fair play'.

Amateurist critiques of commodification involve particular historical claims about sport that are open to serious questions concerning their empirical veracity.[24] The first claim is that during the golden age of amateurism sport was pursued for entirely non-commercial goals. During Victorian and early Edwardian times, a small number of sportsmen (notably jockeys) made similar fortunes, while significant earnings were also enjoyed by a wide range of professionals, including soccer players, cricketers, golfers, bowlers and anglers.[25] In the United States, a similar discourse enables commentators to wax lyrically on the pure motives and financial disinterest of old sporting heroes. Yet in the first two decades of the twentieth century, American sporting heroes were earning sizeable fortunes for their professional endeavours and, in particular, their endorsement of products in a booming consumer culture.[26]

Second, the Amateurist critique is often explicated via the idea that commodification is ethically undesirable because it involves a violation of the non-commercial essence of sport. In other words, sport is, by definition, an activity towards which a commercial orientation is antithetical. However, commerce has long been a part of sporting fixtures. In Ancient Greece, the original organised games were long dominated by athletes who could afford professional training, proper sport diets and travel expenses. Subsequently, wealthy patrons and civic authorities backed lower-class athletes financially, who were well rewarded for victories that brought honour to their city-states.[27] The games themselves were wrapped in commercial activity, including athlete sponsorship, gambling, prostitution and the hawking of food and drink. But in general, if modern sporting disciplines are not really sport because they are commercialised, then much of what we would ordinarily call sport in previous times would also fail to pass muster.

These socio-historical points might well be generalised beyond the Amateurist worldview to all forms of commodification critique. The challenge raised by this socio-historical approach is to provide a critical framework for understanding what is ethically undesirable about commodification which neither rests upon an idealised vision of pre-modern sport nor relies for its ethical force on a view of sport in which certain ideals or virtues are characterised as being constitutive of sport itself. Any plausible form of commodification critique must be able to deal with these criticisms and we explore the issue in some detail in chapter 3.

We should note in passing that a plausible ethical account of what is wrong with commodification must also deal with the vexed problem of amateurism. Over the past half century, there have been a number of quite telling attacks upon the Amateurist movement, as an historical phenomenon rather than just a set of ideas. Nevertheless, it might still be argued that commodification critique is necessarily wedded to Amateurist ideas. The following questions then arise. To what extent can commodification critique distance itself from amateurism? Could it be demonstrated that all forms of commodification critique are in the end just revisions of the old Amateurist attack upon the commercialisation of sport? To what extent does this connection matter? Should commodification critique even bother trying to distance itself from amateurism? In developing our framework for understanding the ethical harm involved in commodification we will also deal in chapter 3

with the relationship between it and the traditional Amateurist approach to commercialism in sport.

The approach pursued

Clearly, the commodification of sport provides moral grounds for concern. Yet
how might one best explicate those concerns? In particular, how might one
explicate them without rejecting markets entirely, without endorsing a return to
amateurism and without making fanciful, ahistorical claims about the intrinsic
nature of sport? This is our challenge.

The approach to be developed here will aim to identify those circumstances or
cases where commodification has morally undesirable outcomes. On this model, it
is not that the commodification of sport is by *its very nature* morally pernicious, or
that it necessarily gives rise to morally pernicious outcomes. Indeed, commodification is often acceptable or neutral in moral terms. Instead, the line of reasoning
here is that there will be cases where commodification is morally pernicious (or
'pathological') and others where it is not. Our task is to isolate such pathologies,
primarily as they arise in elite sport, although we will also consider the influence
upon grassroots sport.

These pathologies involve the violation of what we might take to be fundamental moral values that emerge from or through sporting activity, be it at the elite or
grassroots levels. These values include such items as the pursuit of athletic excellence, community identification, entertainment through genuine competition as
well as aesthetic values, such as the beauty of a sweetly-executed on-drive in
cricket or of a high-jumper effortlessly and elegantly clearing the bar. We show
how commodification might violate these values and where it does we take this to
be morally undesirable. We identify four central instances where commodification
violates fundamental sporting values and it is these pathologies which will be the
focal points of our inquiry.

It is important to note that we make no suggestion that these values are
constitutive of sport itself. Some more romantic sportswriters have, of course,
championed what we take to be the excessive claim that sport is only sport if it
exemplifies certain key moral values. So a dedicated and traditional cricket fan
might say that a game not pursued in the right spirit is not really cricket. Our line
of thinking is somewhat different. Our claim is that a number of important moral
values emerge from sport, rather than being essential to its very being. These
values might be said to *supervene* on sport rather than to be constitutive of it. The
upshot of this is that in criticising commodification we do not need to insist that
the values discussed must always be present in sporting activity. Our claim is not
that these values are always present – for as a matter of historical fact they have
often been sadly absent – nor that they are at the heart of what it is for sport to be
sport (the definitional claim), but that they are at the heart of what matters about
sport.

We should note too that sport itself – whether commodified or otherwise –
might not also be the occasion of moral vice. Although many important moral

values emerge from sport, it must be admitted that sport sometimes generates disvalue.[28] For example, certain forms of sporting rivalry, either at club or individual level, can degenerate into long-term hatred, violence and serious injury. Consider the case of Tonya Harding, an ice-skater whose ambition led her to hire a hit-man to injure a major rival; this criminal act is as ugly in a moral sense as the mob-violence between ethnic groups. When George Orwell famously opined – mistakenly in our view – that international sport led to enmity between nations, he was pointing towards one of the disvalues that sport can sometimes cause. For Orwell, international sport necessarily led to such negative outcomes, but our point is that individual or national enmity is not an intrinsic aspect of sporting competition.[29] Accordingly, in cases of disvalue, commodification which undermines such vices can only be said to be in the general good.

Our first task then will be to identify pathologies of commodification in sport. In pursuing this, we will concentrate primarily on the major elite sports, Association football (i.e. soccer), the Olympics, cricket and American sports (basketball, baseball and gridiron). Through this inquiry we hope to show what might be wrong with certain forms of commodification. Having identified various pathologies, we finish with a discussion of various policy alternatives that might be employed to alleviate or ameliorate any of the pathological consequences of commodification. But first let us begin with a survey of the ways in which moral philosophers and social theorists have treated questions concerning the ethical status of the process of commodification.

2 Moral philosophy, sport and commodification critique

Introduction

The question of what might be wrong with the commodification of sport needs to be explored within a more general framework that considers morally salient features of money and of the market. What, if anything, is wrong with commodifying a thing? Can one develop a critique of commodification that does not commit one to the view that markets should be abolished in their entirety, nor which adopts an aristocratic Amateurist stance?

In this chapter we survey various views on the morality of commodification and how money and markets might change things morally. We consider what various philosophers have said on the issue before developing our own general account of the harm of commodification. On our account it is not always wrong to commodify. Nevertheless, there will be occasions when commodification is *pathological*. We argue that a genuine commodification critique must endeavour to isolate those pathologies and in so doing thereby separate legitimate kinds of commodification from the illegitimate ones.

The commodification and the hyper-commodification of sport

What is commodification? Put most simply, commodification is the transformation of a good or service into a *commodity*, that is, into a thing which is bought and sold. The classical or canonical analysis of a commodity derives from the work of Aristotle.[1] In the *Politics* Aristotle says any article has two possible uses. If we take a shoe as an example, it may be worn or it may be exchanged for something else or for money.[2] Later writers, such as Adam Smith and Marx, have used this claim to provide a definition of a commodity. When there is a market for any article we can say that it has both a *use-value* and an *exchange-value*. Indeed that is what it is to be a commodity. The use-value is its intrinsic worth, whereas the exchange-value is its value on the market – its price if you like. So if we take a simple commodity like a salad sandwich bought at a delicatessen we see that it has both a use-value and an exchange value. The use-value here is the gustatory and nutritional worth we find in, and gain from, the sandwich, while the exchange-value is the price that we have to pay in order to purchase it. This is the distinction as it has been received from the Classical economic tradition.

Following this definition, commodification is defined as the transformation of a thing with only use-value to a good with both use-value *and* exchange-value. A good comes to possess an exchange-value when it is bought and sold on a market of some kind for money or some equivalent. Indeed this is a basic condition for the possession of exchange-value, for without some kind of market in which other goods are bought and sold, a good cannot come to have exchange-value. Markets and money then are central to the process of commodification. A good comes to have exchange value – and thus becomes a commodity – when it is bought and sold, usually for money (although sometimes through barter) in a system where there are many other commodities for sale. Our salad sandwich is commodified when it is part of a social system in which it is exchangeable for money or other goods at a price.[3]

If we apply this model to sport we soon see that a great deal of commodification has occurred in modern sport. Think of Major League Baseball. Such an elite level of sport has both a use-value to players and spectators alike, since they derive value from it, and an exchange value since, for instance, the television rights to a season's worth of baseball can be sold to the highest bidder for a price. In commodifying these games we see that they have come to possess both a use and an exchange value.

When goods are systematically produced as commodities, rather than haphazardly so, then we find a transformation of the incentive structures of those producing the goods. Consider the difference between selling excess and selling a good produced solely with the aim of making a profit. When one produces in the latter manner, then the production of a good which is ultimately sold, is animated by the profit motive at all points in its execution.

There are reasons, however, for wanting to go beyond the classical or canonical analysis of a commodity. Notice that on the classical analysis the focus is restricted to actual buying and selling. However, some of the phenomena in which we are interested are fundamentally 'attitudinal' and concern treating sporting goods as if they were commodities, something Margaret Jane Radin refers to as 'market rhetoric'.[4] For example, consider the case of a sports business official who is only interested in the bottom line. Such a person regards the sport over which he has responsibilities as a mere means to the realisation of profit. Alternatively, think of an administrator who only values athletes in terms of their notional transfer value (despite the fact that those athletes are not 'for sale'), rather than in terms of aesthetic or technical value in playing the game. In general there is something morally pernicious about such modes of regard and our commodification critique should include an account of what might be wrong here.

In recent years a number of theorists have developed broader accounts and included what we might call 'counterfactual commodification' in their definitions of what it is to commodify a thing. Thus the philosopher Elizabeth Anderson suggests that a good is commodified either when it is bought and sold or when it is regarded as a thing with a monetary value (even when no buying and selling goes on).[5] On this model, cost–benefit analysis – which involves the assignation of market values to goods for which there is no actual market – becomes a form of commodification. In a sport such as soccer, players who have been purchased by a club are accorded a notional value on annual balance sheets, despite the fact that they may be on long-term contracts and are highly unlikely to enter the transfer market.

Further, the classical definition of commodification does not fully capture another worrying feature of modern sport. It is not just the buying and selling which occurs that raises concerns, but rather the depth or pervasiveness of market relations in sport. In a sense there has virtually always been some money in elite sport.[6] There is good evidence that ancient Greek athletes were paid handsomely for their efforts and – as we shall discuss in some detail in the next chapter – even in the golden age of amateurism in nineteenth-century Britain, elite sports-people received very high rewards. Equally, promoters of sporting events in the eighteenth and nineteenth century often made enormous amounts of money.

One might be tempted, following the classical definition, to suggest that since there has always been at least some money in sport, no changes have been wrought over the past one hundred years. But such a claim would lead us to overlook the radical intensification of market relations in sport that have occurred over that period of time. A time-travelling English visitor to the Lords Cricket Ground from the nineteenth century would certainly not fail to notice the changes to the way that cricket is now played in response to commercial pressures, from the advertising hoardings that hug the boundary fences to the commercial language of many of the administrators to the entertainment-driven type of game that is played to attract new markets.

In response to these theoretical concerns, we suggest that the focus should be on what we want to call 'hyper-commodification'. By 'hyper-commodification' we are referring to both the substantive increase in the range and number of goods that are bought and sold as well as the intensification of market understandings and attitudes towards sport itself.

There are we suggest four key features of this hyper-commodification: the transformation of clubs and systems into corporations, the emergence of large numbers of highly paid sportspeople, the advent of large scale advertising and merchandising in sport and finally the 'venalisation' of the *ethos* of sport. Let us consider each of these in some more detail, beginning with the corporatisation of clubs.

Elite sports clubs are now explicitly organised as corporate entities. Most have undergone some significant division of ownership and control along the 'joint-stock' model, while some are either capitalised as public limited companies that are listed on major stock exchanges or operate as a franchise, members of expansionist sporting cartels such as the (National Basketball Association) NBA or Major League Baseball (MLB). The corporatisation of sports clubs, and their governing associations, involves amongst other things a change in the *ethos* so that profits are given higher priority within the sporting enterprise over any historical, cultural, social or aesthetic considerations. Many are now transnational entities (think here of Manchester United Football Club), and as such these enterprises experience an increasingly haphazard and accidental relationship to their old, traditional supporter base in the localities surrounding the club stadium.

This represents a considerable transformation for those numerous clubs which had originated as community-based associations. In Latin America, sports institutions such as soccer clubs originated as private member associations and so were constituted as 'leisure democracies'. Each club is owned by members ('socios') who pay a modest subscription every month or year and elect the office-holders on a regular basis. In the United Kingdom, prior to the First World War, most clubs had already become limited companies and were owned by a small group of local shareholders who were keen to sustain their local profile and thus were accessible to the club's (often critical) supporters. With the hyper-commodification over the past twenty years, many clubs were converted into, or maintained their status as limited companies. The new owners are either institutional investors, existing shareholders whose wealth has been multiplied rapidly through the increased value of the club or billionaire business people whose wealth far exceeds that of previous sports team chairmen. In all instances, the social and political gaps between those who run the clubs and those who support them become greater. Indeed, to all intents and purposes they belong to entirely distinct communities.

One important feature of hyper-commodification, then, is the transformation of clubs into corporate entities, and in this change we find more democratic structures or community-tied ownership coming to be supplanted by distinctively impersonal, corporate frameworks of power. Those clubs that do not adopt such corporate structures risk falling behind. The overall effect at the elite level is the homogenisation of club structures with power passing to a cartel of rich investors.

Being corporations, clubs follow similar practices to corporations in the capitalist world beyond sport. Most significantly we find clubs expanding globally. Soccer clubs like Manchester United FC and Real Madrid FC are essentially transnational entities since amongst other things they employ labour from all over the world. Indeed a new international division of labour has become established among players, and this coincides neatly with the transnational marketing ambitions of many top sports clubs. Since the early 1990s, the latter have targeted fresh sports markets in Europe, North American and Asia, in a bid to attract consumers who will buy club products.

In many cases this process of transition into fully-fledged transnational corporations that are entirely decoupled from their surrounding community is still incomplete. This is most clear in the United Kingdom where soccer clubs retain their traditional headquarters in their place of origin (such as Old Trafford in Manchester). However, in both the United States and Australia sports franchises have moved to other cities to play their 'home' soccer fixtures or relocating their business headquarters. For instance, the Fitzroy Lions from Melbourne moved one thousand miles north to Brisbane to become the Brisbane Lions and in the United States the Montreal Expos baseball team played some of its 'home' matches in Puerto Rico before the 'franchise' was eventually moved on a 'permanent' basis in 2005 to Washington DC. Such moves obviously undermine the loyalties and ties of traditional supporter bases.

We also find these corporate clubs engaging in other standard capitalist practices, such as horizontal and vertical integration. 'Vertical integration' means that clubs contract with or have shares in clubs at lower levels both home and abroad. The import of this is that it allows the top corporate clubs to ensure first options on emerging young talents. Horizontal integration on the other hand involves major transnational corporation with sports related interests (such as media and communication businesses) investing in the richest clubs, enabling the former to benefit from greater financial leverage and the marketing expertise of these new investors.

Perhaps the most conspicuous example of such horizontal integration comes from Italy where Silvio Berlusconi's *Fininvest* media empire acquired the ailing giant AC Milan in the early 1980s. Milan soon purchased a huge squad of the world's leading players to become Europe's premier club during the later 1980s and early 1990s. That pre-eminence encouraged Berlusconi to purchase the television rights to the top Italian league (*Serie A*) for his subscription channels.

Media corporations benefit from their role in sports club ownership, since they may sit on both sides of the table when television contracts are negotiated. Moreover, control of televised sport is often a crucial means of expanding into new media markets. For instance, Rupert Murdoch's unsuccessful bid for Manchester United during the 1998–99 season reflected his marketing philosophy that televised sport is a 'battering ram' for penetrating and controlling new television markets.[7]

A second key feature of hyper-commodification is the *professionalisation* of players and athletes.[8] Indeed this is one of the most notable features of modern elite sport generally. Elite players are professionals in the sense that their income from on and off the field activities provides the dominant source of their material wealth. It is important to distinguish here between 'broken time' payments and full-scale professionalism. The former involves payments to working people for wages lost through playing during working hours. This is different to professionalism *per se* where a club pays players to ensure they maintain their services and give their best and where playing sport is best understood as a singular occupation.[9]

In team sports this professionalisation has led to a breakdown of the reciprocal loyalties that had once obtained between clubs and players. This is not to romanticise or misrepresent the earlier nature of the player–club relationship. In most professional team sports in the West until at least the late 1960s, players typically endured highly constrictive industrial conditions that held down pay and minimised their chances of moving voluntarily to other clubs. The legal and political challenges wrought by players' unions and individual athletes served to win many industrial concessions that other workers take for granted. Nevertheless, we should also recognise that, since that period, some crucial aspects of elite sport have been lost unnecessarily, notably the communal relationships that bund players to their supporters and to clubs *qua* community representatives. Social historians have noted how up until the 1960s even the best soccer players in the United Kingdom were often viewed as local heroes, as community representatives who slipped back into the surrounding fold outside of soccer, notably after retirement.[10]

In contrast, the greater professionalisation of athletes has resulted in a more active and flexible labour market. Elite athletes migrate regularly to new towns, cities and countries. Correspondingly, clubs take on fewer responsibilities toward long-serving players. In soccer this trend was accelerated by the so-called 'Bosman ruling'. In 1995 the European Court ruled in favour of the eponymous Belgian player in a civil case and thereby endorsed the rights of players to move, when out of contract, to any willing club without the payment of a transfer fee. At the elite level, 'Bosman' contributed significantly to the massive inflation of player wages, yet weaker ties and responsibilities emerged between clubs and their professional employees.

A third feature of hyper-commodification is the proliferation of *advertising* and *merchandising* in sport. While this has obvious connections to the idea of corporatisation, we consider that advertising and merchandising are worthy of their own category. Walk into any major sports stadium and one cannot but help but be struck by the amount of advertising on the fences, playing surface and stands. Indeed, sporting grounds are no longer open spaces but in the cricket commentator Scyld Berry's words 'diseased by the eczema of logos'.[11] Most sporting broadcasts are also dominated by advertising, sometimes to such an extent that they determine playing times and the structure of games. In the United States, for example, we find the introduction of 'TV time-outs' designed to allow television networks to show advertisements.[12]

Advertising, merchandising and other commercial revenues are now very much a central part of modern sport and as for many elite clubs, essential for their survival. Until the 1980s English soccer clubs derived most of their income from gate-money, however this has gradually changed. In 2005, the top clubs from Europe's largest leagues derived less than 40 per cent of their total revenues from match-day income; in AC Milan's case, the contribution was a mere 13 per cent. In the NFL of North America, an aggressive business strategy by the Washington Redskins has led the way in the new millennium. The Redskins more than doubled their annual revenues within five years, in large part thanks to sponsorship deals with Anheuser-Bush, PepsiCo and Nextel Communications; a 27-year, US$207 million deal with Fed Ex saw the club's home stadium renamed as Fedex Field. So, despite aesthetic objections of the kind made by Scyld Berry, forms of corporate sponsorship will continue to be a part of elite sport and, in the absence of some form of state intervention to prevent it, advertisers will continue to dictate the shape and structure of sport.[13]

A fourth, and final, key feature of hyper-commodification is what we call the 'venalisation of the ethos' of sport. It is not only that an ever-expanding range of sporting events and paraphernalia are available on the market as commodities, but that they are understood essentially as such. In modern sport we find an increasingly explicit market orientation in the actions of players, athletes and administrators. With each passing year their motivational principles become ever more venal. Venalisation arises when the pursuit of money is seen as the sole (or dominant) aim of action. It involves the dominance of financial considerations in a person or organisation's all-things-considered judgements. Sentimental reasons such as pride in the club or the mutual pursuit of excellence become minor motivating forces. In the world of English soccer, for example, we find numerous instances of such venalisation. For example, while supporters buy small share-holdings in clubs for non-trivial emotional reasons, major institutions make significant investments for purely financial reasons.

Thus it is not only the practices of sporting clubs and athletes that have changed, but perhaps not unsurprisingly the self-understandings of those organising and promoting sport as well as those playing it that have been transformed. In a commodified realm, sport is understood either as entertainment or as a form of industry. Central to this is the use of the language of business to describe sporting practices and institutions. Recall the fact that in US sports, major league teams are called 'franchises'. This is part of a much wider trend in which we talk of sport as business – products with customers, workers, brands, market-share, stock-market values and so on. Here we have the emergence of what the North American legal theorist Margaret Jane Radin in *Contested Commodities* calls 'market rhetoric'. 'Market rhetoric' as Radin uses the term involves conceiving of all of human activities as fundamentally oriented towards the pursuit of money.[14] In her book, Radin's attention is directed at those who would apply cost-benefit analysis to all human activities, regardless of whether they are, in point of fact, commodified. In a similar vein, conceiving of any major sports league club as essentially part of the entertainment industry involves a commodified understanding of the nature of human activity. When the organisation of sport comes to be understood within the discursive framework of 'market rhetoric' as either a form of diversionary enter-tainment or as a quasi-industrial commodity, then the ethos has been venalised. Venalised sport represents a considerable shift from a traditional ethos of sport which involves the pursuit of victory in competitive good faith.

These four features, taken in sum, provide reasons for thinking that there is something distinctive about the kinds of market invasions of sport we have witnessed over the past thirty or so years. While it is true that there has been money in sport for a very long time, these features point to an intensification of the degree to which sport has been penetrated by market relations. Any line of objection that wants to claim that there are no grounds for moral concern since sport has always been commodified misses the essential difference between the commodification of the past and the hyper-commodification of the present. There have been distinctly significant changes.

With that thought in mind we turn now to some general theoretical frameworks for assessing the moral status of commodification. If there is something wrong with such changes, then what exactly is it? What follows is not so much an historical account of philosophers and social theorists on commodification as it is a survey of the major critical views on the topic that culminates in what we take to be the correct view.

Marx and abolitionism

Without a doubt the most influential form of commodification critique over the past one hundred years is that associated with the Marxist tradition and so it is here we begin. Even after the demise of Communism, Marxist ideas still influence our ideas on what might be wrong with commodification. According to this tradition, commercial relations are exploitative and morally corrupting and thus should be abandoned in favour of alternative social arrangements. Thus the Marxist advocates a radical programme of decommodification.[15] Not only should we resist any new additions to the market realm, but we should also overthrow the market entirely. In the Marxist utopia there will be no commodities whatsoever.

In Marxism this moral critique is made all the more pressing by the fact that Marx believed that commodification was a necessary consequence of capitalist society. In a society where money in the form of capital dominates, there will be pressure for more and more goods to be allocated by the market. (Marx referred to the degree of commodification in terms of the 'organic composition of capital'). He argued that under capitalism, nothing was sacred and everything becomes saleable and buyable. 'Not even the bones of saints' he suggests in *Capital* vol.1 'are able to withstand this alchemy'.[16]

Marx's moral critique of the commodity form has two key elements, one of which involves a theory of injustice and the other which involves a theory of metaphysical or meta-normative corruption. The injustice strand is based on his analysis of exchange relations and profits within capitalism.[17] The core idea is that in capitalist industries profits are only possible because the capitalist employer of wage-labour does not pay their workers the full economic value of the goods they create. The difference between the money-price paid to the worker (in the form of wages) for producing a good and the price for which it is sold is the 'surplus value' or profit.[18] On this analysis, capitalists do not pay their workers the full value of the commodities they produce and thus they are exploited. Commodity production is morally pernicious since under capitalist relations of production it leads to exploitation. To commodify a good thus is to incorporate it into an exploitative productive system in which those who produce value are not adequately rewarded properly for their labour.

There is a second strand in Marx's thought that is relevant to our topic which concerns the *corruption* of both our systems of value and our understanding by immersion in commodity culture. If we take value, this is undermined by the false view that value and price are synonymous. For instance, in the *1844 Manuscripts* he writes:

> What I am and can do is not at all determined by my individuality. I am ugly, but I can buy the most beautiful women for myself. Consequently I am not ugly ... I am stupid, but since money is the real mind of things, how could its possessor be stupid?[19]

Life in a commodity culture systematically distorts our values. Similarly it infects our capacity for intellectual insight. In his discussion of 'commodity fetishism' he explores how our perceptions of social relations are under the sway of commodity exchange. Marx argues that in capitalism the real source of productivity, which is mutually interdependent labour, is disguised in such a way that we believe the powers are products of the commodity itself.[20] For Marx the thought is that the coordination mechanism is not at all neutral, but influences the way in which agents understand their mutual interdependence. This is but one example of Marx's general claim about ideology that the ruling ideas of any age are those of the ruling class.

The applicability of these Marxist notions to sport should be clear. For instance, the idea that commodification is a necessary part of the 'logic' of capitalism provides a plausible explanation for the changes that have occurred in sport over the past fifty years. The overthrow of sporting traditions and practices in the service of capital is precisely the kind of social upheaval that Marx and Engels were referring to in the *Communist Manifesto*. Equally the rise of a culture in which sport is understood as business reflects the distortion of our values through immersion in commodity culture.

Unsurprisingly, over the past thirty years, there have been a number of radical social theorists who have applied Marxist concepts to sport, most notably and somewhat crudely by commentators such as Paul Hoch in *Rip off the Big Game* (1972) and Jean-Marie Brohm in *Sport: A Prison of Measured Time* (1978). Hoch explores the ways in which sport is used, in the United States in particular, by the ruling classes as an ideological device to further their own military and economic purposes. At one point (p. 69), leaning on the traditional notion of exploitation, Hoch talks of how those who make all of the money do not place their bodies at risk but cream off the profits. More broadly, he views sport as playing an important role in socialising the general public into operating as passive workers and consumers. Hoch's general line is that sport has been taken over by capitalist classes for their own benefit, but he is not antagonistic to sport in itself.

The same cannot be said for Brohm, who views all elite competitive sport as preparing labour-power for industrial labour and of performing the ideological task of stabilising the existing order. In his future communist state all competitive sport will be eliminated and in its place there will be a 'non-alienated culture of the body'.[21] For Brohm sport is the modern 'opium of the masses' that regulates and neutralises any revolutionary energy in the lower orders and in this way occupying the position once said to be held by religion. He believes that it has its origins in imperialism and, further, that the training that is part and parcel of sport involves sexual repression through discipline of the body.[22] Even the victorious athlete cannot transcend his or her alienating industrial position for, according to Brohm: 'The champion becomes a product of performances and records and his labour no longer belongs to him. He is totally governed by his trainer, a veritable foreman, whose sole aim is to increase the productivity of his athletes.'[23]

However, there are problems with the Marxist position, both in general and in the more specific contexts of sport. First, the Marxist commodification critique is abolitionist in nature. It advocates the total elimination of markets and commodities. Yet there are good reasons for wishing to defend market activity as a necessary feature of modern society. Although the arguments may be familiar, it is well-worth restating them.[24] Markets function as both incentive and information systems. In the right circumstances – and, in particular, in the absence of monopoly – the incentives that markets provide for producers can encourage innovation and the production of considerable surplus. Having agents animated by the profit motive leads to the production of surplus and to innovation. Indeed markets are capable of generating a superfluity of goods and fostering innovation to an extent so far unachievable in any other social arrangements. Any plausible social arrangement must, for the foreseeable future, involve at least some degree of market activity. Thus, while commodification is often morally pernicious, our concern with it needs to be placed in a non-abolitionist framework.

Second, the thesis that commercial relations are always exploitative is more-over false. On the Marxist account market exchanges are typically conceived of as being zero-sum games, where one person's gain is necessarily another's loss.[25] The most obvious example of this line of reasoning in Marxism is the wage-labour contract. But there are many cases where exchange benefits both parties. If we consider, as examples, the lucrative contracts elite sports stars sign with their clubs and with sponsors, then it is clear that these athletes are benefiting just as much as their paymasters. Indeed, and *pace* Brohm in particular, it would be absurd to suggest that a highly successful athlete like David Beckham is exploited in some moral sense in his contracts. None of this is to suggest that commercial exploita-tion does not occur. (Indeed it is not difficult to find examples of sports workers, especially those who come from underprivileged backgrounds, being exploited mercilessly.) It is simply to say commercial relations are not always zero-sum. In addition, the Marxist theory assumes that capitalists do nothing whatsoever; they may well do very little, and certainly often do not deserve the rewards they receive, but it is not true that they do nothing whatsoever.

The upshot of this is that commodity exchange is not always morally imper-missible. Thus not only are markets a necessary feature of modern life for the overall outcomes they generate, but the individual commercial interactions on which the market is based are not in themselves *necessarily* pernicious. This is important for it is quite possible to argue, as Mandeville did, that a series of morally vicious actions could have positive overall effects.[26] So the fact that the system is justifiable does not mean in itself that the individual acts upon which it is based are also morally virtuous.

We can go further than this and argue that there are cases where markets are not only permissible but have desirable effects. This is something that the sociologist Georg Simmel (1858–1918) noted in his book *The Philosophy of Money*. Simmel outlined a number of socially progressive aspects of the money economy, an economic system in which commodity exchange predominates. He claimed, for instance, that monetary payment (in contrast to payment in kind) is the form most congruent with personal freedom. Simmel argues that the Lord of the manor who can demand a quantity of beer or poultry or honey from a serf thereby deter-mines the direction of activity of that serf. But the moment he merely imposes a money levy the peasant is 'free', in so far as he can decide whether to keep bees, cattle or anything else.[27] Somewhat counterintuitively, Simmel claimed that the shift from communal to associative relations (to use Weberian language) is a posi-tive development. According to Simmel one of the values of a money economy is the way money frees its owners from entanglements of personality and permits a certain detachment toward social life.[28] However, Simmel does recognise some downsides to this modernisation, notably the rise of a pervasive blasé attitude among urban populations that strikes rural visitors as 'cold and uncongenial' and which can engender some strong feelings of loneliness and desertion within the metropolitan throng.

The relevance of Simmel's ideas to sport should be clear. The professionalisation of sport, for instance, has allowed sports men and women to be freed from many of the semi-feudal ties with their clubs which were part and parcel of the landscape of sport. From the point of view of sportspeople, such freedom of movement can only be seen as progressive. Nevertheless, sport also registers the loss of some important social values within contemporary metropolitan life. These include the diminu- tion of solidarity among fans towards the local club, or the fracturing of communal ties between players, club officials and supporters.

It would seem then that any abolitionist critique is inappropriate if we are to understand what might be wrong with commodification. Markets are not only necessary, but often have morally desirable consequences. Thus, what we need in its place is an account of the harm of commodification that does not lead to abolitionism. In what follows we explore a number of non-abolitionist ethical frameworks for explaining the moral harms of commodification. In considering non-abolitionist accounts of the harms of commodification we begin with Aristotle.

Aristotle, natural exchange and the harms of commodification

One of the first explicit philosophical discussions of the potential harms of trans- forming something into a commodity is to be found in Aristotle. In the *Politics* Aristotle provides an account of different forms of exchange that is antagonistic to the great bulk of market activity. Although elsewhere Aristotle recognises the usefulness of money in allowing people to exchange goods, in the *Politics* he condemns the activities of those whose activities are primarily commercial in nature. As we shall see, this kind of approach is remarkably close to the underlying *ethos* of amateurism.

At the heart of his criticism of what we would now call 'commodification' is the distinction we earlier discussed between use-value and exchange-value. On the basis of this Aristotle contrasts two kinds of productive activity; production for consumption (*economica*) and production for exchange (*chrematistica*). Production for the consumption of oneself and one's household is natural and proper, while production for exchange is unnatural and thereby, for Aristotle, morally perverse. Aristotle thought that all proper activities were by definition in accordance with nature. This does not mean that all commerce is immoral, for it is morally permissible to sell the excess of what one has produced for one's own consumption. It is *systematic* production for exchange which is immoral. Thus, if one had a particularly good harvest of grapes in a particular year and one's household produced more than it could consume, then it was morally acceptable to sell the excess. On the other hand, to have grown the grapes primarily to sell is unnatural.

Clearly, in the modern world this would condemn to the realm of immorality the great majority of market exchanges.

Aristotle's account is not fully abolitionist since there is some legitimate market activity, namely, where the good bought and sold is not *systematically produced* for exchange. To commodify a good which is not systematically produced for exchange is acceptable. However, commodification is morally pernicious when it involves the explicit production of goods for exchange. The morally-relevant feature here is the reasons for which it was produced.

How might this apply to the commodification of sport? Unsurprisingly, given Aristotle's aristocratic background, this fits rather nicely with the Amateurist view of sport. To engage in sport for financial motives, to engage in *chrematistic* play, would be immoral. Following his general line of thought – although obviously he said nothing explicit on the matter – Aristotle would presumably think that one could make some money out of sport, but only in some accidental way. The aims of those engaging in sport should be non-commercial.

Although this approach has the obvious virtue of distinguishing between legitimate and illegitimate forms of commodification, it has a number of serious flaws. The first is the anthropological point that the surpluses generated by those who produce explicitly for exchange free others in society to pursue activities other than the production of material necessities. In modern industrial societies, 'chrematistic' production in agricultural goods has enabled the great bulk of the population to flee a life of rural subsistence. Indeed, one of the main reasons that one might wish to avoid an abolitionist framework like Marx's seems not to be in play here. If we want the surpluses to which the chrematistic production gives rise, then we are not going to get them on Aristotle's system. Elite sport might be seen as one such by-product of surplus, since surplus frees people to maximise their sporting capabilities and thus facilitates what we might regard as outstanding competition.

Second, it is difficult to see exactly what the moral harm in producing, say, wheat for exchange might be. Unless one accepts Aristotle's general claims about the immorality of the unnatural – and on its own this seems an implausible line to take – then there seems no reason to object to producing wheat for exchange. Thus, as a general claim about the harm of commodification it is not particularly convincing.

Finally, it looks, given the reliance on people's intentions, as if this moral framework, if generally accepted, would place grave ethical hazards in the paths of producers. It is always open to any commercial producer, no matter how large, to say that he grew his grapes or made his shoes with his family and household in mind, but that as luck would have it this year he has a tremendous surplus.

Kant on price and dignity

Another source of a critical non-abolitionist moral perspective on commodification derives from the work of the German philosopher Immanuel Kant (1724–1804). Although Kant does not explicitly discuss commodification as such, his work in *The Groundwork of the Metaphysics of Morals* on the relationship between *price and dignity* has obvious implications for the process and, further it has been used explicitly by a number of moral theorists who want to distinguish between legitimate and illegitimate forms of commodification. Since it is the distinction between price and dignity that is central to a Kantian account let us begin there.

Kant's treatment of the distinction appears amidst a discussion of the radical difference between 'things' and 'persons'. According to Kant, 'things' have only a *relative* value; they are valuable in so far as someone happens to desire them, in so far as they are useful for some other ends. Persons, on the other hand, are ends-in-themselves and possess a worthiness or dignity. For Kant, to treat a person with dignity is synonymous with treating her as an end. The value of a person, unlike that of a thing, is unconditional, incomparable and incalculable. It follows, he suggests, that persons cannot have a price – that is, a value in exchange – for things with a price admit of substitutes. Price violates the incomparability of persons since it makes them equivalent. In persons we have beings which by their very nature should not be bought and sold.

The conclusion of Kant's chain of reasoning here is that price and dignity are mutually exclusive, for 'in the kingdom of ends everything has either a price or a dignity'. He suggests that '[i]f it has a price something can be put in its place as an equivalent; if it is exalted above all price it has a dignity'.[29] The implications of this for any proposed form of commodification should be clear. If a being or object is an end-in-itself – that is, if it possesses a dignity – then it should not be commodified, for only 'things' can be commodified. But importantly, unlike Aristotle's account, it does allow for a great deal of useful market activity. Given that the world is inhabited by many objects which are pure means, such as, for instance, saws and hammers, then the proper range of the market is quite broad.

Kant's apparent antagonism towards some market exchanges is certainly not confined to the *Groundwork*. In the *Metaphysics of Morals* he suggests that selling a tooth to be transplanted into another mouth or having oneself castrated in order to get an easier livelihood as a singer are ways of potentially murdering oneself.[30] He does not rule out the amputation of a dead or diseased organ when that organ endangers the amputee's life nor is he concerned with cutting off parts of oneself, such as one's hair, that are not organs, although he notes that cutting one's hair in order to sell it is 'not entirely free from blame'.[31]

Despite all of this it must also be admitted that Kant did not explicitly explore questions about the proper range of the market. Nor did he engage in any detailed discussion of the merits of commodifying particular goods (although he did discuss why it was wrong to sell one's teeth or engage in prostitution). That caveat notwithstanding, over the past thirty years his price-dignity dictum has been routinely invoked to draw conclusions about the impermissibility of various forms of commodification. This is particularly true with respect to debates in applied ethics over the sale of human body parts, sex and surrogate wombs. In each instance the leading thought is that selling such things is wrong because it involves persons and, since price and dignity are mutually exclusive, their personhood or dignity is being violated.[32] For instance, if we ask what might be wrong with selling surrogacy contracts the answer on a Kantian framework is that it fails to accord the woman selling access to her womb the form of dignity requisite of a person.

We can see similar applications in sport. As we will argue later in chapter 4, the treatment of players as *mere means* to the realisation of profit violates some fundamental rules regarding the proper treatment of persons. Equally, treating sport itself as a mere means violates something that should be treated as an end-in-itself. (Again we shall say more about this in chapter 4.)

Despite the usefulness of these applications, there are limits to a Kantian-based critique of the commodification of sport. In the first instance, the price-dignity dictum is insufficiently nuanced to capture all of the different modes of regard with which non-commodities should be treated. Both one's grandmother and one's aged loyal Blue Heeler cattle dog should not be treated as commodities, but for entirely different reasons. Value is more diverse than Kant's two-fold classification would suggest – it cannot do justice to the complexity of the human experience of valuing.[33]

Second, not all of the objections that one might have to the commodification of sport can be understood as violations of the dignity of persons. For instance, one might well be concerned with a distributive issue such as the way that processes of commodification lead traditional fans to be excluded from access to high-profile sporting events. This is not so much a matter of failing to respect persons as ends in themselves, as it is a matter of injustice. So the Kantian story cannot reasonably account for all of the concerns we might have. Yet any plausible commodification critique needs to be able to account for such concerns. So a Kantian critique cannot provide a complete ethical framework for the analysis of the harm of commodification. Thus while a Kantian approach might well be part of the story – and we suggest that suitably modified it is – it cannot provide us with a complete account of what might be wrong with some forms of commodification.

Finally, as it stands, the Kantian account only provides grounds for two policy responses; commodification or blocked exchange. If an entity can be treated as a *mere* means then it is permissible to commodify it fully. If an entity is one that should be treated as an end-in-itself, then any potential exchanges of it should be blocked or prohibited. However, there might be cases where one wants to regulate market exchanges rather than ban them outright. The Kantian account of the harm of commodification in itself does not provide the theoretical resources for explaining why one might wish to regulate rather than prohibit. The only harm it identifies is the harm of assigning a price to things with a dignity and this is a harm that appears to demand prohibition rather than regulation.

Despite these qualms about Kantianism providing the sole basis of a commodification critique, Kantian concerns with treating something as a mere means are certainly part of the story. They simply need to be placed within a broader theoretical framework. In chapter 4 we will return to these issues.

Commodity spheres: Walzer and Anderson

Earlier, in the discussion of Marxism, we noted that one disconcerting feature of the abolitionist opposition to markets is its oversight with respect to the productivity of markets. To commodify is to place in the market and markets have often been very productive. One possible way of reconciling the productivity of markets with certain moral concerns we might have is through the 'spheres approach' that we find in the work of Michael Walzer and Elizabeth Anderson. The idea is to keep certain spheres of goods, such as perhaps political office, from the market. Thus one cannot buy and sell political office. Exchanges in such goods are to be blocked and thus, in this way, we obtain the benefits of the market without some of the disconcerting features of commodification.

This idea is most famously explored in Michael Walzer's book *Spheres of Justice*. There Walzer argues that, although there are certain goods that are properly distributed by money – that is which belong to the 'sphere of money' – for other goods such allocation is inappropriate and thus they should not be commodified. Walzer identifies fourteen such 'blocked exchanges' and his list – which in many ways is a strange list – includes marriage rights, exemption from military service and romantic love.

In sport we see this idea of blocked exchange exemplified in practice with the refusal of certain sporting institutions to commodify particular events or objects (although such examples are increasingly rare). For instance, the Barcelona and Athletic Bilbao soccer clubs have hitherto refused to allow advertising on their club strips because such apparel carries a sacred quality, in symbolically embodying Catalan and Basque identities respectively.[34] In Major League Baseball a controversy arose in May 2004 when it was announced that the MLB had agreed on a US$3.6 million deal with Columbia Pictures, to have the Spiderman logo covering the bases, home plate, pitcher's mound and on-deck area at every game for an entire month. Many fans reacted with fury towards this commercialisation of the 'sacred' sites in their sport. In cricket, the 'baggy green' cricket cap that is worn by Australian international players is also considered to be beyond the influence of mundane commercialism. The only caps in circulation are those that have been awarded to 'capped' players. One cannot buy replicas of the cap as one can say with the one-day uniform. Thus the baggy green is not for sale, although one can buy caps of former players.

The spheres approach is further developed by Elizabeth Anderson who provides a meta-ethical justification for keeping certain goods out of the market. Anderson argues that goods have 'expressive meanings' associated with them that provide means of determining how they are to be properly regarded and hence treated. She outlines a number of different 'modes of regard' which include 'use', 'respect', 'appreciation', 'consideration' and 'love'.[35] Those goods which can properly be regarded as mere instruments can be commodified, while those with different norms or modes of regard might well be violated in doing so. Certain goods, such as love and friendship, for instance, are fundamentally at odds with the use-valuation of the market. It would be wrong to commodify them for their expressive meanings would be violated if subjected to the modes of valuation of the market. For Anderson, determining which goods should be commodified is a matter of determining the mode of treatment appropriate to the good in question. To illustrate her theory she talks of a public park which should be open to all, and for which market fees would be inappropriate. In this way Anderson provides more substantive content to the spheres approach by providing justificatory grounds (notably missing in Walzer) for why certain goods do not belong in the sphere of the market.[36]

The central feature then of a 'spheres' commodity critique is insistence on the maintenance of distinct market and non-market spheres. In this way we have critique without abolitionism. However – just as we noted with Aristotle and Kant – there are also problems with this approach. First, as developed by Walzer and Anderson, it allows for too much unregulated activity within the market. Anderson, for instance, suggests that an economic good (that is a good which can legitimately be commodified) is a good where norms of self-interest and freedom to use goods without constraint are appropriate.[37] Here there is too much sympathy with *laissez-faire* views of the market.

Second, this only provides us with two policy options. Yet it is not true that all of the moral concerns we have with the commodification of sport provide grounds for prohibition of commercial exchange. Some might simply warrant forms of regulation or what Margaret Jane Radin refers to as 'incomplete commodification'.[38] In many cases, such as for instance with regard to questions of access to sporting goods, we might well simply wish to regulate commercial practices. In this way we can ensure access for a greater proportion of the population.

In short, through their partitioning of the sphere of money from other spheres, they appear to have off-loaded all of their moral concerns onto the goods subject to blocked exchanges and thereby excused the sphere of money from any moral obligations whatsoever. Thus while there is much to be said for the idea of quarantining off certain spheres of sport as blocked exchange, any plausible commodity critique also needs to include the idea of regulated commodity exchange as a possible policy option. Our desired approach then would have both blocked exchange and regulation (or as Radin calls it 'incomplete commodification') as part of the policy menu.

Alasdair MacIntyre – internal and external reasons

Before presenting our own preferred account, we should also briefly consider a form of commodification critique that derives from the work of Alasdair MacIntyre and which has been extremely influential in the Philosophy of Sport (especially with respect to criticisms of markets in sport), especially as a result of William Morgan's use of these ideas in his *Leftist Theories of Sport*.

MacIntyre's work itself is pitched at a much more general level than our own commodity critique. His theory is concerned not only with commodification but more generally with the relationship between social institutions and practices. MacIntyre regards institutions and practices as quite distinct phenomena that are very much in conflict with one another. The distinctive feature of practices is that they involve what MacIntyre calls 'internal goods'. Internal goods are those which cannot be enjoyed other than through engagement with the practice in question and which can only be recognised and specified as the goods they are by those involved in the practice. Assessment of their goodness is internal to the practice in which they arise. Institutions, on the other hand, are typically concerned with external goods. They are 'involved in acquiring money and other material goods; they are structured in terms of power and status and they distribute money and power as rewards'.[39] This is in contrast to practices in which internal goods are pursued and which are vulnerable to corruption by institutions through the latter's focus on external goods. Without wishing to appear too cynical, the picture MacIntyre paints is of a rather Manichean universe in which the forces of good (i.e. practices) are pitted against the evil forces of institutions.

In his influential work *Leftist Theories of Sport*, William Morgan draws on MacIntyre's distinction between practices and institutions to provide a critique of commodification. Commodification is understood here, as it was for MacIntyre, as primarily consisting in a shift from practices to institutions. For Morgan the morally salient feature of the mass commodification of sport is that it involves a 'capitulation of the practice side of sport to its business side'.[40] When we com-modify sport, we corrode the goods and ends pursued in it as a practice.

Morgan outlines three reasons why this capitulation of sporting practice to business should be regarded as corrupting. First, it *distracts* sporting participants from realising the goods internal to the practice. External goods have a tendency to dominate internal goods, if for no other reasons than they are the goods that institutions ordain and endorse. So the idea is that once one pursues external goods (such as money and status) in sport, these displace the internal goods (and this has some considerable plausibility). Second, it *degrades* the internal goods by subordinating them to external ones. The point is that replacing internal goods with external ones does not provide an adequate substitute. The external goods endorsed by institutions cannot 'adequately reflect the value of the internal goods they displace'.[41] Here Morgan approvingly cites Robert Nozick who suggests that goods such as money are not a 'vehicle for nuanced expression'.[42] (Although one imagines this is one of the few elements of Nozick's rather right-wing philosophy which Morgan endorses). Third, the domination of practices by institutions ultimately undermines the kinds of preferences and attitudes required if the practices are to *sustain themselves* and flourish. It harms practices of sport by corroding the basis of their own reproduction. Morgan's concern clearly is with the maintenance of the goods of sporting practices. But with the commodification of sport we find people coming to regard sport as 'synonymous with the external ends it subserves'.[43]

There is much that is valuable in this approach. Nonetheless there are still some genuine problems. The first concerns the initial distinction between practices and institutions. Once we move from the requisite level of abstraction to everyday human institutions and practices, we find that it is not so easy to distinguish institutions from practices. Are there pure practices and institutions in everyday life, if we define them as MacIntyre does?[44] Is modern elite sport, for instance, a practice or an institution? Whilst it still maintains a practice side where internal goods are pursued, it is also clearly institutional in MacIntyre's sense. Moreover, if, as we suggested earlier in the chapter, there has long been money in sport, to what extent can sport be genuinely called a practice, in MacIntyre's sense of the term?

Second, there are questions about whether this approach allows us to isolate the morally salient features of markets and commodification. A market is understood on this account as an institution which is focused on external goods. In this regard, market institutions are not different from the institutions of the old state socialist societies, such as the Soviet Union. But this is odd since surely the kinds of moral concerns that emerge in a market context are very different from those that arise under socialism. The model does not really allow us to distinguish between phenomena that are entirely distinct. It seems that MacIntyre's framework is too broad to capture the fine moral detail that we require of an adequate commodification critique.

Finally, not all of the concerns we have with the commodification of sport can be understood as violations of an internal good. Later in this book we shall consider various undesirable distributive consequences (such as the exclusion of traditional fans from access to sporting events) to which commodification gives rise. But can such concerns *really* be understood as examples of internal goods being displaced? We suggest not, for one would need to build an awful lot into the idea of a practice and an internal good to demonstrate that excluding traditional fans is a violation of the internal goods of sport. It is not that the internal meanings have been violated but that traditional fans are excluded from a good to which they once had access.

Commodification and moral pathologies: our preferred approach

Having provided a brief survey of some of the major moral frameworks for assessing what might be wrong with transforming goods into commodities, it is now time to provide an outline of the commodification critique to be developed in the remainder of this book. This critique will be non-abolitionist since, as we noted in the section on Marxism, there are good reasons for wanting to maintain markets. This is true in sport just as it is in other areas of social life. At the same time – as should be clear from the introductory chapter – we believe that hyper-commodification in many cases provides genuine grounds for moral concern. Our task then it to provide a theoretical mechanism for distinguishing legitimate from illegitimate forms of commodification.

In developing such an account we do not attempt – as say a Kantian might – to isolate a *single* way in which commodification can go wrong, but instead isolate a series of *distinct* 'moral pathologies'. The central idea here is that the market goes wrong in ways that cannot be reduced to an individual moral concern. Accordingly, we identify four such pathologies herein, which concern: (1) the illegitimate transformation of the structure of our motives by the market, (2) the corrosion of our attitudes towards the intrinsically valuable aspects of sport, (3) distributive injustice and (4) practical ways in which the market might undermine the long-term health of sport. (We will devote a separate chapter to each of these pathologies.) In each case the pathology under review involves some injury, violation or damage to an important value that we believe supervenes on sport as it is currently played. These are values we suggest that survive even in the midst of the hyper-commodification of sport, but which are nonetheless threatened by it.[45]

In pursuing this line of thought it is important to note that we do not claim that commodification is the only route to such undesirable states of affairs. To take an example of one of our pathologies which involves the Kantian concern with objectification, there are other social forces that might well lead us to regard sport as a mere means. Thus, for example, in a state socialist society, sport might be seen as a mere means to the glorification of the homeland. So other social forms may give rise to these or similar pathologies. Our position is simply that insofar as markets give rise to these pathologies then they are morally pernicious.

At this point it is important to emphasise that talk of pathologies does not commit us to the view that commodification is always, and in every way, morally pernicious. It is not true that commodification critique of this kind entails rejection of the market as some critics have suggested. For instance, Robert L. Simon in his recent book *Fair Play* asks whether 'commercialisation' is defensible.[46] He notes that some critics of the commercialisation of sport adopt what he calls a 'corruption thesis'. The corruption thesis, as Simon explains it, states that the commercialisation of sport, the transformation of elite sport into a product that can be bought and sold, corrupts sport. In response to this, and in defence of the market, he argues that commercialisation needs to be judged against the benefits it produces, such as the way that it has made athletic contests available to people all over the world.[47] Since these benefits are many, the corruption thesis must be false.

However, this line of reasoning does not touch our commodity critique. The fact that commodification often gives rise to benefits does not provide evidence against our account. Simon fails to distinguish between the question of whether all things considered the market should be retained and the question of whether the market ever gives rise to undesirable outcomes. That we accept the necessity and desirability of markets in sport, does not rule out the possibility that the market is often morally pernicious and that we might wish to avoid some elements of it. We do not argue that the market is corrupting of important values *simpliciter* but rather it is corrupting of important values, for instance, when it leads us to regard sport as a mere means to the realisation of commercial gain. If a corruption thesis is committed to the view that commercialisation always gives rise to bad outcomes and only gives rise to bad outcomes, then our commodity critique is clearly not a corruption thesis.

As well as developing a moral critique of commodification, we also provide some policy prescriptions. In line with our discussion thus far we advocate a variety of *distinct* responses to the presence of market pathologies. In some cases a pathology will merely warrant moral censure. In more serious cases it will warrant either regulation or the blocking of exchanges in the goods in question. Unlike

Anderson and Walzer we do not believe that it is enough simply to separate some goods from the market and this is as true in the world of sport as it is in other spheres of life. In chapter 7 we will spend some time exploring detailed policy responses to our various pathologies.

Let us turn now to the first of our pathologies which concerns undesirable transformations of the *motives* of sportspeople through the influence of money.

3   Financial motives, venality and the ideals of sport

Introduction

The first pathology of commodification we explore concerns the quality and nature of the motives of those professional athletes and administrators involved in commercial sport. Various ideals, such as the pursuit of individual excellence, sportsmanship and community-mindedness are no small part of what it is that makes sport morally valuable. Yet while these values survive in professional sport, they are threatened by the tendency within commercial society towards what eighteenth century moralists called 'venality'.[1] In the previous chapter we defined venality as the dominance of financial considerations in one's all-things-considered judgments. In sport this occurs when both players and administrators making decisions predominantly with respect to the 'bottom line'. The danger with such venality is that the ideals of individual excellence and sportsmanship will be evacuated as financial considerations become increasingly dominant.

What is at issue then is the *motivational structure* of those directly involved in sport and, more specifically, how commodification might affect their aims and attitudes towards sport. The person or organisation motivated solely (or predominantly) by financial considerations excludes significant values that can and should be realised in sport. In so far as commodification leads to such venality, then it is morally pernicious.

We begin our discussion with a closer analysis of some of the important performative ideals of sport.

Intrinsic value and the autotelic goods of sport

The suggestion then is that commodification can detrimentally affect the motivational structure of those participating directly in sport. But before considering how it might do so we need to say something about the nature and good-making features of the motivational structures we wish to defend against commodification. Why should we think that a 'venal' transformation of the goals and aims of those playing sport is ethically undesirable? What kind of motivational structures is it that we wish to defend and why might they be of value?

Our central concern here – as the reader will recall – is with the pursuit of sport for its own sake. This is the motivational structure that we wish to defend and which we suggest realises morally valuable goods when actions are performed in its name. The goods realised are of a special kind since they are realised in the performance of the activity itself, rather than being consequent upon it. We shall call such goods 'autotelic' (from the Greek meaning simply self-purpose). An absorbing activity which is enjoyed for its own sake is described in the philosophical literature as being 'autotelic' and accordingly an autotelic good is a good realised in an activity by the participant. Autotelic goods involve value that is realised in the very performance of an action.[2]

Alasdair MacIntyre provides a useful account of such goods. In *After Virtue* MacIntyre discusses the case of a parent who pays his child fifty cents worth of 'candy' to play chess (with another fifty cents worth if the child wins). Eventually, through habituation, the child comes to value the game in itself; the child comes to value the opportunities chess provides for the 'achievement of a certain highly particular kind of analytic skill, strategic imagination and competitive intensity'.[3] In this case money is a conduit to pursuing the game as an end in itself. Whilst the child's initial motivation is pecuniary, given familiarity with the game's intricacies, the child learns to appreciate the activity as an end-in-itself. Autotelic goods then are those goods realised when an agent performs an action for the sake of that action not for anything consequent upon it, though that of course does not rule out the idea that the action might also give rise (and often will) to other goods beyond the activity in itself.

The relevance of this to sport should be clear; indeed sport and games are often used to explain the notion. One realises autotelic or participatory goods in sport when the sporting activity is an end itself. Here value arises through participation in the activity itself, not through whatever other goods, such as fame, money or social status, might come the way of the sportsperson. Autotelic goods are realised in sport when the agent pursues sport-for-sport's sake; that is when the motives of those playing sport are realised by the very performance of it rather than through outcomes consequent upon it. To value sport for the autotelic goods one might realise is to value sport for reasons which are intrinsic to it. To value it for other reasons, such as money or status, is to value it for reasons that are extrinsic.[4] The pursuit of autotelic goods is one way of regarding sport as intrinsically valuable.

This is an idea expressed, in different ways, by a number of philosophers of sport using different theoretical frameworks or idioms. Steve Overman speaks of the 'ludic spirit' of play and (to confuse matters) of the 'intrinsic spirit of competitive play'.[5] He suggests that pure play, which he takes to be an expression of the proper spirit of sport, is its own end, an activity purposeless outside of itself. Here he follows the philosopher Michael Novak who suggests, in a very Kantian explication of the idea, that to participate in play is to dwell in the 'kingdom of ends'.[6] All of these are merely so many ways of making the point that the good is realised in participation in sport rather than through any consequences of such participation. (Although it should also be noted that Overman and Novak have very different political orientations.)

It is important at this point to distinguish the autotelic from *internal goods* which rather than being internal to a single activity are internal to a social or cultural practice. In the philosophy of sport in particular, there has been considerable discussion of the relationship of the goods of sport to the social practices out of which they arise. Writers such as William Morgan have argued that the goods of sport are 'internal' to the practice of sport in that understanding the nature of their goodness requires an understanding of the practice itself.[7] Morgan claims that it is the practice-specific character of these goods that warrants their being labelled 'internal'. This practice-specific nature has two elements. First, they can only be realised through engagement in the practice. Second, only those with experience of the practice are in a position to assess these goods; as Steenbergen and Tamboer note those who lack this experience of participating in the practice '... are not competent to judge the internal goods of the practice in question.'[8] These goods are to be contrasted with 'external' goods which are those goods which are not 'inextricably bound up with engagement in a particular practice'.[9] External goods are merely instrumentally related to any practice, for there will always be other ways of achieving such goods. Examples of external goods that are commonly given are money, power and status. (There does seem to be a conflation here between the fact that the goods are external to the activity and external to the practice.)

As we noted in the previous chapter, this line of thought regarding internal and external goods is derived from the work of Alasdair MacIntyre who described internal goods as goods which cannot be achieved other than through engagement with the practice and which can only be recognised and specified as the goods that they are by those involved in the practice.

Our point is much simpler than that explored by Morgan and MacIntyre and simply involves the claim that certain goods (the 'autotelic') are realised in the *very act* of playing sport, rather than the stronger claim that the meaning and value of the goods realised in sport can only be determined and understood within the practice by practitioners. It is not that we wish to deny that there might be goods of this kind or that we do not believe that the goods realised within sport might be internal in this sense. Rather it is that for our purposes debates over the extent to which assessment of the good of a practice might be external to that practice are an unnecessary diversion. One can hold that goods are realised in the very act of playing sport, regardless of whether one believes that sporting goods only acquire their meaning within the practice of sport.

Whilst we are in the business of clarification, we should also distinguish the idea of autotelic goods from another related notion, namely the *internal logic of games*. This term – which will be of some import in later chapters – refers to the idea that games have a developmental logic of their own and which external considerations might well disturb. This idea of a distinctive way of changing that reflects internal history of the sport is particularly clear with respect to rule changes. Such changes are often a response to internal developments in the game. So for instance, in response to concerns in cricket that uncovered pitches were allowing results to be overly determined by the weather – and hence being more a function of luck than skill – the relevant authorities decided to cover the pitches overnight and whenever it rained. This reflects views (which are of course subject to change) about the proper goals of the sport, what skills should be being tested and how well the rules reflect those goals and skills. Similarly in soccer, the practice of simulating a serious foul or injury became so common that the game's authorities were eventually compelled to act by penalising players whom referees considered to be guilty of such intended deception. Given certain socio-historical views about what sporting skills and virtues are to be exemplified in the game, we can see how it would naturally follow (as a matter of 'logic' as it were) that certain changes to the rules might be introduced. We can contrast these internally generated changes with those which come from considerations outside of the game itself. For instance, if a socialist sport authority changed the rules of a game so that no one came last, and the pressures for change did not come from the practitioners themselves, then this would presumably be an example of an external consideration. Equally when sports-rules are changed to make them more entertaining for television audiences, this again is an example of changes which are not determined by the game's internal logic.[10]

The next question we need to consider concerns the *content* of our favoured motivational structure. Thus far we have been speaking in rather broad terms of the idea of sport-for-sport's sake. It is possible (and for the purposes of explication desirable) to be more specific about the content of the desirable motivational structure; that is, we can say more about some of the aims or goals that might animate agents pursuing sport-for-sport's sake. There are four aims that spring readily to mind here (in no particular order): (i) competing at one's best against other similarly skilled athletes (ii) the development of skills (iii) exhibiting the virtues of sportsmanship and fair play and (iv) community and national representation. We are not suggesting, in a romantic vein, that these are the reasons all athletes do in fact compete, but rather that these are aims that we suppose animate some athletes and when they are so animated they pursue sport for its own sake. Moreover, as we shall argue later, sport is devalued when it is not so pursued. Let us say a little about each of these in turn.

First, athletes might take satisfaction in competing to the best of their abilities against relevantly skilled competitors. For instance, an Olympic runner might take pride in having competed to the best of her ability. Here it is partaking in the competition that matters. Even when they do not win or take a prize, athletes often feel some sense of achievement in having competed against their peers and having 'done their best'.

Second, athletes might value sport for the opportunities it provides to develop their skills. Here one might, in the spirit of Aristotle, view the realisation of one's sporting potential as an end in itself. Thus a cricketer might aim to increase the speed and direction of his bowling and find satisfaction in the realisation of such goals. An archer might enjoy learning to shoot more accurately. A runner might feel satisfaction in completing a marathon, after months of training for the event. In all of these cases, the athletes in question view the development of skills as an end in itself.

A third autotelic aim that one might find among athletes – though perhaps this is a thing of the past in elite sport – is to compete according to the norms of sportsmanship and fair play.[11] (Here the excellence aimed at is more specifically moral than the previous two.) An athlete might find value in sport through their capacity to compete fairly, even under trying circumstances. She might take pride in the fact that despite the pressure of competition – and in particular the pressures to succeed – she did not succumb to the temptation to engage in unfair or 'unsporting' behaviour or take unfair advantage of her competitors. Interestingly, this is a virtue that might only be evident to others counter-factually – we might only notice that an athlete is playing according to an ideal of fair play when and if she encounters a circumstance in which her moral fibre is tested. Despite the fact that it might rarely or never be evident to observers, it is nonetheless an ideal that can be motivating for the sportsperson involved. For the athlete so motivated, pursuit of sport in this way can be an end in itself.

A final motivation that one commonly finds amongst sportspersons who pursue sport-for-sport's sake is representation of one's community, be it at a club, regional or national level. This is the idea of pride in one's jersey that is spoken of by many sportspersons. The thought is that one plays amongst other things because one is proud to represent the relevant community. When the test cricketer Michael Slater had the number 361 tattooed to his ankle because he was the 361st cricketer to represent Australia he was making it clear that he took great pride in playing for his country. This is just one example of public display (such as kissing the badge or wrapping oneself in the flag) in which athletes aim to demonstrate that they are motivated (at least in part) by pride in representing one's club or country. Interestingly, such displays will often draw criticism from fans if they feel that the display of attachment is insincere.

If any of these aims are understood as ends in themselves then they are in our terms, 'autotelic' and their pursuit realises what we call autotelic goods. To be sure, this list of autotelic goods is not exhaustive of the autotelic – and indeed it is not intended as such – for there are other possible candidates which will presumably occur to the reader. But our discussion is illustrative of a more general point regarding the pursuit of sport-for-sport's sake; there are a number of motives that might animate those who play sport for its own sake. It is also important here to recognise the possibility of mixed motives when one pursues sport for its own sake. Pursuit of any one of these aims need not preclude the simultaneous pursuit of other goals, such as the pursuit of money. Too often in ethical discussions of motives it is assumed that animation by a specific motive means that no other motives are present in an agent's motivational set. But more than cursory examination of one's own reasons for action soon reveals that this is false. One might go to the soccer to support one's club, meet friends and relax after a week of hard work. The mere fact that one can demonstrate the presence of one of these motives does not mean that one is not animated by the other motives. This point regarding the non-singularity of motives will be important when we explore the relationship between these internal goods and commodification.

The final point we need to consider concerns the sense in which we regard autotelic goods of sport as being valuable. Our suggestion is that they are *intrinsically valuable*, although this is a term which we need to approach with some caution for it has a number of closely related but distinct meanings. When we use the term we mean to employ it as a synonym for non-instrumental value. *Intrinsic value* we thus define as value for itself: a thing is intrinsically valuable when it is valuable for itself alone and not for some other goal consequent upon it. Accordingly, *extrinsic value* is value for something else.

However, there are, as we suggested above, other common uses of the term. John O'Neill, in 'The Varieties of Intrinsic Value', distinguishes three central meanings, the first of which is the one listed above.[12] What are the other two? In the first place, 'intrinsic value' is sometimes used to refer to the value an object has in virtue of its intrinsic properties.[13] Thus we might talk of the value that a diamond ring has in virtue of the intrinsic property of hardness that comes with being a diamond. Its hardness is thus an 'intrinsic value'. On other occasions the term is used as a synonym for objective value in the sense of value that an object possesses independently of the valuations of valuers. However, neither of these senses is what we intend by the term. By 'intrinsically valuable' we mean simply something which is non-instrumental or, to cast it in a Kantian manner, which is 'an end in itself'. Accordingly, an intrinsically valuable good will be a good that is valuable in itself. Many of the goods that emerge in and through sport are intrinsically valuable in our sense. They are good in themselves rather than for other ends.

Our suggestion is that the autotelic goods of sport are intrinsically valuable. As we shall argue later, they are not the only intrinsically valuable goods to be found in sporting activity but they are one important source of intrinsic value in sport. When sportspeople engage in sport in this way, then we might say that the activity itself is intrinsically valuable.

Our concern now is with the moral status of this motivational structure rather than with attitudinal descriptions. What we are saying – and at great risk of becoming prolix – is that pursuing sport-for-sport's sake (i.e. regarding sport as intrinsically valuable) realises goods that are intrinsically valuable. It realises goods that are ends in themselves and which are therefore constitutive of human flourishing. Interestingly, some theorists in the philosophy of sport have tied the notion of 'regarding as intrinsically valuable' to that of internal goods, as described above. Steenbergen and Tamboer argue that an activity is valued intrinsically if motives are given which flow from the 'internal goods associated with that activity', that is if the motives are not derived from goals outside of the activity itself. This sounds as if it is merely another way of saying that it is intrinsically valued if our aims in sport are autotelic. Perhaps we might just talk of internal goods. However, there is one important difference; in our account we do not tie the goods realised in an activity itself to more radical claims about how such goods gain their meaning through their embeddedness in social and cultural practices.[14] Recall that internal goods are defined as internal to a cultural or social practice not a single activity. If by internal goods one simply means those goods realised within an activity itself, then we have no quarrel with the definition. However, if one ties it to MacIntyre-style claims about internal goods then it seems that the definition buys unnecessarily into contentious metaphysical claims about the very nature of human goods. For these reasons we shall persist with the use of the term 'autotelic'.

Let us leave such definitional questions to one side and turn our attention to the ways in which processes of commodification might undermine the autotelic goods of sport.

Financial values, commodification and venality

Our claim is that via the rise of a venal social context, commodification threatens the production of the autotelic or participatory goods of sport. This immediately raises two questions. First, what is the connection between commodification and venality? Second, how might such venality threaten the autotelic goods?

In answering these questions the first point to make is that commodification involves amongst other things a transformation of the incentive structures associated with the production of a good. By commodifying something, we incorporate that good into a market structure and in so doing change the incentives of the agents who produce it. In a market agents undertake their activities for financial reward. They are animated (perhaps amongst other things) by the profit motive. By commodifying sport we ensure that those associated with its 'production' have as at least one of their goals the pursuit of profit. They come to engage in sport for commercial benefit. And this has a number of morally salient consequences which we shall consider shortly.[15]

In saying this we do not wish to give the impression that this transformation of our incentive structures means that all other motives for undertaking an activity are *necessarily* eliminated once money enters the picture. To commodify sport is not thereby to evacuate all non-commercial reasons necessarily. Indeed there is an unfortunate tendency when speaking of money and the profit motive to make two closely related mistakes. The first is the view that to be animated by commercial self-interest is to exclude all other incentives. The second is the view that for non-commercial incentives to provide a reason for one to act requires that one possess not the slightest hint of commercial self-interest. These lines of thought are mistaken for they exclude the possibility of *mixed motives*. It is possible for one to be motivated both by commercial self-interest and other considerations.[16] Thus consider the motivational set of a well-meaning general practitioner. She might well do what she does to receive financial rewards (and she is paid well for her efforts) but she also wishes to benefit the wider community through the exercise of her medical skill. Antony Flew makes a similar point in his article 'The Profit Motive' when he dismisses the identification of self-interest and selfishness:

> This [identification] is wrong. For, although selfish actions are perhaps always interested, only some interested actions are selfish. To say that a piece of conduct was selfish is to say more than it was interested, if it was. The point is selfishness is always and necessarily out of order. Interestedness is not, and scarcely could be.[17]

He then goes on to say that when his daughters eagerly eat their dinners they are pursuing their own interests, for he thinks that 'it would be monstrous to denounce them as selfish hussies, simply on that account'.[18] The pursuit of one's interests is not, on its own, sufficient to label one selfish. What is missing in any such inference is an understanding of the possibility of our motives being mixed.

The second mistake involves the idea that the slightest hint of commercial self-interest evacuates other non-commercial goals. According to this line of thought the pursuit of non-commercial goals, such as the pursuit of excellence can only appropriately be attributed to another *if, and only if*, their action or decision is untainted by self-regarding concern(s). One is reminded here of the debate about the relationship between the non-commercial goal of altruism and self-interest. In the eighteenth century Bishop Butler wrote that ' ... there is generally thought to be some peculiar kind of contrariety between self-love and the love of our neighbour, between the pursuit of public and of private good; insomuch that when you are recommending one of these, you are supposed to be speaking against the other'.[19] Butler acknowledges that love of oneself and love of one's neighbour are distinct *principles*, but points out that does not make them exclusive of one another. As he says, disregard of the interests of others is no part of the *idea* of self-love, just as disregard of self-interest is no part of the *idea* of benevolence or altruism. Self-love is not exclusive of 'all regards to the good of others', and 'neither on the other hand does benevolence . . . exclude self-love'.[20] Having considered self-love and benevolence, Butler proceeds to explore the relationship between the pursuit of private interest and the pursuit of public good, arguing again that the two need not diverge. His point is not the modern claim that selfishness has good public consequences, but that self-interest, not being at odds with benevolence, means that pursuing self-interest need also not be at odds with the public interest.

Butler's discussion fits neatly (*mutatis mutandis*) into debates about the relationship between the non-commercial internal goods of sport and self-interested financial aims. Like Butler we suggest there is no necessary conflict between commercial self-interest and ideals such as the pursuit of excellent, although, as a matter of fact, the two do often diverge.

We can see the relevance for sport. First, it is clear that players have a right to pursue self-interest without being labelled 'shameless hussies' as it were. In the mid-1970s, the world of cricket was thrown into turmoil when the Australian media mogul, Kerry Packer, signed many top players to establish a 'rebel' international tournament (World Series Cricket). While the business motives of Packer were transparent, many cricket commentators attacked the players for allegedly betraying the game for money. However, in defence, the players justifiably argued that their earnings from existing cricket authorities were insecure and highly seasonal.[21] As Mr Justice Slade noted in the High Court in London in 1977 in the Packer World Series Cricket case:

> A professional cricketer needs to make his living as much as any other professional man. It is straining the concept of loyalty too far for the authorities to

expect him to enter into a self-denying ordinance not to play cricket for a private promoter during the winter months merely because the matches promoted could detract from the future profits of the authorities, who were not themselves willing or in a position to offer him employment over the winter or guarantee him employment in the future.[22]

Accordingly he found in favour of the players.

Second, there is no reason to think that self-interest and the goals of sport are necessarily at odds. During the period of Steve Waugh's captaincy of the Australian cricket team, his players were rewarded handsomely. Indeed they made more money than one could ever hope to make in an ordinary salaried job. But during that period the players were also motivated by the desire to become the best cricket team in the world. They worked on their individual skills and teamwork in the hope of becoming clearly the dominant team in the world. And this they nearly achieved (however their failure to win in India prevented them from achieving this goal). Similarly, the world's leading golfers, such as Tiger Woods, VJ Singh, Annika Sorenstam and Michelle Wie, must practice intensely to maintain levels of professional excellence. Certainly they are richly rewarded for their efforts, but much of their competitive motivation derives not simply from the desire to make money but the personal goals of testing their potential and achieving the greatest possible success in the world's major tournaments.[23]

What then are the grounds of criticism of financial motives in sport? A radical critique would have it that the *mere presence* of financial motives evacuates the kinds of internal goods we discussed above. Here venality is a necessary consequence of sport's incorporation into commercial society. But if mixed motives are possible – and financial motives can co-exist with our valued internal goods – then this line of criticism fails.

A more moderate critique – and one which is endorsed here – focuses on the dominance of financial motives in one's motivational set.[24] The moral vice here is the predominance of financial considerations. This is the vice of venality and it is a vice to which activities performed within commercial society are all too prone. It is not that athletes should not be financially motivated but that they should not allow such commercial considerations to be the sole or predominant aims when they engage in sporting activity. This explains a large part of, say for instance, the moral viciousness of crooked promoters of sporting events.

This more moderate critique allows for the possibility of elite athletes possessing mixed motives (and for the good realised by such activity to be mixed as well).[25] At the same time it is critical of cases where, as a matter of fact, commercial considerations are so dominant that the internal goods of sport no longer feature in the aims and attitudes of athletes. Thus we wish to endorse the conditional moral claim that whenever commodification leads to venality it is morally pernicious. In so far as the commodification of sport leads to the elimination of such admirable goals as the pursuit of excellence then it is morally pernicious.

A second feature of this more moderate critique is the *causal claim* that there is a tendency within commercial society towards venality. While there is no necessary connection between commodification and venality there are pressures for it to become so.

What reason might there be to believe that commodification will give rise to such venality? The first concerns what we might think of as the gravitational pull of money first noticed by the ancient Greeks. In a passage in *The Laws* Plato writes:

> There are not many of us who remain sober when we have the opportunity to grow wealthy, or prefer measure to abundance. The great multitude of men are of a completely contrary temper – what they desire they desire out of all measure – when they have the option of making a reasonable one they prefer to make an exorbitant one.[26]

Plato does not suggest it is impossible to 'remain sober', that money necessarily corrupts, it simply has an over-whelming tendency to do so. For Plato money is 'ethically hazardous', and clearly he thinks the hazards are extremely high. Aristotle thought that because the pursuit of money was an activity without a *telos* or 'end goal,' one could never satisfactorily complete it. Unlike many other goal-oriented activities, such as the successful building of a sea-worthy boat, it has no 'satisfaction conditions' and endlessly iterates. This endless iteration means that there is a tendency towards the obsessive pursuit of wealth.

For the ancient Greeks the moral corrosion involved greed, the desire to go beyond the satisfaction of need, not the elimination of other goals, such as our internal goals of sport. But the gravitational pull here is similar. When money is present, the same psychological forces that lead one to avarice also place pressure on one's non-financial motivations.[27] Thus while it is entirely possible (and often is the case) for the profit motive to be one motive amongst others in a person's motivational set, there is a clear and present danger of the profit motive becoming either the sole or overwhelmingly predominant element in one's reasoning. Although commodification need not lead to venality, the incorporation of sport into a commercial world means that it is difficult for the aims and goals of sports-people not to be affected. Hansie Cronje, the former South African cricket captain who took money for match-fixing from Indian bookmakers, might provide us with a particularly telling case in point. Cronje, who at one press conference claimed it was the Devil who led him down the path of corruption, became obsessed with money, despite the fact that he was, by ordinary standards, handsomely recompensed.[28] Once exposed he admitted that his love of money affected his love of cricket. At one point he frankly conceded, 'I had a great passion for the game, my team-mates and my country. But the problem is the unfortunate love I have for money. I do like money.'[29] We should not think of the case of Cronje as the exception which proves the rule, for as the inquiries into match-fixing in international cricket at the time demonstrated, corruption was widespread.[30]

Cronje seems to have fallen victim to venality. For the venal agent the pursuit of money is either the only or the dominant motive in his or her motivational set and, accordingly, other goals are subordinated to the desire for financial reward. In pursuit of money it seems that Cronje was willing to sacrifice the sporting standing of his national cricket team and to encourage the players under his charge deliberately to play poorly.

Perhaps the most notorious incident involved Cronje's role, as captain of South Africa, in fixing a Test match against England in February 2000. On this occasion, a match that would normally be played over a period of up to five days was actually decided in a single day. On the scheduled final day of play, after several days of rain, both Cronje and England captain Nasser Hussain were faced with a match that seemed to be petering out into a deadly boring draw. In an act of apparent sportsmanship and innovative captaincy, before play commenced, Cronje offered to set England a victory target that would provide the game with an entertaining climax. While many commentators at the time praised Cronje's spectator-friendly suggestion, no one guessed at the venal motives behind his actions. Perhaps this is a case where Mandeville's dictum that 'private vice gives rise to public benefit' rings true, since the final day's play was indeed an exciting experience for spectators. However, in truth, Cronje had given England more than a fair chance to win the game, an objective which they duly met. When Cronje's collusion with bookmakers was subsequently exposed, most commentators bemoaned the fact that their enjoyment of the game had been based on a deception; that they had in fact been duped.

The philosophical point then is that *commodification is pathological* if incorporation into the commercial world of the market leads athletes and sports administrators to regard the pursuit of wealth as their primary aim, thereby evacuating or subverting the internal goals mentioned above. Although commodification need not necessarily lead to venality, there is in the commercial world a pressure towards such venality that generates moral concern about the incorporation of sport into the market. As Lincoln Allison notes what we find with the rise of commercialism is a blurring of non-commercial and commercial motives and a weakening of the capacity of ideals of sport to provide an independent incentive for action.[31]

Disturbingly, there is evidence that the aims of those running sport are increasingly dominated by commercial ends. For instance, the business 'chief executives' who now run sporting clubs, governing bodies and tournaments, usually prioritise the financial rather than the on-field performances of their institutions. In some circumstances, gaining wealth can have a severely corrupting effect upon sport. During the Indian betting scandal surrounding cricket in the late 1990s, the former India pace-bowler Manoj Prabhakar noted: 'Commercialisation of cricket has changed its face – it's no longer just a game; it's a game where money is the main motivator. Sponsors and bookies have started exerting pressure and games are now increasingly being fixed.'[32] If Prabhaker is right, then it would seem that the commercialisation of cricket has had morally undesirable consequences.

There is more at stake in the dominance of money than just the ideals of sport, for the rising venality of commercial sport can affect the general moral dispositions of sportspeople. Think of the cricket 'rebels' who toured South Africa during the latter stages of the Apartheid era in contravention of the Gleneagles Agreement.[33] The angry crowds who greeted the rebels on their return from South Africa were not protesting against the violation of fundamental norms of sport, but rather because the rebels' love of money was such that they were willing to deal with a murderous regime despite sporting boycotts. The anger here was directed at the violation of what we might think of as society-wide moral norms, rather than those specific to sport.

We have thus far considered the connection between commodification and venality. Let us now turn to a discussion of how venality might undermine the autotelic or participatory goods of sport. How does commodification threaten the pursuit of sport-for-sport's sake? How might it threaten the autotelic goods of sport?

One obvious line of response is to say that it does so *by definition*. To pursue sport-for-sport's sake is necessarily not to pursue money and *vice versa*. If one is pursuing money, then how could one be pursuing sport for its own sake? Here the two are thought to be mutually exclusive, so commodification since it involves the transformation of our motivational structures threatens the autotelic goods necessarily. Given that we assume, for whatever reason, that these ideals are morally valuable – or more strongly at the very heart of what is valuable about sport – then clearly we can see why commodification stands condemned as morally vicious. The very moment that one commodifies, and participants come to be animated by the pursuit of profit, then these valuable ideals are evacuated.

The moral harm of commodification with respect to the autotelic ideals of sport then might be understood as violating the essential meanings of sport. There are ideals appropriate to the conduct of sport and since the profit motive is incompatible with those ideals then commodification of sport is morally vicious, and is so necessarily. Unsurprisingly, especially given the preceding discussion of the profit motive, we are not impressed with this definitional approach to the problem. Once one admits the possibility of mixed motives in this area then it looks as if simply pursuing wealth is not a guarantee that our autotelic goods will be evacuated.

To be sure, when commodification leads to venality then clearly our ideals will not be present. If the pursuit of money is the sole or dominant motive in one's motivational set then as a matter of definition one is not motivated in any significant sense by these ideals. But the relationship between commodification and venality is not one of entailment; commodification does not necessarily lead to venality.

The reasons for rejecting the idea of mutual exclusivity here become vivid if and when we undertake a more fine-grained analysis and consider the incompatibility between particular ideals (such as the mutual pursuit of excellence) and the profit motive. If we consider the claim that one cannot at the same time be engaged in the pursuit of excellence in competition with others and also pursue wealth, the mutual exclusivity is not at all obvious. It seems entirely possible for sportspeople to be animated by both motives and not at all a logical impossibility. And one need not look too far for sportspersons who do so; one need only think of the participation by many in charity matches to find living examples. It would seem that pursuit of the profit motive and our ideals are compossible.

The definitional line of critique then is too strong. Given that it is venality we regard as morally vicious, what is the connection of commodification to the evacuation of our autotelic ideals? Another approach – and the one we wish to endorse here – is to talk of the corrosion or displacement of the ideals of sport with the advent of the profit motive. Pursuit of the profit motive by sportspeople does not evacuate the autotelic ideals as a matter of logic, but rather there is an empirical tendency for it to do so. The relationship between commodification and the evacuation of these ideals is *causal* rather than *logical*.

Our claim, accordingly, is that the profit motive gradually pushes out ideals such as the mutual pursuit of excellence or representation of a specific civic location. When one commercialises sport and athletes compete for financial rewards then there is a tendency for the autotelic ideals to gradually disappear. This is not to say that the profit motive cannot co-exist alongside our ideals nor that there will not be any athletes for whom the ideals are still significant motivating factors. In this we are simply following a significant body of psychological literature, starting with Lepper and Greene's famous study in the 1970s, that explored the way that financial rewards undermine intrinsic reasons for pursuing an act.[34] Lepper and Greene examined the effects of financial rewards on children's motivation to play. They found that when children were paid to play games they had once undertaken spontaneously, over a reasonable period of time those children were no longer motivated to do so if they were not paid.[35] Subsequent studies have explored in great detail the ways in which rewards can undermine the pursuit of activities for their own sake. The point is that pecuniary incentives are 'imperialistic' and often come to dominate other motivations once they are in place in an agent's motivational set. We suggest that the same holds for the autotelic goods of sport.

Commodification does then threaten the ideals of sport-for-sport's sake and the threat is morally significant. The pursuit of sport for its own sake is part of what makes sport an occasion for the realisation of value. It is not that there is some essential meaning or structure of sport that is sacrosanct, but that sport pursued in this way has a role to play in human flourishing. If commodification crowds out the ideals of sport for its own sake and the pursuit of such ideals is part of a flourishing human life, then commodification can be said to be pathological in such circumstances. Commodification is in this way ethically hazardous.

In response, it might be argued that all of this could also be captured with the framework of internal goods and practices outlined by Morgan in his discussion of corruption and distortion in *Leftist Theories of Sport*. Whilst there will often be more than one true description of any phenomenon, one description might well have more explanatory power. What advantages are there in our approach?

At the heart of Morgan's commodification critique is Alasdair MacIntyre's distinction between practices and institutions. As the reader will recall from our earlier discussion, 'practices' are defined in terms of the internal goods that they realise (such as our autotelic ideals), whilst 'institutions' are defined in terms of external goods (such as money, power and status). Pursuing sport for its own sake is an internal good and is thus part of a practice whilst playing for money is not an internal good and thus to play for money is to partake in an institutional activity rather than a practice. Commodification is understood, as it was for MacIntyre, as primarily consisting in a shift from practices to institutions.

Notice here that we are not simply talking about the ideals of sport-for-sport's sake, but all of the non-instrumental good-making features of sport. The term 'internal goods' is intended to capture all of the goods that are intrinsic to the practice. The concerns we have expressed regarding the loss of the ideals of sport-for-sport's sake are thus subsumed within a more general critique of the loss or corrosion of internal goods.

Morgan outlines three reasons why this capitulation of sporting practice to business should be regarded as corrupting. First, it *distracts* sporting participants from realising the goods internal to the practice. Second, it *degrades* the internal goods by subordinating them to external ones. Third, the domination of practices by institutions ultimately undermines the kinds of preferences and attitudes required if the practices are to *sustain themselves* and flourish.

However, whilst there is much insight in this approach, there are good reasons for preferring our commodification critique. First, as we noted in our discussion of MacIntyre in chapter 2, there is a genuine question as to whether the categories used here are themselves *sufficiently nuanced* to capture all of the moral issues raised by the commodification of sport. If we consider the description of the process of commodification we find that Morgan's critique is not specific to money and the market, but is a generic critique of *all institutions*. This is in contrast with our critique which begins with the specifically morally-salient features of money and the market to determine what might be morally undesirable about some forms of commodification. This is a more perspicuous approach for the very idea that we can isolate a single account of the harm to be found in the expansion of such diverse institutions as commodity markets, state-capitalist welfare agencies and Soviet-style bureaucracies almost beggars belief. The external goods that corrupted the practice of sport in the old Soviet Union are very different from those that do so in contemporary Western capitalist nations (a point we noted in the previous chapter). And if we consider the moral harms associated with such commodification, we find that vastly different phenomena such as for instance, on the one hand, athletes playing solely for money and, on the other, administrators treating players as mere objects fall under the general rubric of actions driven by external goods. In the first case the moral vice involves no longer pursuing acts for their own sake whereas in the second it consists of failing to respect persons. Within Morgan's framework such distinctions between moral harms are lost.

Second, there is a tendency in Morgan's criticisms to adopt an unwarranted 'moral essentialist' approach to the moral value of sport. There is an essential nature to the practices and the harm of allowing the institutional side to dominate the practice side is to fail to recognise that practices are not 'essentially devices for attaining external goods'.[36] As Morgan says: 'Money and power can be said to be dominant when they are able to command a wide range of other goods to which they have no intrinsic connection, when, that is, they can be converted into other goods without regard for their intrinsic meanings'.[37] The moral focus here is on the violation of practices themselves rather than the frustration of possible human interests which might be realised. This strikes us as a mistaken way of characterising the harm of commodification. It is not that there is some meaning or ideal that is essential to sport and which we should regard as sacred and inviolable in itself. Instead it is that there are human interests which are realised through the pursuit of the ideals of sport for its own sake and these are what is of value.

It would seem to us then that our approach, which focuses on the corrosion of the ideals of sport, has more explanatory power. According to this approach, the commodification of sport is pathological when it transforms the motivational structures of sporting participants to such an extent that the profit motive becomes the sole or significantly dominant motive in the athlete's motivational set. In such circumstances the ideals of sport-for-sport's sake and the goods they realise are no longer a part of sport. This is an important way in which commodification is ethically hazardous. (In chapter 4 we shall consider the related vice associated with regarding sport merely as a means to the generation of revenue.)

Amateurism and four objections to sport-for-sport's sake

One might object that the line of reasoning above buys too heavily into what we might call 'Amateurist ideology' and in particular the ideals of the nineteenth-century aristocratic Amateurist movement associated with figures such as Baron de Coubertin and for these reasons it should be rejected.

What force might such objections have? It is true that the notion of sport-for-sport's sake (or at least sport-for-sport's sake amongst other things) was a central pillar of amateurism. We find these ideals expressed in the writings of many famous Amateurist icons such as Thomas Arnold and Baron de Coubertin as well as being explicitly endorsed by leaders of many sporting organisations, especially in the Olympic movement and English cricket.

If we take the Olympics, we find numerous examples of this ideal. For instance, the former President of the IOC Avery Brundage argued that sporting activity must be pursued solely for its own sake:

> The ancient Olympic games ... were strictly amateur ... and for many centuries, as long as they continued amateur, they grew in importance and significance ... Gradually however abuses and excesses developed. Cities tried to demonstrate their superiority ... by establishing special training camps ... by recruiting athletes from other communities, and by subsidising competitors. Sports prizes and awards and all sorts of inducements were offered and winners were even given pensions for life. What was originally fun, recreation, a diversion and a positive became a business. The Games degenerated, lost their purity and high idealism, and were finally abolished ... sport must be for sports sake.[38]

Other Olympic writers describe the Olympic garland as the 'wreath which bespeaks the symbol of genuine disinterestedness.'[39] Or consider D. Stanley Eitzen's ethical definition of amateurism:

1   The amateur derives pleasure from the contest.
2   The activity is freely chosen.
3   The process is every bit as important as the outcome.
4   The motivation to participate comes from the intrinsic rewards from the activity rather than the extrinsic rewards of money and fame.
5   Because there is a love of sport for its own sake, there is a climate of sports-personship surrounding amateur sport.[40]

In their historical sociology of rugby union, Dunning and Sheard examine the male 'public school elite' who developed amateur sport in Britain during the late nineteenth century. This privileged group developed an amateur ethos with three defining characteristics:

1   pursuit of the activity as an 'end in itself', i.e. simply for the pleasure afforded, with a corresponding downgrading of achievement, striving, training and specialisation;
2   self-restraint and, above all, the masking of enthusiasm in victory and disappointment in defeat;
3   the norm of 'fair play', i.e. the normative equalisation of game-chances between contending sides, coupled with a stress on voluntary compliance with the rules and chivalrous attitude of 'friendly rivalry' towards opponents.[41]

Again we find a clear connection between the idea of sport-for-sport's sake and amateurism.

Amateurist ideology was also a mainstay of traditional English cricket, where Amateurs played alongside Professionals. As Mike Marqusee notes for the English amateur, 'to play cricket for a living, to turn the game into a species of labour was demeaning'.[42] Accordingly, they developed a sporting ethos in which emphasis was placed on style and the muffling of competitive strife in so called 'fair play'. Central to this was the idea that commerce was antithetical to the true spirit of the game. The legendary English cricket captain, C.B. Fry, who captained the England cricket side and held the world long-jump record before the First World War, once suggested that to vulgar merchant minds, the *profanum vulgaris*, cricket is a 'cult and a philosophy entirely inexplicable'.[43]

It was within cricket that we find the even stronger claim that non-commercial ideals are an essential or constitutive element of the game itself. The idea here is that if one is not following the true ideals of the game then one is not only violating the game, but that it is in fact a different game. To play cricket is to be motivated solely by the ideals of sportsmanship and competition for its own sake. Ironically, perhaps the most famous expression of this idea that the pursuit of certain noble ideals is definitive of cricket came from a colonial rather than an

Englishman himself. The 1932–33 cricket Test matches between Australia and England became known as the 'Bodyline' series, because the visiting English side employed the highly intimidating tactic of bowling fast deliveries directly towards the batsmen's bodies. The Australian public and many English commentators were outraged by this exceptional and dangerous strategy. The Australian cricket captain Bill Woodful, is said to have declaimed bitterly following one session of play that there were two sides out on the field, but that only one of them was playing cricket. To play cricket, rather than some aberrant variant of the game is, amongst other things, to adhere to certain tacit or unwritten rules of fair play. One can presume that Woodful would not have thought cricket played specifically for profit would meet the definitional requirements for being properly regarded as cricket.

The moral content of amateurism was sufficiently explicit and present in the minds of the leaders of amateurism as to inspire a tradition of casuistical questioning that would not have been out of place amongst the more notorious Scholastic philosophers. At the International Congress of Amateurs which met in 1894, the delegates considered such questions as: 'Can a professional in one sport be an amateur in another?', 'What should be the limit on the value of medals and prizes?' 'Does betting on himself disqualify an amateur?'[44] Over time many other questions of a similar nature were raised. For instance, amateur authorities worried over whether an amateur could charge for an interview or whether he or she could be paid to appear on a television discussion. There is no doubting then that many of the founders of amateurism had high-minded ethical ideals in mind. Further it is not as if they were blind to the philosophical issues raised by their endorsement of the Amateur ideal.

If we concede the connection between the ideals of sport-for-sport's sake and the Amateurist movement, then what follows? What might be wrong with amateurism?

The sport-for-sport's sake view of amateurism has been subjected to four main lines of criticism. First, there is the claim that is it is historically inaccurate being based on idealised accounts of how sport has been conducted. Second, there is the claim that it contains (often explicitly so) various aristocratic prejudices against the lower orders. Then there is the claim that it fails to recognise the material necessity that leads many less well-off to seek remuneration in sport. Finally, there is the claim that the hazards of amateur sport are far worse than those that mere commercial sport presents when the commercial element is explicit. Let us explore these in greater detail and consider, in particular, whether they provide any grounds for repudiating critiques of commodification based on the internal goods of sport. Are those who object to commodification on the grounds of the importance of sport-for-sport's sake really just Amateurs in disguise?[45]

Perhaps the most common line of objection to amateurism is that the suggestion that sport was once played for noble ideals alone is simply historically inaccurate. Whilst those Amateurists who oppose commodification yearn for a long-gone era, their complaints are based on an entirely mistaken portrayal of sport's past, and hence they are in fact yearning for a mythical past. In the first place if we look closely at the activities of the amateurs of the golden age of amateurism, we soon find that many were not at all averse to financial reward. (Indeed it was this pre-dilection of so-called amateurs for pursuing wealth that gave rise to the *bon mot* 'shamateur'.) Consider for instance, the doyen of nineteenth-century English cricket, Dr. W.G. Grace (1848–1915). It is estimated that as an amateur he earned more than £120,000 from cricket over his 43-year career. For a tour of Australia in 1873–74 he received £1,500 plus expenses. This is to be contrasted with the rewards of the so-called professionals who received £170 plus expenses (nearly one-tenth of the amount of the amateur pursuing sport for its own sake!). Again on a subsequent tour of Australia eighteen years later he asked for, and received, £3,000 for a return visit.[46]

One might well be tempted to dismiss this since Dr. Grace was a well-known rogue – for there are stories of him refusing to leave the wicket when bowled first ball on the grounds that the crowd had come to see *him* bat – and thus not regard it as hard evidence that amateurism was rife with financial reward.[47] Or else one might, noting Grace's unprecedented popularity and influence on English cricket note like Shakespeare's Henry V after the Battle of Agincourt, that 'nice customs curtsey to kings' and that such stories should be seen as exceptions to the more general rules.[48] However, there is good evidence that such 'shamateurism' was a common element of the nineteenth-century scene. Many amateurs at the time earned a great deal of money. For instance, another famous amateur cricketer of the period, A.C. MacLaren (1871–1944) was employed by Lancashire as a cricket instructor for £450 per annum, twice what the clubs leading professionals received.[49]

Further, it might be argued that the idea these amateur ideals are essential to sport is contradicted by the history of sport since the Victorian era. Any suggestion that sport has, in the recent past, been entirely free from the taint of commercial self-interest is simply mistaken. If we were to make the amateur ideal definitive or constitutive of sport, then much of what we would ordinarily think of as prime examples of the activity would fail to pass muster. For instance, the traditional Highland games in Scotland always offered cash prizes to the victors.[50] And Association Football (i.e. soccer) legalised professionalism in 1885. Allegedly the first paid player was James Long who came from Scotland to join Sheffield Wednesday in 1876. When the Association formed the Football League in 1888, its aim was, as Wray Vamplew notes, 'specifically to promote the professional game'.[51] Rather than being antithetical to its essence, from its very beginnings such large-scale organised sport had a commercial element. One might thus think of Association Football's move to professionalism as simply legalising what was going on, via under-the-counter payments, already.

If this was true in England then commercialism in organised sport was even more pronounced in the nineteenth century in the United States. If we take base-ball as an example, we find the domination of money being warmly welcomed rather than deplored during its rapid expansion in the 1870s. Ian Tyrell suggests that part of this enthusiasm stemmed from the experience of semi-professionalism immediately after Civil War which undermined and corrupted the ideals of amateurism.[52] To many it seemed that only full and open professionalism could rescue the game from its bad reputation. But also it was due to the general *laissez-faire* attitude after the war. As Tyrell notes '[p]rovided the influence of money on sport was, like everything else in the society, subject to the discipline of market forces, only good could result'.[53] There are even some critics who believe that sport-for-sport's sake, entirely devoid of self-interest was not even true of the ancient Greek Olympics. David C. Young refers to this as the 'heterodox thesis' (though given its prevalence we might well now think of it as the orthodoxy). Amateurism, he argues, was alien to ancient Greeks. His claim is that while such myths were important in the formation and development of the modern Olympics – think of long-term Olympic President Avery Brundage's claim that the ancient Olympics were always amateur – they do not reflect the historical reality.

But, whatever the truth of amateur sport in ancient Greece, it seems clear that modern amateurism was not as commercially pure as its advocates would have us believe. The first objection then is that the commodification critique of commercial motives in sport is historically inaccurate with respect both to modern amateurism as an historical phenomenon and to the nature of sport itself.

A second line of criticism of the Amateur Ideal focuses on the aristocratic prejudice that it is claimed was an essential element of amateurism as an historical phenomenon. There is some considerable evidence of this in nineteenth-century British sport, the details of which are particularly interesting. (Indeed much of our discussion here will consider Imperial Britain since the ethical ideals of amateurism were forcefully and clearly proclaimed during this period.) At that time, members of the so-called lower orders were deliberately and explicitly excluded from amateur competitions. Thus, many rowing clubs and athletic clubs banned men who had undertaken manual labour from competing in amateur events. For instance, in 1846 at Lancaster there was a dispute following a Manchester crew's victory in the Borough Cup rowing competition. Two of the crew, a cabinet maker and a brick-layer, were not, it was alleged acceptable entrants on the grounds that 'they were not known as men of property.' The debate continued until in 1853, when the category of 'gentleman amateur' was distinguished from the pure amateur for the Lancaster Rowing Club's purposes. Other clubs followed suit stipulating that those who worked as mechanics, artisans or labourers would not be eligible for competition as their employment, 'being physical in nature, equipped them with advantages'.[54] In the regulations for the Henley Regatta of 1879 we read: 'No person shall be considered an amateur oarsman or sculler ... who is or has been by trade or employment for wages, a mechanic, artisan or laborer.'[55]

We find athletics clubs also excluding competitors who had worked in manual trades. For instance, the British Amateur Athletic Association in 1866 officially defined an amateur as a person who had either never competed (1) in open competition; (2) for prize money; (3) for admission money (4) with professionals; (5) never taught or assisted in the pursuit of athletics exercises as a means of livelihood; or (6) was not a mechanic, artisan or labourer. Condition 6 was removed in 1880.[56] The British delegation to the meeting that formed the modern

Olympics had wanted to bring in similar requirements for Olympic amateurism, but were overridden; they had wanted amateurism formally limited by social class.[57]

What is striking about all of this is how the term 'amateur' is defined in terms of one's occupation rather than in terms of whether one plays sport for money: it was thought during this period that the lower social orders should always be counted as professionals. As *The Times* noted: 'The outsiders, artisans, mechanics, and such like troublesome persons can have no place found for them [in amateur sports]. To keep them out is a thing desirable on every account.'[58] We can see why Allen Guttmann was moved to suggest that '[T]he amateur rule was an instrument of class warfare.'[59] There was a desire amongst the English authorities to ensure, as the cricket writer Mike Marqusee put it, 'that the hierarchies outside the field were reflected and respected on it'.[60] Amateurism, as an historical movement at least, was not really about whether or not one played for money but about one's social class. The ideal of Amateur was reserved for gentlemen.[61]

Perhaps the most interesting sport for observing these class distinctions in action is English cricket. Unlike other sports, such as rugby union, athletics and later tennis, where professionals were barred from amateur competitions, in cricket, professionals and amateurs played alongside one another and so the machinations of the class system are thus more transparent.[62] At first sight this might appear to represent a departure from the class exclusions of other sports. But that would be a mistake because a system of class apartheid operated in English cricket for the best part of a century.[63] Amateurs and professionals had separate entrances to the field, separate travel, accommodation and dining arrangements. Their dressing rooms were segregated, for fear that changing and showering with professionals might somehow corrupt the amateurs.[64] Amateurs were addressed by professionals as 'Sir' or 'Mr' at all times and any failure to follow this protocol could result in either a fine or a dismissal. On the other hand, professionals were addressed by professionals simply by their surnames.[65] In one incident in the early 1950s, Sussex's David Sheppard, the future Bishop of Liverpool, had batted superbly against Gloucestershire. At the close of play, a Gloucestershire professional congratulated him with the words, 'Well played David!' only to be strongly censured by his captain for over-familiarity and causing serious offence to Sheppard.[66] Even in 1961 one could find English cricket officials making public announcements to correct mistakes over the amateur status of players that might have been printed on team sheets.[67]

These class distinctions carried over, not unsurprisingly, into the choice of captain for the English cricket team. Until the middle of the twentieth century only an amateur could be named as captain. It was not until 1952 that we find Len Hutton being chosen as the first non-amateur skipper of the English. From contemporary perspectives it is anomalous that Hutton was chosen for this role so late in his career, since he was a prolific run-scorer and had for fifteen years been the holder of the record for the highest score in Test cricket.

The Hutton case indicates how recent in historical terms is the decline of the influence of the Amateurist movement on sport and in particular, English sport.

The class attitudes remained well into the twentieth century. Thus, the actor Grace Kelly's father, J.H.B. Kelly, was excluded from the 1921 Diamond Sculls at Henley because he had once laid bricks for a living.[68] And as late as 1960 we find an English authority defending the exclusion of mechanics, artisans and labourers as 'the only way to keep the sport from the elements of corruption. ... It is argued, with much show of truth, that the average workman has no idea of sport for its own sake'.[69] And while this might well be anomalous, for the explicit class bias had long disappeared in most cases by this time, the anti-commercialism of the amateur rule persisted in many sports. Tennis (or at least traditional tennis events such as Wimbledon), for instance, held out against professionalism until 1968 at which time it became 'open' to all, professionals and amateurs alike. Full acceptance of professionalism in rugby union did not come until 1995, although shamateurism had long been rife prior to then and was regarded as an acceptable means of recruiting and retaining players.[70] In athletics, it was not until 1983 that the International Amateur Athletics Federation adopted a new approach.

Not only might it be argued that amateurism reflected a class prejudice of the wealthy aristocratic class, but that amateurism was not the original state of our organised sport. David C. Young argues that amateurism was a system devised as an 'ideological means to justify an elitist athletic system that sought to ban the working class from competition.'[71] Young claims that while most people nowadays think that amateurism was somehow the original state of our own organised sport, and that professional sports encroached on an earlier amateur system, the reverse is true. 'Amateurism itself was the late-comer and amateurs as a matter of practice tried to displace existing professional institutions'. He suggests that '[T]he amateur generally usurped the place of the professional, not ... the other way around.'[72] While amateurism may well have functioned as a unifying force for the dominant social classes during the latter half of the nineteenth century, as John Hargreaves argued, what Young suggests is that it is not some original *ur*-version of sport.[73]

Whatever the truth of Young's claims about the pre-modern history of organised sport, what is clear is that amateurism as an historical movement explicitly sought to exclude working class participants. But what is most surprising about this is that they even felt the need to do so via explicit exclusionary mechanisms. One would have thought that the rule against rewarding financially from sport would have been enough, for without financial recompense what working class athlete would have had either the time or the resources to train for and compete in such events. This brings us to the third objection to amateurism. Leaving aside the explicit class bias of much of the Amateurist movement, there are questions which can legitimately be raised about an anti-commercialism that fails to acknowledge the consequences of material necessity. On this line of reasoning, athletes without sufficient resources will be effectively excluded from competition because of their inability to travel, to train full-time and make use of modern training facilities. It is perhaps no accident that Olympic swimming, which is a sport that requires expensive training facilities, is dominated by competitors from wealthy Western countries such as the United States, Germany and Australia.

The third objection then is that amateurism, and its concomitant sport-for-sport's sake ideology, fails to acknowledge material necessity. Elite sports persons require money to train and compete and for many the only means of obtaining sufficient funds is through sponsorships and prize money. The amateur rule which bans commercial reward would effectively exclude such competitors from actively participating in elite level events and thus would effectively leave sport open only to those with sufficient financial wherewithal. In the Olympics, for instance, if the no money rule were strictly adhered to, then the cost of international competition would discourage the working class as a matter of course. As David C. Young notes, what working class person could afford the time needed to train and to compete without any hope for remuneration. [74]

The final criticism of amateurism concerns the 'ethical hazards' associated with amateurism. It might be argued that whatever hazards commercialism presents to players and sports administrators, those occasioned by amateurism when this ideal is pursued in an otherwise commercial world are significantly worse. Here doubts are expressed about whether it is possible for amateurs to remain untainted by money, given the highly commercialised context we now inhabit and it is thought that explicit up-front commercialism is preferable to its under cover counterpart.

The first kind of ethical hazard involves the possibility of hypocrisy where one espouses values to which one does not adhere. The hypocrisy here is the hypocrisy of the 'shamateur': the athlete who publicly espouses the ideals of non-commercialism whilst lining their pockets with gold. Whilst amateurs might engage in all kinds of casuistic subterfuges to justify the taking of back-handed sponsorships and so on, such sophisms typically bring sport into disrepute rather than convincing anyone that their behaviour is still amateur in point of fact, let alone in spirit. For instance, in 1983 the International Amateur Athletics Federation took a new approach, recognising that competitors were being paid, and insisted that any money athletes received should go directly to a trust fund and dispensed later to cover expenses.[75] The idea was that covering expenses did not count as remuneration in the full sense, and perhaps it does not, but one can see how that could easily be manipulated and viewed as a mere 'work-around' by the public at large.

There are a number of different reasons why there might be pressure towards shamateurism for the amateur athlete. In the first place, athletes need to provide for themselves materially and the expenses of travelling to international competition and taking time off work to train and so on means that unless they are independently wealthy, they will always be in need of some extra cash. Further, outside the stadium, athletes live in a world dominated by commercial values. It would be odd for athletes not to be tempted by dreams of material goods given the high status that Western societies place on the acquisition of such goods. Moreover, elite athletes are highly regarded in society in general and are highly attractive to advertisers and related commercial organisations. Thus there are likely to be offers of endorsements and other commercial opportunities that will make a mockery of their amateur status.

The danger here is of bringing the very principles that they espouse into disrepute and by association sport itself. The critic of amateurism might well say it would be better if the amateur simply admitted his or her commercial interest and ended the pretense of following principles that clearly he or she does not follow. It might even be thought that such sham ethics brings morality itself into disrepute.

Of more concern is a second kind of ethical hazard which involves pressures for illegality. The thought is that amateurs, by virtue of not being rewarded, and being, like all of us, subject to material necessity, are likely to be more receptive to corruption in the form of bribes and match-fixing than they would have been if they were receiving a reasonable income from sport. Without adequate recompense, or so the argument goes, athletes are more likely to be tempted by illegal money than they would otherwise be, and with that corruption sport itself is corrupted. In particular, match-fixing – which is deadly for a sport – is much more likely to arise.[76]

Sport in the United States has endured some particularly graphic instances of this problem. The most notorious concerns the 1919 'Black Sox Scandal' in baseball when eight players on the brilliant Chicago White Sox conspired with gamblers to lose the World Series and receive a pay-off in return. The team's owner, Charles Comiskey, was renowned for his miserliness in paying the players, notably star performers like Eddie Cicotte and Shoeless Joe Jackson, who took the disastrous step of trying to cover the shortfall through illegal earnings.[77] In recent years, the 'amateur', billion-dollar enterprise that is known as the NCAA has issued leaflets and warnings to college athletes to advise on its prohibition of wagering in sports. Several athletes in the past have wagered on their team's results, or played poorly to win bets or pay off bookmakers. Critics argue that if the NCAA paid these amateur athletes a mere fraction of the revenues that they generate, such corrupt practices would be far less likely to occur.

This is not to say that amateur athletes are always tempted to engage in corrupt practices in sport, but simply to say that there will be pressures upon them to which many will succumb. They are, after all, hazards not immutable laws of logic. But they are sufficiently tempting to give rise to moral concerns.

Responding to the four objections

These four objections to amateurism (concerning historical inaccuracy, aristocratic prejudice, material necessity and ethical hazards), however, do not, in any sense, provide the grounds for a repudiation of the importance of sport-for-sport's sake as a fundamental value that emerges in and through sport. Whilst the historical record of amateurism might tempt us, like David C. Young to regard the 'intrinsic pleasure of sport for its own sake' as a bittersweet phrase, that in no way should lead one to the conclusion that it is to be rejected.[78] If it is bittersweet, it is so because of that which is done in its name and also because of a misunderstanding of what it implies or entails rather than because of any in principle immorality or wrong-headedness. We need to acknowledge that as an historical phenomenon amateurism had numerous morally pernicious features. Indeed, even a grand defender of amateurism such as Lincoln Allison concedes that the movement was tainted by aristocratic elitism and hypocrisy on a grand scale.[79] But to think that that provides a knockdown objection to sport-for-sport's sake would be, for reasons that we adumbrate below, a serious error.

First, there is a general question that needs to be asked about the bearing or relevance of these four criticisms on the very idea of sport-for-sport's sake. This is really just a matter of undertaking some informal logic – rather than engaging with the historical details of the objections – and teasing out the line of reasoning that connects our sporting value with the historical phenomenon of amateurism. After doing so, one might well come to the belief that the two are being injudiciously conflated. Though it is quite common for these mainly socio-historical issues to be raised when one makes mention of the intrinsic value of sport for its own sake – and to thus cast doubt on the latter – it is not clear on closer examination how one might tease out the connection between the two. Is it mere guilt by association? How plausible is the connection? We believe much depends here on how the argument against sport-for-sport's sake is actually developed. Whether or not any plausible connection can be drawn depends on what kinds of logical connections are posed between the two.

One way of explicating the claim is in terms of some kind of entailment. Amateurism, it is claimed, has various morally objectionable and historically specious features and because the idea of sport-for-sport's sake was a central theoretical plank of amateurism, then those features can be inferred also to be ascribable to sport-for-sport's sake. Let us lay this out schematically:

1   A central element of amateurism was the idea of the intrinsic value of sport played for its own sake.
2   Amateurism was elitist, morally hazardous and failed to acknowledge material necessity.
3   Therefore, any theory that is based on the idea of the intrinsic value of sport played for its own sake will be elitist, morally hazardous and fail to acknowledge material necessity.

Laid out in this deductive formulation the objection begins to seem a little less plausible. Indeed, the reasoning is fallacious. To see this consider the following chain of reasoning:

1   The theory of natural selection was a central plank of Social Darwinism.
2   Social Darwinism was elitist and morally objectionable.
3   Therefore, the theory of natural selection is elitist and morally objectionable.

Similarly, one might argue that because Nazi scientists believed in the existence of gravity or in germ theory, that therefore these theories are also morally suspect.

If the objection to sport-for-sport's sake then is that the morally objectionable features of amateurism carry across as a matter of logical necessity to any theory that endorses the intrinsic value of sport, then this is simply a *non sequitur*. What we might want to endorse is a much weaker thesis that on the basis of the historical record regarding amateurism we should be naturally suspicious of theoretical positions that rely on the value of sport-for-sport's sake. But this does not make for an objection to the value of sport-for-sport's sake.

But perhaps this is all a little too swift and the analogies just a little too cute. A critic of sport-for-sport's sake might argue that it is not just that amateurism and our commodification critique share an admiration for the value of sport played for its own sake (just as at a general level modern scientists and Nazi scientists might share a belief in germ theory); rather the value has its origins in amateurism. Part of the objection to sport-for-sport's sake is that it is an ideology that has its roots in the Amateurist movement of the nineteenth century and thus, as far as organised sport goes, it is a relatively recent phenomenon and one which is part of a morally suspect social movement. These are then not just two arbitrarily related entities that have some ideas in common, but rather one has its very origins in the other.

This reformulated objection to our commodification critique is but a species of a more general socio-historical approach to cultural phenomena. Rather than asking direct normative questions about the normative justifications of practices or ideas, the socio-historical approach aims to explore their origins (or 'genealogies' if we wished to place an explicitly Foucauldian slant on the approach). This kind of approach is very common in sports studies. Lincoln Allison in *Amateurism in Sport* calls it 'contextualising' and contrasts it with what he sees as a philosophical approach. And while it is very different from a strictly philosophical approach in Allison's terms, it is valuable in many ways. Such approaches have been very useful in demonstrating the recent origins of ideas and practices that we might well have thought to be essential, necessary and atemporal elements of any human culture whatsoever.

But while there may well be much to be gained theoretically from analysing the socio-historical origins of the idea of sport-for-sport's sake, this kind of approach does not provide us with a knock-down objection to the idea of sport-for-sport's sake and accordingly of our commodification critique. To see why this is so, let us once again tease out the objection schematically. Consider what the objection says:

1   Sport-for-sport's sake has its origins in the Amateurist movement of the nineteenth century.
2   The Amateurist movement was morally objectionable because it was elitist and hypocritical.
3   Therefore, sport-for-sport's sake is also morally objectionable.

Now, let us assume for the sake of the argument the truth of the historical claim that sport-for-sport's sake has its origins in the Amateurist movement. (Although one could well imagine many taking issue with its accuracy.) Even if we accept that claim and we accept the second premise regarding the moral status of amateurism, we need not accept the conclusion. The thought that demonstrating the origins of an idea (or practice) provides us with grounds for repudiating that idea rests on a fallacious line of reasoning. Indeed it is a sufficiently common *non sequitur* to warrant a title, namely the *genetic fallacy*. This is the fallacy of inferring that because the origin of *x* is F, therefore *x* is F. To use a standard example, a water lily has its roots in slime and mud. But we should not infer from that fact that the water lily is ugly or lacks beauty. To apply this reasoning to our own case, the mere fact that sport-for-sport's sake has its origins in the aristocratic Amateurist movement does not, on its own, show that we should reject it.

To see in greater detail why it is fallacious to move from origins to repudiation consider the following. Imagine that a scientist discovers a fundamental law of the universe whilst engaged in some morally objectionable activity. The morally questionable origins of the theory do not undermine its truth-value. Similarly, that the Amateurs were morally vicious – if indeed they were – does not demonstrate that they did not pick out in the idea of sport-for-sport's sake some fundamental sporting value. Nor is it enough to demonstrate the existence of dubious motives at the point of origin. One might be tempted to argue that the Amateurist move-ment was not only morally objectionable in itself, but that it explicitly conceived of the idea of sport-for-sport's sake as a means of excluding the lower orders. The idea might be that the aristocrats in the Amateur movement recognised at the outset the effects that a no-money rule would have on working class competitors and thus their support of this ideal was entirely disingenuous. Or alternatively, it might be, as Mike Marqusee suggests, that the ideals of amateurism were driven by a desire on the part of the aristocratic amateurs to 'redefine the manliness associ-ated with the game in ways that suited those who did not work with their bodies'.[80] This might all well be true, but this again does not show that the ideas are wrong. One might well conceive of an idea with the worst of motives, but that does not mean that it is incorrect. To think that the dubious motives of those who are the originators of an idea entails that the idea is itself thereby incorrect or that a proposed value is not a genuine or fundamental value is once again to commit the genetic fallacy.

In a sense we are pointing to a more general failing of a certain style of socio-historical critique to engage with philosophical ideas in themselves. Imagine a Marxist critique of the views of John Locke along the lines that Locke's political views simply reflect an attempt to defend the property rights of an emerging bourgeoisie class. That might well be true, but it does not demonstrate that his arguments in defence of property are not valid. There is often an unfortunate tendency amongst those committed to socio-historical critique to reject entirely questions of the content of beliefs.[81] That an idea has a history might take away some of its aura but it does not show it is incorrect. We find similar fallacious reasoning at play in Jean-Marie Brohm's work where he criticises sport for its imperialist origins.[82] The fact that those who promoted sport in the nineteenth century had imperialist aims, if indeed it is a fact, does not show that the practice they promoted has no value outside the value it putatively has for the project of imperialism. Moreover, the historical record would seem to suggest that countries under imperial domination often rejected or refashioned imperial sports to suit their particular cultural identities. For example, British sports such as cricket and rugby were spread across the old empire, and these were quickly seized upon by indigenous populations to become effective ways of challenging and beating the former colonial powers (a prime example being cricket in the West Indies).[83]

We also find a failure in these approaches to develop the ethical content of their critiques. All too often such critics point to the origin of an idea without explaining – as we did in premise 2 above – what might be morally salient about that origin. The argument thus relies on hidden ethical assumptions. In the case of the critique of sport-for-sport's sake objections too often rely on hidden moral assumptions about the immorality of the class system without saying what is wrong with that system (my concern is not with the content of such hidden moral assumptions but with the fact that they remain hidden or suppressed).[84]

Further, while the putative aristocratic origins of sport-for-sport's sake are typically read as having negative connotations, a case could be made to the contrary. It might well be argued – though it runs contrary to the prior discussion of origins – that because aristocrats were freed to a great extent from the realm of necessity, they were able to pursue sport in the spirit that it should ideally be pursued. Indeed, the sports historian Steven J. Overman runs just this very line when he writes: 'For a point of time, following its colonial age, sport enjoyed an unfettered freedom which allowed it to be true to its own values.'[85] He suggests that the sports of the leisure class reflected the true spirit of sport. Without accepting the essentialist assumptions here about the true nature of sport, one might well agree that leisure can provide grounds for genuine exploration of human values and ideas. For instance, Aristotle was able to develop his informal logic – which is still used today – in part because he was freed from menial chores by the existence of a slave class in his society. And Marx's sketchy vision of how life would be in the future communist utopia seems modelled on lives lead by aristocrats. When he envisages that under genuine communism we would be free to engage in well-rounded self-developmental activity, hunting in the morning, fishing in the afternoon and philosophising in the evening, the life pictured sounds very aristocratic. It would seem that even Marx thought that the way of life of the aristocrat – if not the economic arrangements which made it possible – provided us with a vision of how all human lives could and perhaps should be led. We might think that their sporting values have a similar status. It is not so much that freedom from menial labour necessarily enables a group to develop sport more ethically, but simply that it provides the space for such developments.

At the same time, we should not think that the origins of the ideal of sport-for-sport's sake, if they are indeed aristocratic, should give us no cause for concern whatsoever. Our claim is simply that its putative origins in amateurism do not in themselves provide a knockdown argument against sport-for-sport's sake. It is a question of intellectual warrant. But equally, in pursuing any line of reasoning based on ideas that have an aristocratic lineage we would do well to examine them critically and see to what extent they might carry aristocratic biases or have anti-egalitarian implications. The origins thus provide us with a caution, if not a reason for rejection.

What we are suggesting then is that we should treat the origins of sporting values such as sport-for-sport's sake as grounds for caution. A model for this approach might be the work of the Marxist literary theorist C.L.R. James (1901–89) in his classic commentary on cricket *Beyond a Boundary*.[86] James was a revolutionary Marxist who spent much of his life campaigning for social change. As well as being the leader of the movement to have a black West Indian appointed captain of the West Indian cricket team (and this campaign was successful with Frank Worrell being appointed in 1960).[87] James' writings, most notably *The Black Jacobins*, were read by revolutionaries throughout the Caribbean and were said to be the inspiration for a Marxist uprising in Granada in 1983. James was well aware of the imperialist and class-biases of cricket as it was played in his time for he had played cricket at first class level for Trinidad in the Red Shield Competition in the West Indies. However, he also felt that cricket was a social practice in which many important and fundamental values were given room to be expressed. He was one for whom the ideals of fair play and the pursuit of athletic excellence were of great significance, despite their origins. While he hated the racism and imperialism of cricketing institutions, he could still find in the sport beauty and moral purpose. Mike Marqusee notes of C.L.R. James despite his Marxist radicalism his highest claim on behalf of the black West Indian cricket captain, Sir Frank Worrell, was that he was a worthy inheritor of the tradition of *Tom Brown's School Days*.[88] Certainly, like James we consider the origins of the values we endorse in sport are worthy of close historical inspection. Indeed it is imperative that socio-historical accounts of sport explore how these values connect to matrices of power within specific social settings. However, in this context we merely seek to confirm that discovering the exact origins of these values does not establish a normative case for their repudiation. It is the values themselves that we must assess.

Let us turn now from questions about the relationship between sport-for-sport's sake and the Amateurist movement to an objection that directly concerns the ideal of sport-for-sport's sake, regardless of its connections to amateurism, namely the Objection from Material Necessity. The claim is that sport-for-sport's sake is in itself (irrespective of any necessary historical or conceptual links to amateurism), a flawed ideal and thus should not be employed in the service of any critique of commodification. It is a flawed ideal because it fails to acknowledge the need of human beings to provide for themselves. By defending the value of sport played for its own sake we are thereby simply re-invoking the old amateur no-money rule. This not only involves an unrealistic assumption about the human situation – we are after all material beings – but ultimately favours those who are independently wealthy. If athletes are not permitted to make money from their sporting activities, then only the independently wealthy will be able to compete at an elite level. This would seem to be a serious criticism, if it could be sustained. How should we respond? Is our commodification critique based on faulty philosophical anthropology? Are we defending the No-Money rule?

At this point we should step back and recall the way in which the objection to money as a goal in sport was formulated. First, we did not argue that commodification is pathological *simpliciter* whenever sport is pursued for goals other than those internal to it. Instead, our conditional claim is that commodification is pathological when external goals exclude or come to dominate the internal goods of sport. Accordingly, the advent of money as a motivational end for sportspersons does not mean by itself that commodification is pathological here. Rather it is pathological in those cases when the internal goods of sport are excluded or dominated by financial concerns.

Second, we did not argue that money necessarily excludes other goals. Our approach allows for the *compossibility* of financial goals and the goals of sports-for sport's sake. Our motives can as a matter of logic be mixed. Accordingly, we can draw distinctions between different forms of professional sporting activity based on the different roles that financial motives play in our motivational sets. For instance, one might be a venal sportsperson for whom there are no goals other than money. Alternatively one might be an accumulator for whom the internal goals of sport co-exist alongside the financial motives. The moral force of this is that the pursuit of money is only pernicious with respect to our motives when it is the sole or dominant motive in a sportsperson's motivational set. So long as money is not the sole or dominant goal of the sportsperson's action then moral vice does not arise.

Note the difference here between our approach and the way sport-for-sport's sake has traditionally been interpreted. The Amateur rule that absolutely prohibited any financial reward, in order to defend the pursuit of sport for its own sake involves a hidden assumption that the mere presence of money eradicates the internal goods of sport. Thus the objection was to money itself. Our objection is not to money *per se* but venality.

If we allow the possibility of these mixed motives then mere defence of the fundamental value of sport-for-sport's sake need not lead us towards the No-Money rule. We are not thereby guilty of founding our critique of commodification on a faulty philosophical anthropology; our approach allows for financial reward in the service of material necessity. (Interestingly Lincoln Allison suggests, though he does not spell out in detail how it would work, that amateurism itself need not be thought of as involving the total rejection of payment.)[89] Moreover, our approach can allow for remuneration in the service of more than just material necessity. This is in stark contrast with the motivationalist accounts of various Medieval philosophers, like Aquinas, concerning those cases where the pursuit of profit is morally admissible. These Medieval philosophers – against a background of earlier Church hostility towards business – thought that although commerce was morally hazardous, it was acceptable when one was pursuing gain to provide for oneself and one's family. In today's world that sounds like a call simply for a minimum wage. Our approach is far more permissive. It does not matter whether one is seeking wealth for material necessity or is in pursuit of what we would call luxury, so long as the internal goals of sport survive, and the action is not venal, then it is morally admissible.

But equally our approach provides reason for caution. While motives can be mixed we need to be wary of commodification since there is a natural tendency towards venality within capitalism. It is not that we should not be rewarded for sporting excellence, but that such rewards should not become the sole or dominant motive in our athletes' motivational sets.

The final objection to our commodification critique to be addressed concerns the historical accuracy of the picture of pre-modern sport upon which our critique is based. The suggestion is that our critique involves a romantic and inaccurate view of the nature and history of organised sport and, accordingly, this provides grounds for rejecting it.

Recall in the discussion of amateurism the following objections were outlined in some detail:

1   Amateurism was far more commercial than is often portrayed.
2   There is a pre-modern sporting tradition that existed prior to the advent of amateurism and which had a significant commercial component.
3   There is no reason to believe that any particular ideals such as the No-Money rule are somehow essential to or constitutive of sport as it has been pursued in history.

Certainly we can see the importance of these claims for amateurism. It looks, if these claims are true, as if amateurism was neither as pure as its advocates would have us believe nor are its ideals constitutive of sport as it has been played. Notwithstanding these truths, we must still ask what is the relevance of such claims to our commodification critique, given that we can distance the ideal of sport-for-sport's sake from amateurism?

The suggestion is that these claims undermine *any* commodification critique that is based upon or wishes to defend the ideal of the intrinsic value of sport undertaken for its own sake. If we wish to reject the commodification of sport on moral grounds then *ex hypothesi* we must have in mind some earlier non-commercial practices that were ethically superior. (In this case our concern is with the motives and ideals of those playing and administering sport.) An ethical critique then rests *necessarily* on either one of the two following claims:

M1   Commodification involves the violation of what has been historically the case with respect to sport, namely the pursuit of non-commercial internal goals and this is a reason why it is ethically undesirable.

M2   Commodification involves the violation of ideals concerning the pursuit of non-commercial internal goals that are constitutive of sport and this is a reason why it is ethically undesirable.

Moral criticism of commodification, of the kind developed here, rests then on claims about either the history or essential nature of sport.

The objection is, just as was the case with amateurism, that these claims are undermined by an examination of the historical record and since our commodification critique must rest on either one of these two, our critique is also undermined. Consider M1. There has always been money in sport, even in the ancient Greek Olympics. (David C. Young even goes so far as to suggest that the word athlete in ancient Greek meant one who competes for money.[90]) The historical record then tells us that commodification cannot be ethically undesirable because it breaks with the tradition. If we consider M2 we find similar problems arising out of the historical record. If non-commercialism is essential to sport, then a great deal of what we would ordinarily call sport will not count, since so much sport has been undertaken with commercial reward in mind. The existence of commercial elements in pre-modern sport seems to create insurmountable difficulties for M1 and M2.

What should we take from this? Is the historical record fatal to our case? We suggest not for it is possible to develop a moral critique of the corrosion of the ideal of sport-for-sport's sake by commodification for which the existence of commercial elements in sport in earlier periods is not at all troublesome. M1 and M2 are not the only options.

Let us begin by considering the relationship of the ideal of sport-for-sport's sake to sport itself. We do not claim that the values we wish to defend here against commodification are constitutive of sport. In our account the good-making properties associated with the pursuit of sport-for-sport's sake supervene upon sporting activity; they emerge in and through it rather than being essential to its very existence. Where sport is undertaken for the sake of sporting ideals such as the pursuit of athletic excellence, value is generated. But there may well be sporting practices where such intrinsically valuable ideals are not pursued and yet which still warrant the title of 'sport'. Our criticism here is not that sport, where sport is not pursued for its own sake is not sport, rather our criticism is a moral one. Sport where such ideals are pursued is morally preferable to sport where they are absent. For whilst these ideals might not be constitutive or definitional of sport, they are central to what matters about sport. It is through the pursuit of such ideals that part of the value of sport emerges.

There have of course been many critiques based on this notion that sport has some definitional essence which is being violated. Take, for instance, Lincoln Allison's *Amateurism in Sport*. In this book Allison aims to defend amateurism against the dominant commercialism of modern sport. He claims that the moral and philosophical meaning of amateurism remains fundamental to our definition of sport, and must still apply to professional sport if it is to survive into the twenty-first century.[91] This is one example of a more general ethical strategy by theorists who wish to provide an ethical framework for criticism of commodification. As we noted in chapter 2, writers like Elizabeth Anderson and Michael Walzer have criticised commodification for its violation of what they take to be the intrinsic meanings of goods. Our approach is somewhat different. It is not that its essence is violated but that the values that emerge in and through sport are suppressed and the space for their expression limited.

The relevance of this to commodification should be clear. Any institution that diminishes or eliminates the possibility of pursuing sport for its own sake is morally undesirable with respect to that diminution; that is to say, diminishing or extinguishing the opportunities of pursuing sport-for-sport's sake is a bad-making feature of a social institution. Accordingly, in so far as commodification lessens or eliminates the opportunities for the pursuit of sport-for-sport's sake then this is a bad-making feature of commodification; commodification is pathological when it does so. We can formulate our moral critique as follows:

> M3   Commodification is ethically undesirable when it leads to an elimination or significant limitation of the epistemic space available for the pursuit of non-commercial internal goals that supervene on sport and which are an essential element of the moral value that sport generates.

This is a non-essentialist moral critique of commodification that outlines one set of conditions under which commodification is pathological. It is non-essential in the sense that it does not rely upon claims about the essential historical nature of sport.

What philosophical or argumentative import might historical claims about the existence of commercial elements in earlier epochs have for our moral critique of commodification? The first point to note is that our concern in this chapter is with the existence of the ideal of sport-for-sport's sake rather than commercial elements *per se*. Historically, commerce has undermined this ideal, but equally the mere existence of commerce does not show that sport-for-sport's sake was non-existent, for as we noted earlier, it is possible for sport-for-sport's sake and commerce to co-exist. Too often the evacuation of the ideal of sport-for-sport's sake and the rise of commerce are wrongly conflated as being somehow logically equivalent. (On our model there is a causal relationship between the two.) Any historically based objection to our commodification critique would need to isolate cases where these commercial elements had evacuated the ideal of sport-for-sport's sake. Pointing to commerce in earlier epochs is not enough.

However, clearly there are such cases in pre-modern sport where commerce has meant that the ideal of sport-for-sport's sake is absent. Might not such cases count as counter-examples to the claim that commodification is pathological because of its role in eliminating the ideal of sport-for-sport's sake? This is where it is important to note the shift from an essentialist to an emergent picture of the ideal of sport-for-sport's sake. Such cases would only count as counter-examples if we adopt an essentialist view according to which the pursuit of these ideals are necessary for the every existence of sport. To be sure, if sport was never pursued with ideals such as the pursuit of athletic excellence in mind, then this would create problems for our account because then we would be suggesting that one important value that emerges from sport is something that as a matter of historical fact has never existed. (It would be equivalent to suggesting that what matters about horse-racing is the opportunities for participation it offers to unicorns.) But unless it can be shown that sport has never (or even rarely) been pursued with these ideals in mind, then the historical evidence does not undermine our critique. Our line of thought is not that sport has always exhibited such ideals because it is an essential feature, but rather part of its moral value emerges through their pursuit.

This leads us to our final point about such historical evidence. Sceptics regarding commodification as a genuine moral problem might employ it to attempt to demonstrate that there is no problem because sport has always been commercial. On this line of reasoning the search for a framework for morally evaluating commodification is Quixotic since the problem is imaginary. However, as we argued in chapter 2, this overlooks the radical differences between sport in earlier epochs and sport today. There may well have always been commercialism but not of the systematic and extensive kind we see today. It does not show that there is no need for a moral framework for assessing the commodification of sport.

Our conclusion is that it is fallacious to claim that because one can find evidence of money in sport throughout history – if indeed one can – then this undermines either the basis of the critique or the need for such a critique in the first place. Unless one can show that sport has never been pursued for any reasons other than money, then our approach withstands such a line of objection.

The upshot of all of this discussion in this section is that critiques of amateurism do not undermine the very idea of sport-for-sport's sake as a fundamental value and hence do not undermine this arm of our commodification critique. We should not allow our legitimate concerns with the exclusiveness and hypocrisy of the amateur movement to lead us to lose sight of an important value in sport.

Summary

The person or organisation that is only motivated by financial considerations subjugates important values (such as the competitive ethos of sport) to the logic of the market. Whilst financial motives are not morally vicious in themselves and a society in which people are animated by the profit motive receives many material benefits, such motives should not be dominant in the all things considered reasoning of those who play sport and those entrusted with its administration and development. If financial motives dominate then other important internal goods associated with sport will be evacuated from the sporting arena. The commodification of sport then is pathological when it leads to such venality. In so far as the transformation of the incentive structures that comes with commodification generates venality it is morally pernicious. It does not do so necessarily but within commercial society there will always be a pressure towards such an undesirable form of sport.

4 Commodification and objectification

Treating athletes and sport itself as *mere* means

Introduction

One common complaint about modern commercial sport is that athletes come to be viewed as mere commodities, both by those who pay for their services and by sports fans. Soccer players are traded in end-of-season negotiations between clubs like cattle at a market. Fans regularly talk of whether a player was a good buy or represents value for money. And it is not only players who are so regarded; as we have noted, North American major league sports clubs are termed 'franchises', while the phrase 'sports industry' has become part of the popular vernacular. It is not so much the attitudes of the players themselves, which are at issue here (which was the theme of the previous chapter), but rather the attitudes of those who buy and sell sporting commodities towards athletes and sport itself.

For those who find such talk repugnant, the moral concern is with a commodified *mode of regard* in which things that are valuable in themselves are treated as mere means of making money. It is this moral concern that we wish to explore in this chapter. In our intuitions here it is possible to discern strong echoes of the Kantian objection to commercial exchanges in intrinsically valuable entities. In the *Groundwork of the Metaphysics of Morals* the German philosopher Immanuel Kant (1724–1804) famously argues that it is wrong to treat intrinsically valuable things as commodities, for to do so is to rob them of their dignity. According to Kant, putting a price on something is incompatible with treating it with dignity. It involves an incorrect mode of regard. To use a more contemporary lexicon, it involves a form of 'objectification'.

The relevance of this critique to commercial sport should be clear. What is wrong with commodification, on this line of reasoning, is that it leads us to regard athletes as the mere means to the realisation of profit, rather than, as they are entitled by virtue of their status as persons, as ends in their own right. If Kant is correct about the price-dignity relation, then clearly commercial sport violates the moral rights of athletes. There are reasons for being cautious here, however, for the relationship between commodification and treating something as a mere means is a little more complicated than the orthodox Kantian tradition in applied ethics would have us believe. While we believe that the basic thrust of the approach is correct, below we develop a modified Kantian model according to which commodification has a morally significant causal influence on our attitudes to things that are commodified. As we shall see, on this model, commodification is patho-logical (*inter alia*) when it leads us to regard athletes as mere means.

What is perhaps not so clear is the relevance of this to sport itself. Sport is not a person in any recognisable or ordinary sense of the word. Nonetheless, despite initial appearances, it is possible to identify the ends of sport and to show how these are undermined by commodification. Indeed this Kantian-inspired critique provides us with a remarkable explanatory grip on what it is that many find objectionable about commodification. What is pernicious about commodification phenomena – such as rule changes aimed squarely at television audiences rather than players or spectators – can be understood in terms of our failure to respect the ends of sport. Much of this chapter then involves an examination of how, through a transformation of our attitudes towards sport, commodification corrodes many of its intrinsically valuable features.

We might say then that with this chapter our moral attention shifts to the *demand* rather than the *supply-side* of commercial relations in sport. It is not so much the motivational structures of those sporting participants who sell their labour that is of issue here, but rather the mode of regard that those who pay for sporting goods have towards the goods they buy. Hence it is the attitudes that commodification fosters towards athletes and sport itself that we shall now examine.

Commodification, objectification and corrosion: a brief survey

In the *Groundwork* Kant argues, as we have seen, that everything can have either a price or a dignity but not both simultaneously since the two are mutually exclu-sive. We are told that persons should not be given a price because this violates their dignity. To be treated with dignity is to be treated as an end in oneself. Ascribing a price to a person leads that person to be regarded as a mere means and this is morally pernicious since all persons should be treated as ends in them-selves.

The concern about the difference between persons and things, refers not just to markets and commerce, but is at the heart of his general moral theory. Kant's Respect for Persons formulation of the Categorical Imperative implores the moral agent to act in such a way as always to treat humanity 'never simply as a means but always at the same time as an end'.[1] We should note the importance of the modifier 'means' in this formulation. Kant's principle does not rule out making use of other people, for if it did it would make demands of us that would render social life impossible. In any single day we necessarily treat others as means to our ends. The bus-driver who provided transport for me to travel to university, the hairdresser who cut my hair, the librarian who checked out the books I borrowed from the university library and the shop assistant who made me a coffee have all functioned as means to my various ends. Kant does not rule out such instrumental interactions, for he does not regard treating as a means and treating as an end as necessarily incompatible. What is at odds with treating persons as ends is treating them as *mere* means, as mere instruments to our own ends. On this formulation of the Moral Law, instrumental treatment and treating-as-an-end are not mutually exclusive, for it is entirely permissible to treat another as a means so long as one also simultaneously treats that person as an end.[2] We should not treat others as mere instruments for our own ends, but recognise that they are ends in themselves. This is at the heart of the Kantian approach to moral life.

Kant's moral framework then is one important way in which one might flesh out recent moral concerns with 'objectification'. Many feminists, for instance, have objected to pornography on the grounds that it objectifies women. Here one might re-describe this concern, using Kantian terminology, as treating women as mere means. What is wrong with pornography on this line of reasoning is that it leads men to regard women as mere means to gratification and fails to recognise that women have ends of their own, over and above whatever role they play in male fulfilment. We find similar concerns about objectification in sport. Marxian and Weberian criticisms of sport have drawn particular attention to this objectification of athletes and spectators.[3] Theodor Adorno viewed sport as an element of the mass culture of monopoly capitalism, in which the athlete's personal virtuosity is sacrificed in the interests of efficiently serving the collective; in brief, the 'compulsive repetition' of sport that is endured by the athlete mirrors her experiences of the disciplinary injustices of industrial capitalism.[4] Jean-Marie Brohm argues in *Sport: A Prison of Measured Time* that with modern training techniques elite athletes are treated as mere things. Sport involves, according to Brohm, a mechanisation of the body. The sportsperson is: 'treated as an automaton, governed by the principle of maximizing output. The organism is trained to sustain prolonged effort and maintain the necessary regulatory of pace'.[5]

Brohm approvingly cites Jurgen Habermas' comment on the close similarity between production line work and the process of training for sport and remarks that in the guise of a game that is supposed to freely develop the strengths of the individual, sport in fact reproduces the world of work. Underpinning Brohm's objections is the moral claim that it is wrong to be treated as a thing. We might re-describe this (without necessarily endorsing Brohm's broader political views) in Kantian terms and argue that what is wrong with being treated as an automaton is that we are regarded as mere means to others' ends. The sportsperson trained through mechanical processes is not treated as an end in themselves.

One advantage of Kant's price-dignity relation is that it provides critics of markets with an unambiguous framework for demonstrating what is wrong with the commodification of sport. If price and dignity are mutually exclusive then *as a matter of necessity* anything which is commodified no longer possesses the dignity that is due to persons. If the potential commodity is something which should be regarded as an end in itself, then it follows as a matter of necessity that commodification of that entity is morally pernicious. One of the appealing features of Kant's dictum for many of those who would use it in public policy settings is the necessary conclusions one can draw. If we think about it in the context of sport, the professionalisation of athletes is wrong *necessarily* since it evacuates their dignity as a matter of moral logic.

Yet those who would straightforwardly apply Kant's price-dignity relation to the commodification of sport would do so overlooking a *lacuna* in the argument. The suggestion that commodification necessarily means that the commodified object is treated as a mere means is open to counter-example. It is not true that in all instances placing a price on something means that one views it as a mere means. For instance, imagine that the owner of an ageing racehorse decides that it is time for the horse to retire. He has loved the horse and would like to see it enjoy its final years in a pleasant and relaxing environment. He decides that the best option would be for it to be owned by a family with young children and, no longer having young children of his own, he decides to advertise the horse. He comes to the conclusion that in order to ensure that the horse will be taken by a family who really wants it and will love it, he should sell the horse at its going market price. While there are no guarantees here, he hopes that this process will weed out those who are not committed to looking after a horse properly. Thus he is not motivated by the money from the sale, but by his concern for the horse's welfare. What we have here is price with dignity.

There are, in fact, many counter-examples like this. One need only look to the world of work to find cases where price does not prevent a person from regarding the commodified object as an end in itself. A university biologist may do what she does in part for the money, but also in large part because she loves investigating biological phenomena. Her work is a commodity but she does not regard it purely as a mere means to an end. Here once again we have price with dignity. Similar stories can be told in the sporting context.

The upshot of this is that placing a price on something does not necessarily mean that the commodity in question, be it labour, a racehorse or the sporting performance, is regarded as a mere means. If we are to show how commodification might give rise to some form of objectification then it would seem that we need to think more carefully about how it might do so.

Second, in the sporting sphere there are independent reasons for eschewing the price-dignity relation as traditionally conceived. Think of the radical implications of Kant's claim for sport. As we noted in chapter 2, if commodification necessarily leads to objectification, then it would seem commercial sport is necessarily morally bankrupt. Since athletes in commercial sport are, as a matter of fact, paid for their efforts, it must follow as a matter of logic on Kant's dictum that they necessarily are not accorded the requisite dignity. They must necessarily be treated as mere means. But if this is true, and given that we agree that people should not be treated as mere means, then commercial sport is not morally permissible. Kant's commodification critique would be abolitionist with respect to professional sport; and commerce in sport should be abolished entirely. This we take as a reason in itself for rejecting the approach.

It would seem then that Kant is wrong about the nature of the relationship between price and dignity. Why did Kant believe that putting a price on something must lead to regarding it as a mere means? A rational agent will certainly recognise that a thing that is bought and sold is a commodity, but will she necessarily view it *merely* as a commodity?

It turns out that this conflation of commodity with mere commodity is a consistent feature of his work on money. We find related puzzling comments about the pernicious role of money in the *Lectures on Ethics* when he discusses the evils of prostitution:

> But to allow one's person for profit to be used by an other for the satisfaction of sexual desire, to make of oneself an Object of demand, is to dispose over oneself as over a thing and to make of oneself a thing on which another satisfies his appetite, just as he satisfies his hunger upon a steak.[6]

But why should making oneself an 'object of demand' mean that one is *only* an object of demand – a mere thing such as a steak? Kant suggests that in commercial sex the 'inclination is directed towards one's sex and not towards one's humanity'.[7]

What is particularly perplexing about all of this is how his claims about money and intrinsic value sit with the compatibilism of his Principle of Respect for Persons. That principle allows for instrumental and non-instrumental modes of regard to coexist. Yet when Kant attends to the market context such compatibilism appears not to be a live option.[8] Given his prior discussion in the *Groundwork* one might have expected Kant to proclaim that everything has either a *mere* price or a dignity. Here the compatibilist option seems unavailable to the potential commodifier, for Kant assumes that in the commercial realm to be a means is necessarily to be a mere means.

One possible response at this point would be to abandon the idea that commodification has consequences for how commodified goods are treated and regarded. We believe that such a response would be a mistake. There is an important connection between commodification and treating as a mere means. Recall that the Kantian line is that commodification of an object *necessarily* leads us to treat it as a mere means. But we need not conceive of the relationship in such strong modal terms. It need not necessarily lead to purely instrumental regard but instead has a corrosive tendency to do so. Let us call this the 'Corrosion Thesis'. The idea here is that if one incorporates a good into the market, then there is a strong tendency for it no longer to be valued intrinsically.[9] According to the Corrosion Thesis, money or commodification has a strong tendency to corrode our attitudes towards commodified goods such that we will often come to regard the commodity as a mere means. In doing so we come to disregard the ends of the commodified entity.

The Corrosion Thesis thus involves a causal claim rather than a logical one. This causal claim we might conceive of analogously with the kind of connection that is drawn between smoking and cancer. It is not that smoking necessarily leads to lung cancer. Nonetheless there is a causal relationship between the two.

On this model it is not that commercial sport is ethically impossible or necessarily wrong, but that it provides us with 'ethical hazards'. Commercial sport, if left to its own devices, might well give rise to objectified modes of regard. Our aim is to ensure that we do not succumb to such attitudinal states.

Commodification and athletes as *mere* means

How might athletes come to be regarded as mere means? In sport there are many routes to such 'depersonalisation'. It can arise through competition itself, through cultures of violence sometimes associated with sport as well as through commodification.

Let us begin with competition itself. In elite sport, athletes and teams compete against one another, ideally in a mutual quest for excellence. However, competition can lead to depersonalisation. Scott Kretchmar, in his book *Practical Philosophy of Sport* outlines three main ways in which athletes come to treat other athletes or themselves as mere means, these being 'excessive survivalism', 'runaway individualism' and 'oppressive rationalism'.[10] (Although the terms he employs sound slightly odd, they mark out three important forms of depersonalisation in sport.) 'Excessive survivalism' describes cases where one is so obsessed with victory that one will do anything to win. One will cheat, tamper with rules or even play ludicrously weak opponents just to ensure that one does not lose. (It is said that the chess champion Bobby Fischer stopped playing chess when his obsession with not losing took over from his desire to win.) Kretchmar suggests that in the first place this involves a failure to respect persons because it treats one's opponents as mere means to victory. One's opponents' ends of desiring victory are not respected here as being in any sense a legitimate outcome. In the second place, excessive survivalism leads athletes to fail to use sport to develop their talents and abilities, instead sacrificing those opportunities to the cause of victory.

Kretchmar's second category, 'runaway individualism', describes cases where the competitiveness of sport leads one to view sport simply as an arena for self-aggrandisement. In such cases one fails to see sport as an opportunity for cooperative enterprise and instead one simply focuses on one's own achievements and level of fitness and exhibits an insensitivity to the ends of others.[11] Here the athlete is disinterested in (and perhaps incapable of recognising) shared ends that are part and parcel of a great deal of sport. For such egoists, all other persons with whom one plays, be they team-mates or opponents in team sports or fellow competitors in individual pursuits, become mere means to one's own end of self-glorification.

Kretchmar's final category, 'oppressive rationalism', concerns excessive training regimes that we discussed earlier in which athletes are treated by coaches and by themselves as machines. Recall Brohm's comments that the sports person is treated as an 'automaton, governed by the principle of maximizing output'.[12] This is precisely what Kretchmar is concerned with. In oppressive rationalism, every activity in which the athlete engages must be oriented towards ensuring an optimal outcome and this leads the athlete's body to be treated as an object of scientific inquiry. Such scientific training techniques involves an attitude that 'truncates and diminishes the individual' because athletes and their coaches are more interested in records, personal bests and anything else which can be measured, rather than the development of the person as a whole. These techniques objectify athletes as mere performance machines.[13]

Kretchmar's categories clearly mark out some significant ways in which competitive sport can lead athletes to be regarded as mere means, either by their opponents, coaches, administrators, fans or by the athletes themselves. One important form of depersonalisation not included here is that of violence in sport. One striking feature of many elite sports is the violence involved. This is particularly true in the various soccer codes where, to varying degrees players, inflict great injuries on one another. It is difficult to see how such violence involves respecting opposing athletes as ends in themselves.[14]

Despite the widespread acceptance of the deliberate infliction of harm on others, sporting cultures that accept and promote such violence violate the principle of respect for persons and are to be condemned on these grounds. There is of course the view that sporting arenas are special spheres where the rules of every-day life do not apply. Behaviours which would not be acceptable on the street are often accepted as common practice in sport and players who engage in them are not condemned as they would in the world outside of sport. In sport, be it at an elite or amateur level, it is not uncommon to encounter the phenomenon colloquially referred to as 'white line fever' where ordinarily mild-mannered, civilised and cultured citizens become vicious thugs once they cross into the playing field. Sport is outside the rules of everyday life and those who exhibit symptoms of white line fever are not treated as criminals or psychopaths as they would undoubtedly be if they acted so violently on the street.

So inured are many sports fans to this idea of sport as a special or exceptional sphere that any mooted intrusion by the law into its jurisdiction is regarded as outrageous. For instance, many Australian Rules football fans were shocked in the early 1980s when police attending a game threatened to charge a particularly violent player for the Hawthorn football team with assault. Sport is sport and criminal statutes were regarded as out of place in the world of sport.

Such violence might be justified by the claim that it is directed 'at the jumper' and not at the player or person. Opposition players who engage in violent behaviour towards one another do not hate each other, but rather hate the teams that their opponents represent. In this way it might be argued that sporting violence does not violate the Principle of Respect for Persons. One can hate a team without hating the human beings who make up the team. Indeed some sports cultures continue to promote an ethic among players that terminates match enmities (and often promotes forms of social bonding) at the end of play. Up until the 1980s in amateur Australian Rules football matches, it was not uncommon to see players who had inflicted great injury on one another walking off arm in arm after the final siren sounded. In contact sports such as rugby and soccer that are played in the United Kingdom, one common ethic promotes respect for players who can 'take it' as well as 'give it' without complaint. Yet there is also evidence that in increasingly rationalised and competitive sports, the maintenance of fraternal sociability is on the wane. At many fixtures, the post-match handshake between opposing players seems to have become little more than an archaic ritual.

Defenders of sporting violence might argue that it has to be remembered that nearly everyone who plays rough sport does so of their own free will. In this sense, then they have consented at least to the possibility of being harmed, even if they do not consent to any particular harm. Let us call this the 'justification from consent'. Given that we should respect the freely chosen decisions of all competent adults, then we cannot morally condemn the violence that such agents consent to inflict upon one another.

While there is some sense in which these lines of justification are correct, there are limits to their applicability. White line fever is in the end morally wrong, at least in its extreme manifestations. Although it is possible in theory to distinguish the person from the jumper, such distinctions are hard to maintain when one is actually directly harming another person. Such distinctions are psychologically unstable, particularly when one is not just hurting a jumper but inflicting pain and perhaps permanent injury on another human being.

The 'justification from consent' is a slightly more complicated argument with which to deal. Can people consent to have their persons violated? To what extent does respect for persons require that we respect the choices, no matter how self-destructive, of autonomous agents? There are good Kantian grounds we suggest for rejecting choices which might lead to extreme forms of harm to oneself as being worthy of respect, for the person who submits to such violence fails to respect the humanity in him or her self. Kant himself discusses the immorality of the male who submits to castration in order to improve his singing voice. Following this line of reasoning we might say that the mere fact that a person consents to an extremely violent sport in no way means that it does not involve a violation of the principle of respect for persons. Respect for consent does not mean concerns with serious physical harm being inflicted on a person are thereby irrelevant. Extreme violence is wrong because it damages the person upon whom it is perpetrated and the mere fact that a person consents to the violence, if they do so, does not mitigate the harm.

Thus, while there is a case for keeping separate ordinary laws of assault from body-contact sports, this does not give rough players *carte blanche* to inflict serious life-long injuries on other players. Any sporting culture that encourages extreme violence fails to respect the persons who wear the jersey and this is a reason for condemnation of that culture. This obviously has implications for the sport of boxing. Boxing often inflicts long-term harm on boxers, as anyone who has witnessed the plight of Muhammed Ali suffering from boxing-induced Parkinson's will be well aware. Boxing clearly seems to violate the principle of respect for persons and on these grounds such a sporting culture stands condemned. Unless boxing officials can find ways to minimise the long-term harms suffered by boxers, then appeals to either the claim that boxers freely consent to any injuries they receive or to the claim that boxers only hate their opponent *qua* opponent, cannot be thought to override our legitimate concerns with the failure of boxing as a sporting practice to respect persons as ends in themselves.

Commodification is another important way in which athletes might come to be objectified. In addition to sporting violence and Kretchmar's three categories, the professionalisation of sportsmen and women can lead to a situation where they are treated as mere means by those who purchase their services. This is most obvious in the case of player markets. As professional sports become increasingly commercial in orientation, players often come to be regarded by clubs as mere commodities to be traded on markets in much the same way that one would trade wheat, iron or any other fungible item. As Robert Simon notes, this can also affect the relationship between players and fans. Players come to be regarded by team supporters 'less as persons and more as products who are defective if they do not produce high performances on the field'.[15] Here the advent of price certainly seems to have evacuated their dignity as persons.

In some ways players in team sports are responsible for such attitudes from fans. Many players are highly transient, moving from one team to another in search of the best financial deal and their peripatetic ways have had an effect on how they are regarded by fans. Fans in many elite sporting competitions are now less likely to view individual players as representatives of their club and its community of supporters and instead regard them as hirelings brought in for the specific task of improving their club's fortunes. Fans feel little loyalty towards and have little empathy with the players because they know the player has played for rival clubs in the past and will in all likelihood play for other rivals in the future. The players' lack of club loyalty means that the fans simply see them as mere instruments of success.[16] Players are thus evaluated entirely in terms of their success-rate. If the players fail to help the club succeed, then the players have failed full stop and fans are not slow to make the players in a failing club aware of their shortcomings. This is vastly different from the more traditional situation where player and fans alike share in clubs' successes and failures. In this way, players are thus no longer regarded as ends in themselves.

Commodification can also be responsible for a 'ratcheting up' of competitive pressures. Since there are great sums of money involved in many sporting competitions, this means that the pressures to succeed often become greater than would have been in the case in less commercially oriented competitions. For example, in British soccer it has become common for the mass media and sports officials to discuss competitive successes in financial terms. The achievement of winning the Scottish Premier League, or taking fourth spot on the English Premiership, is typically reckoned in financial terms, as guaranteeing entry to the lucrative European Champions League tournament. In English soccer, the annual match between two lower division sides is often referred to as the 'richest game in world soccer', since it enables the winners to gain promotion to the lucrative Premiership. In 2005 it was estimated that West Ham United earned around €50 million by beating Preston North End to win promotion. Hence, the financial rather than soccer prize associated with entry to the Premiership has become more dominant in the popular imagination.

In this context the forms of objectification outlined by Kretchmar are more likely to arise. If we consider each of his categories in turn we can see how commercialisation might intensify any pressures in their direction. His first category concerned the obsession with victory such that one will do anything to win. Clearly the great sums of money involved in sport increase this tendency towards 'excessive survivalism'. Equally, the imposition and acceptance of oppressive training regimes in which athletes are treated as mere machines is more likely to occur when great sums of money are involved. Kretchmar's 'oppressive rationalism' is a common feature of much highly competitive commercial sport. Finally, the high sums of money not only increase the competitive pressures but also create grave dangers of hubris for successful players. Kretchmar's 'runaway individualism' in which sports people focus simply on their own achievements is more likely to occur in a highly commercial context. When one is earning great sums of money for one's sporting prowess, the temptations to think that those sums of money are indicative of one's ultimate standing in the cosmos are quite high.[17] In each of these cases we find players being treated as mere means.

However, it might be argued that the line of reasoning explored above misses the point, for Kantianism really should be thought of as providing a more thoroughgoing critique of competitive sport. After all, isn't all competitive sport about thwarting the ends of others? The claim here is not that commercialisation leads to the violation of the Principle of Respect for Persons, but that *all competitive sport* necessarily involves athletes treating each other as mere means. If one engages in competitive sport then one aims to defeat one's opponent. Given that the aim of one's opponent is to win, then in aiming for victory one must be aiming to thwart the ends of one's opponent. How could willing the defeat of one's opponent be anything other than a failure to respect his or her ends? And following this line of reasoning, it must also be true that one's opponent aims to thwart your ends. Since in competitive sport the pursuit of victory is typically the aim of all competitors, then surely all competitive sport fails to live up to the Kantian standards of moral permissibility.

On the face of it this looks like a serious attack upon elite competitive sport. If one takes Kant's maxim seriously then it looks as if, not only highly commercialised sport, but all competitive sport is immoral. Much depends here upon the spirit in which sport is played. If competitors engage in sport under the influence of the ideal of the mutual pursuit of excellence then this allows for all competitors to pursue victory and simultaneously to respect the end of their opponents. To see how this might be, let us think about competitions in which all competitors aim to excel in whatever skills or talents it is that the sport demands. For instance, in basketball a player's aim might be to develop whatever potentials she possesses to their fullest extent. Such potentials are most fully realised when she competes against other basketballers also aiming to develop their abilities to the outer-limits. In pursuing her abilities to the utmost, an aspiring basketball champion does not thwart her opponents' ends (since her aim is also to excel in her chosen sport), but rather she creates a context in which they can both pursue their chosen ends.

This might initially sound counter-intuitive, since we are now so accustomed to regarding sport as being primarily about victory and it is true, as we noted above, that in many sports the mutual pursuit of excellence has given way to victory at all costs. But to see the continuing relevance of the mutual pursuit of excellence to sport consider a contrary case where one's opponent gives up and does not compete whole-heartedly. In this case one cannot develop one's skills to the greatest extent possible since one's opponent does not provide one with any challenge. One feels a strong sense of disappointment at the completion of the game for the very reason that one has not been challenged and there is little opportunity for one's skills to develop. If victory were one's sole aim then one should not feel that sense of let-down. But one does and that is because one's opponent has not provided one with a challenge that allows one to pursue one's end of developing skills. One's ends are in fact thwarted by one's opponents choosing not to compete properly.

The more general point here is that if sport is played in a spirit in which competitors challenge one another and in so doing develop their skills and abilities, then genuine competition is not only compatible with the Kantian principle of respect for persons, but it would seem necessary for the realisation of all competitors' ends. Indeed it is against this understanding of the ethos of sport that we can appreciate what is wrong with sport when victory becomes the sole aim.

Our conclusion then is that sportspeople do not fail to treat one another as ends when they compete against each other as such. When competitors lose sight of such ideals as the mutual pursuit of excellence, then they will violate the Principle of Respect for Persons. And, as we noted above, commodification is one important means via which such violations will occur and in which athletes come to be treated as mere means.

Commodification and corruption of the internal developmental logic of sport

Consider now the harm that occurs when we regard *sport itself* as a mere means. At first sight this application of the Kantian formula might appear a little strained. We are talking about a cultural practice and the Kantian principle was formulated with rational conscious agents in mind. Sport is clearly not a person in any sense, let alone a Kantian one. Moreover, there is the question of what ends it is that commodification could possibly corrode. In what sense can we sensibly speak of sport having its own ends that are undermined if it is treated as a mere means?

We need not let ourselves be overly restricted, however, by the Kantian origins of the critique. If sport is intrinsically valuable when it allows persons to realise certain autotelic goals, as we argued in the previous chapter, then sport is an end-in-itself. Whilst it is not a person, the human activity of people pursuing appropriate goals can sensibly be thought of as being valuable in itself. Accordingly, the Corrosion Thesis will apply to sport just as surely as it does to persons.

If we think of sport in Kantian terms, as an end-in-itself, then it follows on the Kantian line of reasoning that as such it should not be treated as a mere means to instrumental ends such as the pursuit of profit. Mike Marqusee expresses this idea with regard to cricket beautifully, when he writes:

> Cricket is its own end. It is not, nor should it be a means to an end: to private profit or national aggrandizement. The baggage of higher purpose, a telltale sign of English capital's perennial need to seek a noble rationale for its beastliness, weighs down the game, suppressing its beautiful pointlessness.[18]

Marqusee directs our attention to the intrinsic value of sport being pursued for its own sake. Sport should not be regarded as subordinate to other external ends. This is no more than another way of saying that people engaging in sport for its own sake is a valuable thing and that external purposes should not be imposed upon such activity. It is not that sport has a meaning or value over and above the value that is realised by those who participate in it – we do not need to engage in 'reification' here to make our point – sport should be regarded by external agents as an end in itself precisely because of the value that is realised by people engaging in sport for its own sake.

Commodification obviously is one mechanism via which sport might come to be regarded as a mere means. As we noted earlier, it is not that commodification necessarily leads us to regard sport as a mere means. There is a tendency for com-modified entities to be regarded as mere means to profit. Those who commodify will often come to see sport itself as a mere financial instrument.

In just the same way we can think of sport as having ends of its own. The ends of sport are nothing more than the elements we spoke of in chapter 3 and would include such things as the mutual pursuit of excellence and fair play. It is against these ends that we may judge any changes and against these ends that we might come to the conclusion that commodification is sometimes corrupting of sport.

Any corrosion of attitude on the part of those who buy and sell sporting commodities is morally significant not simply because of the inappropriateness of the fully commodified mode of regard but because it leads to fundamental changes to sport itself. In regarding sport as a mere means, one becomes disposed to contemplate changes which corrupt sport and which one would not be so disposed if one regarded the sport as an end-in-itself. In the modern world, treating sport as a mere means to profit, in many sports, has led to undesirable changes to their very structure and rules and to the interpretation of those rules, all of which ultimately make sport less a site for human flourishing.

The first of such undesirable changes involves cases where the *very structure* of a game is reorganised along commercial lines in some fundamental way. So, for instance, in cricket we find in recent times the introduction of 20–20 cricket, in which twenty overs, rather than the traditional fifty, are bowled by each side. The aim of this extremely abbreviated version of the game was to halt the decline of interest in one-day cricket. In many North American sports the authorities have introduced 'TV time-outs' which are designed to allow television networks to show commercials even though such time-outs will often involve considerable disrup-tion to the flow of the game.[19] We also find the extension of seasons to maximise the profit returns of the sport, often to the detriment of the player's fitness and the quality of the home and away games. At the time of writing, there were consider-able concerns amongst many first class cricketers about the effect the extended playing schedules were having on players' long-term health and their capacity to recover from injury. In South America, under the influence of television networks, players are regularly moved from one team to another within a single season, in an attempt to create more exciting television spectacles, but in so doing destroying any sense of camaraderie within teams and undermining supporter loyalty.

We also find the rules of sport being transformed as a result of the increasing influence of commercial forces. Changes are sometimes introduced to make a game more entertaining for a mass audience and, in particular, for television audiences. This trend is evident in international cricket, where under the influence of commercial interests, we see an increase in the amount of one-day cricket being played. One-day cricket is an abridged version of the game which appeals to a much broader audience than the traditional five-day Test cricket. The rules of one-day cricket are significantly different from those of the five-day game, most of these changes being designed to make one-day cricket more appealing to non-traditional fans. Thus, we see for example, the introduction of fielding circles to prevent tactics that would frustrate exciting stroke making and coloured uniforms to make the sport more visually appealing on the television. Robert L. Simon notes similar changes in baseball. He suggests that the introduction of a designated hitter into Major League Baseball may have made the game more exciting for those fans that wanted more home runs and more action generally.[20]

Another example where such rule changes have been made is snooker. Here the introduction of more generous pockets and thinner cloth has made for faster games and higher breaks which ultimately are more appealing for television audiences. But there are questions about whether it has diminished the skills required to play the game.

We should not think that such commercially oriented rule-changes are a recent phenomenon. Ian Tyrell, in his study of the professionalisation of American baseball, discusses how in the nineteenth century commercialisation transformed the game as played on the field.[21] Tyrell notes that originally the pitcher had to deliver the ball with a straight-arm action, just as currently is the case in cricket. This action was exceedingly difficult to master and this factor limited the number of pitchers. In the 1870s, however, there was an expansion in the number of professional clubs and this increased the need for good pitchers. According to Tyrell this demand could not be met under the old rules which restricted the type of delivery which was acceptable. In response to this problem in 1884 the owner of the league had those restrictions concerning the bending of the pitcher's arm removed from the laws of the game. But once the pitcher could throw the ball with a bent arm, this shifted the balance of power in favour of the pitcher because it allowed the development of various unorthodox deliveries including the curved ball. As Tyrell noted the end result of the changes was to transform baseball matches into low-scoring duels between pitchers.

Commercial pressures can also influence how sporting officials interpret rules. In the British Premier League there is evidence that refereeing decisions are sometimes made in favour of the rich and popular teams.[22] We are not speaking here of straightforward corruption in which officials are bribed to ensure that certain individuals or teams come first but rather 'loose-officiating' that is oriented towards pleasing the crowd. Robert Simon notes that many critics believe that such loose officiating is rife in the National Basketball Association in the United States. The charge is that NBA officials allow stars to get away with what would ordinarily be seen as rule violations, such as travelling with the ball, in order that the crowd's favourites might score more points.[23] This obviously makes good business sense, since audiences often come to see their favourite players do well and by allowing these rule-violations to go on, crowds are more likely to watch the sport on television or to attend games in person. But clearly such loose officiating, if indeed it does occur, involves a partial and discriminatory application of the rules.

All of this sounds like it involves some kind of corruption of sport, but what exactly is the nature of the harm? The answer is simple. The kinds of changes towards which we have adverted are corrupt because they undermine the ends of sport. For instance, discriminatory loose officiating is corrupt because it undermines sport as the mutual pursuit of excellence. In such cases, some athletes are being rewarded or alternatively not being punished for play that does not meet the standards of excellence achieved by other (less commercially valuable) athletes or teams.

Similarly, rule changes that are oriented towards increasing the mass entertainment value of sports are corrupting when they undermine the nuance of the game. In order to attract mass audiences sporting administrators sometimes eliminate aspects of the game that only appeal to knowledgeable, long-term fans. In so doing they often down-grade the kinds of subtle skills required on the part of players and thus corrupt the game as an opportunity for the development of such skills. The rule changes of snooker discussed above would be an obvious example of such a corrupt change. When a sport becomes less demanding in terms of the skills it requires on the part of players, then all other things being equal, this involves a corruption of the game.

Robert Simon makes the further suggestion that this kind of athletic deskilling has what he calls a 'steam-roller effect'. As fans less educated in the nuances of the game are drawn to it, the sport will be changed more and more frequently to ensure that it is increasingly entertaining, though this Simon says is at the cost of 'important principles that make the game challenging and important traditions that have been part of its history'.[24]

It should not be thought that the objection here is to change itself. It is not that change itself is corrupting, but rather that change driven by external demands for profit often rides roughshod over the ends of the particular sport. To see this, we should contrast the kinds of corrupt changes noted above with those directed by the ends of sport. There is legitimate change that is a response to the *internal developmental logic* of sport. Sport has a developmental logic of its own in which rules are modified in response to internal demands for change that is in response to needs that arise from a desire to further the internal ends of sport itself.

The difference between rules changes motivated by the internal logic of a game and by money can be seen by thinking of some of the changes which have been made in soccer. In the early 1990s, the rising efficacy of defensive and destructive tactics needed to be challenged in order to reaffirm the value of attacking, skilful play. The world governing body FIFA contributed significantly towards meeting those ends by banning the time-wasting 'pass-backs' to goalkeepers and empowering referees to clamp down strongly on cynical fouls. However, many soccer fans reacted furiously to reports that FIFA were considering more radical rule-changes in order to sell the game more easily to American audiences, notably when the United States hosted the 1994 World Cup finals. Mooted rule changes had included widening the size of the goal area to increase goal scoring, and having games divided up into four quarters rather than the existing two halves in order to attract more advertising revenues. Such proposals were criticised explicitly for their monetary orientation. In this case, the views of established soccer followers were heeded and these suggested changes were quietly deflated.

In his book *The Battle for Human Nature* Barry Schwartz provides another useful discussion of this internal developmental logic as it arises in the game of basketball. To be sure, Schwartz's aim is to explore the notion of goods internal to a practice rather than an examination of the values inherent in sport, but nonetheless his discussion is pertinent to our own topic. Schwartz suggests that the value realised in basketball was once thought to involve skills in dribbling and passing, accurate shooting and above all coordination amongst members of the team.[25] Over time, basketball came to be played by some very tall people who had sufficient coordination and could simply stand at the goals and place the ball in the basket from a very close range. The aim of the game changed; all that teams had to do was to pass the ball to a very tall person positioned near the goals and he would shoot. In this way, sporting skills such as accurate shooting and so on came to be less important and the value realised in the game for players was also diminished. To allow such value to continue to be realised the rules were changed. Restrictions were placed on the amount of time an individual player could camp beneath the basket; each player was only allowed beneath the basket for a brief period of time. Now success required skills in addition to height. It still remained that the most effective way of playing was to get the ball to the big men near the basket, but now 'exquisite timing, planned movement and sharp passing' were also required to do that well. In this way, the values realised in the sport were preserved.

What is significant about this passage is the claim that changes to the structure and rules is morally desirable when it is driven by the desire to preserve goods internal to the sport itself. These *internal demands* for change are to be contrasted with those that do not arise from within the sport, but are due to external forces, such as money. Schwartz contrasts the case with an example of *external demands* for change that involve money. He suggests that changes to rules about the length of time one could camp under a basket are to be distinguished from the introduction of a time limit within which a shot could be taken. This rule he suggests was introduced to increase the speed of the game, so as to make it more appealing to spectators and in this way more commercially successful. However, he claims that it diminished the time available for passing and coordinated team play and led to players launching shots from a long way out as soon as they could. While skills at long distance shooting were eventually developed, it diminished the opportunities for developing skills in passing and cooperating. Schwartz's point here is that, even if other skills developed, the impetus for change came from outside of the sport itself and not from any desire to preserve or enhance the pre-existing good-making features of the game.

At this point we should note that commodification is not the only conduit to corruption. As the quote from Mike Marqusee would suggest, when sport is treated as a mere means to national aggrandisement, then it is also corrupted. For instance, when, in the name of national glorification, States engage in systematic doping of their athletes, then sport is corrupted. It is corrupted because the important goal of the mutual pursuit of excellence is subordinated to winning at all costs so that national pride can be asserted. Equally, the 1936 Berlin Olympics were corrupted because the Games were regarded by the German government of the time as a mere means for glorifying the Third Reich. When Hitler refused to attend the ceremony in which the black athlete Jesse Owens was awarded a gold medal, it was simply the most egregious example of a more general attempt on the part of the German state to use sport as a tool of political propaganda. Hitler's racialism meant that he was not at all disposed to attend a ceremony in which a black – and in his eyes inferior – athlete was honoured. But in so doing Hitler and his fellow Nazis failed to follow accepted norms of good sportsmanship that are an integral element of such events.

Accordingly, we should acknowledge that there are means other than the market via which the proper ends of sport might be undermined or violated. But our point was not to claim that the market is the only such mechanism, rather it was simply that in our modern capitalist context commodification is an important, and in all likelihood the primary, means through which sport is objectified and often thereby corrupted.

Commodification then is pathological with respect to sport itself when it gives rise to either of the two following phenomena. First, it is pathological when it leads us to regard sport as a mere means for the pursuit of profit rather than an end-in-itself. (Here the concern is with modes of regard.) Second, it is pathological when it leads to the corruption of the ends of sport so that the very structure and rules of sport are transformed to accommodate the needs of capital. As we noted above, this is not the only way in which sport might be corrupted, but in the modern world it is a dominant and perhaps the primary way in which corruption occurs. If elite sport is to be commodified then we must be vigilant that it does not come to be seen as a mere goldmine. We should also guard against the logic of its development being driven by factors external to sport rather than those that fit with what we might properly think of as the ends of sport.

Summary

Commodification of sport is pathological, amongst other things, when it leads us to regard either athletes or sport itself as mere commodities and, in this way, 'objectifies' them. In pursuing this line of argument we do not claim, as Kant famously did, that commercialisation *necessarily* denies dignity, but rather that there is a strong causal tendency for commercial entities to come to be regarded by those who buy and sell them as mere means to the realisation of profit. With respect to athletes, it is not uncommon in our commercially-oriented sports to see them treated as if they were cattle in a stock market, their respective sporting qualities being compared and evaluated with little respect for the persons that are the bearers of such properties. With respect to sport itself commodification can lead those in charge of its development and administration to regard it as a mere vehicle for financial reward and in this way the internal developmental logic of sport is corrupted.

Of course, none of this is to rule commercial sport morally objectionable in itself. As was the case in our earlier treatments, we do not regard the commercialisation of sport as intrinsically morally pernicious. Instead, it is simply that the commodification of sport often leads to instrumental or objectified modes of regard and when it does so it is rightly censured.

5 Sport, commodification and distributive justice

Introduction

In the British film *Purely Belter* two young Newcastle United fans ('wannabe' members of the so-called 'Toon Army'), driven by a desire to buy season's tickets, engage in a series of somewhat implausible illegal escapades to gain the necessary funds. The subtext of the film is that the entry prices to what was once the people's game have become so high as to exclude many of the traditional fan base. The film reeks with a sense of basic injustice.

This leads us naturally to another area of moral concern upon which commodification impinges; namely that of *distributive justice*. Markets are amongst other things distributive mechanisms; in the market goods are allocated via the price system from buyers to sellers. Thus, when we commodify, we not only transform the incentive structure; we also transform the mechanism via which social goods are distributed. In pathological cases such a transformation will have morally undesirable effects because the outcomes will be unjust and this is as true in the sporting realm as it is elsewhere. In this chapter we explore circumstances in sport in which commodification leads to distributive injustice.

Let us begin however with a general survey of the theoretical terrain; what it is that theories of distributive justice examine, how it is that problems of distributive justice arise and how it is that markets and money function as distributive mechanisms.

Distributive justice, distributive principles and scarcity

Our concern in this chapter is with justice. Since Aristotle's canonical treatment of the topic in the *Nicomachean Ethics*, it has been conventional for political philosophers to distinguish between two central categories of justice, rectificatory justice and distributive justice. Rectificatory justice concerns restoring fair shares when some unfairness has come about and hence covers justice in punishment and justice in contracts. Distributive justice concerns the allocation of social benefits and burdens: it is concerned with ensuring among the citizens a proper distribution of honour and wealth as well as unpleasant tasks that no one wishes to perform.[1] Our interest herein is primarily with the effects of commodification on allocation of the benefits and burdens to be found in sport and so when we use the term 'justice' we will mean the distributive variant.

Let us consider distributive justice in a little more detail. In general it concerns itself with the proper allocation of *social goods* such as honour, money, rights and privileges as well as *social burdens*. When people argue about who should have access to irrigation water, how low a minimum wage should be, whether basic medical services and housing should be provided by the State or what rate of taxation is fair, they are arguing about questions of distributive justice. In sport, as in all spheres of human life, there are important questions about the just allocations of benefits that are debated and resolved. Examples would be, for instance, debates about the principles upon which sporting trophies should be awarded (should they be for the best or the best and fairest), or how tickets to major sporting events like the Olympics should be allocated.

Of course, all of the examples we have given thus far have involved benefits produced by the community. But distributive justice also concerns the allocation of social burdens. In *Spheres of Justice* Michael Walzer famously discusses the case of the rich Northerners buying their way out of conscription during the American Civil War. The rule was quickly rescinded after an enormous outcry on the part of the population that threatened to derail the Northern war effort. The evidence from those protests suggests that the population at large believed that the social burden of military service (with its attendant risks of death) should be shared by all of the adult male population, rather than being something out of which the rich could buy their way.[2] Decisions about where polluting industries should be located or where a new highway should run and whose houses will have to be demolished to make way for it or who should undertake dirty and dangerous occupations and how much they should be paid all concern the allocation of social burdens. In sport there are also such decisions to be made regarding burdens: how often teams must play away from home, who is responsible for injured players, who gets the outside lane in a relay race or what fans will lose their seats when stadia are redeveloped.

In delineating the basic elements of philosophical debates over distributive justice, we should also consider the circumstances that give rise to the problem in the first place. Central to the problem of distributive justice is the phenomenon of *scarcity*. Distributive problems arise in large part because of scarcity. There is a distributive problem, for instance, over the allocation of tickets to major sporting events because in such cases demand exceeds supply and thus not everyone who wants a seat at the event can have one. Such seats might be said to be scarce. Where goods are not scarce, there is rarely disputation over how they should be allocated. Fresh air in pristine mountain regions is not at all in short supply and hence it is unlikely that anyone would argue over who should have access to particular cubic metres of oxygen, or for that matter to any of the oxygen in supply. We might further distinguish between two forms of scarcity, namely between *moderate* and *hard* scarcity. Moderate scarcity covers cases where all relevant members of a community can have access to a good but not in the amounts they might desire. Delicacies such as mangoes might be thought to be moderately scarce in that there is sufficient for everyone to regularly eat them, but not enough for everyone to eat them whenever they like. In cases of moderate scarcity it is possible to allocate goods equally. Hard scarcity refers to cases where it is impossible to allocate the goods in question equally. Think of a lifeboat situation. When we have ten people and only five can board the boat without it sinking, then the good of a life-saving spot in the boat cannot be distributed equally. Some potential beneficiaries will have to miss out. Similar examples arise with medical equipment, such as kidney machines where perhaps 20 people need a machine that can only be used by one. These are all cases where demand outstrips supply in such a way that some persons will be excluded from access. In cases of hard scarcity a theory of distributive justice determines in effect who will be excluded. A meritocrat would give a seat in the lifeboat to the most deserving, which might include aged community members who have contributed a great deal in the past. A utilitarian on the other hand would allocate seats according to what will most benefit the community in the future and thus might well favour the young and potentially socially productive over the aged. Thus we see different ways in which the central distributive theories will deal with conditions of hard scarcity.

Some philosophers have thought that scarcity is tied so closely to the problem of distributive justice that if scarcity were to be eliminated then the problem of distributive justice would also be eliminated. The thought here is that if all goods were in such abundance that any human interests we wanted could be realised then there would be no need for the community to make decisions about how goods should be allocated. Certainly Marx thought this was reason enough for ignoring questions of distributive justice altogether. In his future Communist Utopia, when the wheels of industry had eliminated scarcity, questions of distribution would simply not arise.

But one imagines that even in such a society of material abundance there would be what are sometimes called 'positional goods'.[3] Positional goods are things such as honours, prizes and status items that are only the kinds of goods they are because they are scarce and not everyone can have them. If everyone were awarded a Nobel Prize at birth, then it goes without saying that it would not have the value it currently has for recipients. The point is that while distributive questions arise because of scarcity, merely bringing about material abundance would not by itself end the need for mechanisms for distributing goods and would not end discussions over the justice of any particular mechanism.

These claims about scarcity also have implications for what we demand of a theory of justice. It can be no criticism of a theory of distributive justice *in itself* that it leads to some human interest not being satisfied or that it excludes some people from accessing the good, for given the fact of scarcity this will be true of any theory of justice. There will necessarily be some human interest that is 'sacrificed' when we make a decision about distribution. For instance, when we fund hospitals rather than Olympic stadiums, this obviously means that the human interests realised when people play sport will not be realised in this case. (Presumably most readers will not find this kind of sacrifice entirely unpalatable.) What needs to be shown is that the interest not realised is in some relevant respect one that should be realised. When one is forced to choose between public hospitals and Olympic facilities, the sacrifice of the opportunities to encounter Olympic sport, is one that many would be willing to make. The fact that one theory of distributive justice, say perhaps a utilitarian one, advocates hospitals over Olympic facilities and its implementation means that some interests in Olympic sport will not be realised is not in itself a criticism of the theory.[4]

The upshot is that when we consider the distributive implications of the market and thereby the moral status of the process of commodification we need to show two things. First, we need to show not only that it will lead to certain human interests not being realised but that these are morally significant human interests, such that failing to realise them whilst realising other interests is morally pernicious. Second, we need to show that there are other ways of distributing these goods that do not have such morally undesirable effects. Simply demonstrating that certain interests are not realised when one commodifies will not by itself provide us with a knockdown objection to this process. We need to consider what alternatives are available. As the economist Bruno Frey notes in a related context: 'Confronted with an excess demand situation, the fairness of pricing should be judged relative to the alternatives which could be used in lieu of a price increase'.[5]

Theories of distributive justice then are concerned with the proper allocation of such benefits and burdens in the context of scarcity and attempt to provide general moral rules for determining a just allocation. Traditionally the main contenders here have been egalitarianism, meritocratic proportionalism, utilitarianism and libertarianism. According to *egalitarian* theories of justice social goods should be governed by the principle of equality. Sometimes this is interpreted as meaning an equal allotment of whatever good it is that is being distributed should be given to each member of the community. Sometimes egalitarianism is interpreted in terms of the notion of 'need' so that goods are allocated according to need, rather than in terms of a straightforward mathematical notion of equality. Marx's famous dictum from *The Critique of the Gotha Program* that in his future communist society goods would be governed by the dictum 'From each according to his ability, to each according to his need', is standardly thought of as embodying an egalitarian ideal. Another tradition, that of *meritocractic proportionalism*, urges that social goods be allocated on the basis of desert or merit. Goods should be distributed in direct proportion to the relative merits of respective members of the community. So, for instance, on this theory relative wage levels should reflect the relative skills, talents or effort (and these bases will each lead to different outcomes) of employees. Other distributive theorists believe that the allocation of goods should be determined by social utility. Decisions about distribution should be governed by an interest in the overall welfare of society as a whole. Here the focus is forward-looking – unlike the meritocrat whose focus looks back in time to see what people deserve on the basis of what they have contributed in the past. However, there are some similarities with desert-based theories, in that both allow unequal distributions. On this theory unequal distributions will be justified when it brings the greatest benefit to society as a whole in the future.

What is common to all of these theories is the idea that the aim of a theory of justice should be to find a single principle that will govern the allocation of all goods. In more recent times, a number of political philosophers have developed *pluralist* theories of distributive justice which attempt to make use of a number of different principles simultaneously in different areas of human social life. The most well known of these is the pluralism Michael Walzer develops in *Spheres of Justice*. Walzer argues social goods should be divided into different spheres, such as the sphere of education, the sphere of bureaucracy (or 'office' as he calls it), the sphere of membership, the sphere of money and commodities and so on. He then provides three distributive principles – free exchange, desert and need – which are to be implemented in the different spheres. The idea is that in some spheres, such as that of the affections, free exchange will be the appropriate principle of allocation, whilst in others either the principle of need or that of desert will be appropriate. Thus prizes and public honours are to be allocated by the principle of desert, while security and welfare are to be distributed on the basis of need. Walzer characterises his pluralism as ultimately being motivated by a concern with what he calls 'complex equality', where equality is realised overall through inequality in different spheres. Part of the aim of the pluralism is to ensure that while a person or group can dominate in one sphere no one person or group dominates in all spheres. According to Walzer the aim of political egalitarianism should be a society free from domination.[6] Whilst he will allow inequality in different spheres, he argues that by maintaining the integrity of different spheres we can achieve equality across the spheres. The goal is to ensure that no one is able to dominate all of the spheres of social life and hence no one will have unequal access to all social goods. This is a complex form of equality. Here money presents special dangers because if everything is commodifed, then those with money can dominate in all social spheres.

This pluralist approach has many advantages. For instance, and perhaps most notably, one of the principal difficulties for any monistic theory of distributive justice is to demonstrate (in a plausible manner) that its single principle is applicable to all relevant cases. Thus, for example, a challenge for an egalitarian – or at least a simple egalitarian if we adopt Walzer's thesis – is to show that equality is applicable to such goods as public honours and prizes or to the realm of romantic love. It is a genuine challenge, for there is something counter-intuitive about the idea that one's love should be distributed equally or that sporting prizes should be handed out to everyone in the same amount. In these cases it is not even clear that they would be the goods that they are if they were distributed equally. Similar puzzles arise for those other philosophical traditions that employ a single principle to cover all distributive goods. The pluralist does not have these difficulties since he or she is not committed to the thought that there is a single distributive principle that must govern the distribution of all social goods.

There are however difficulties with this approach. One question which arises quite naturally here concerns the philosophical basis of such a pluralism. What is it about particular spheres that means they should be governed by the principle of need whilst others are to be governed by free exchange? Without some kind of philosophical justification it looks rather *ad hoc*. Walzer's argument is that different goods have different essential meanings and those meanings are varied in such a way that different principles are appropriate to them. For instance, the meaning attached to the goods of the sphere of romantic love and friendship are such that they must be distributed according to the ideals of free exchange. Similarly with honours and prizes, we find that their meanings are such they must be allocated according to merit, that is to those who deserve them. Many have found this response plausible, however, it does require that commitment to the idea that there are essential meanings that are somehow part and parcel of the very nature of the goods themselves. One might well object that there is no reason for thinking that the meanings we currently attach to goods are somehow sacrosanct and to be respected. What, for instance, would be the harm if society democratic-ally decided that, in the future, marriages were to be arranged by lot, rather than by free exchange as is currently the case? It would of course mean that marriage would become a very different social good, and would carry different meanings. But unless one thinks that the current meanings somehow reflect something about the essential nature of the universe – and this would be a remarkably ahistorical view – then it is hard to see that the mere fact we have in the past allocated these goods in a certain way by itself justifies continuing to do so.

There are other justificatory bases for pluralism. For instance, one might argue that certain ways of allocating goods are more amenable to human flourishing than others. We will say more about this in the next section. Thus we might argue that the goods to be gained in marriage are optimally realised when marriage partners are chosen through the ideal of romantic love according to the principle of free exchange. The reason that we require a plurality of distributive principles is that human goods are varied and human flourishing requires satisfaction via access to these varied goods. In this way, we are not committed to any claims about the essential meanings of human goods. All that is required is endorsement of the view that optimising human flourishing involves amongst other things distributing social goods via a variety of distributive principles.

Commodification and distributive justice: domination and the violation of appropriate distributive principles

Thus far we have said very little about markets and distributive justice or about the distributive implications of commodification. The aim is to show ways in which commodification might distributively be pathological. What then might be wrong about commodification from the point of view of distributive justice?

The first point to make here is that the market is, amongst other things, a *mechanism* for the distribution of social benefits and burdens. Goods are allocated in the market through the price system. Producers of commodities place prices on their goods and through this pricing mechanism various potential buyers (and eventually consumers) decide whether or not they will acquire the commodities in question. If one has the desire to acquire a good, the financial resources to do so at the given price and the willingness of the owner to sell, then the commodified good will be yours. Through millions of such exchanges goods are distributed across a society.

Notice the difference here between market allocation and the principles discussed in the previous section. While the principles of justice outlined above will typically be determined by bureaucratic authorities, the market allocates goods in a much more decentralised and, many would say, principle-free manner. The market allocates goods to those with money, instead of on the basis of some principle like 'first come first served' or equality or desert.[7]

There are some who would dispute the claim that we should (and can) place the market outside of the range of principle since they regard it as in fact embodying salient principles of distributive justice. For instance, there are those who see the market as an arena in which players are rewarded according to their merits. Advocates of *market desert* believe that the differential outcomes of the market simply reflect the relative worth or merit of different market players. Highly productive employees command higher wages than the less productive, just as highly talented sportsmen earn more than their less talented peers. We see this thought at play in the writings of the Italian economist Vilfredo Pareto (1848–1923) who claimed that the constancy of inequality in the distribution of income reflects inequalities of human ability, 'which is a natural and universal category'.[8]

There are two obvious objections to this rather rose-coloured interpretation of market distributions. First, in the market there are such large elements of luck involved in the success of an enterprise that it is hard to see that the relative rewards of different enterprises can always be seen as an exclusive marker of their respective merits. Second, often differential rewards in business are simply a function of differential initial endowments. The son of a tycoon is much better placed to make his way in business than the son of a fish and chip shop owner. The fact that one son earns billions of dollars a year whilst the other scrapes a mere living from his business can hardly be taken seriously as reflecting their respective merits as businessmen. Hence, the idea that the distributive patterns brought about by the market reflect patterns of merit in the community has serious flaws.

Other critics claim that market distributions are principled because they are underpinned by the important ideal of freedom. Here one might draw on Robert Nozick's work to make good the claim. In *Anarchy, State and Utopia* Nozick develops an 'entitlement' theory of justice in which there are three main principles. First, there is a 'principle of transfer' such that whatever is justly acquired can be justly transferred. Second, there is a principle of just acquisition which provides an account of how people come initially to own the things which can be transferred in accordance with the principle of transfer. Third, there is a principle of rectification of injustice which details how to deal with holdings if they are in violation of the first two principles and were not justly acquired or justly transferred. Nozick says that his theory is *historical* and *unpatterned*. It is historical in that it respects the history of how goods come into being in determining a just distribution. It is unpatterned in that there is no particular distributive pattern that his theory advocates must be directed. So long as the distribution of goods across a community is a result of a series of just acquisitions and just transfers then that distribution is just. What underpins all of this is a concern with the free and uncoerced transfer of holdings. He summarises his theory of distribution with the slogan 'From each as they choose, to each as they are chosen'.[9]

The relevance of this to the market as a distributive mechanism should be clear. The market provides us with a system for the distribution of goods which is historical and unpatterned, just as Nozick desires. The idea would be that although it is unpatterned it is not unprincipled because as a mechanism for distributing goods it reflects the important value of freedom.

There are many criticisms that one might raise against Nozick's theory. Notably, one might take issue with the notion of freedom he employs, since it is not one that takes into account the material circumstances in which people find themselves. On Nozick's line of thinking when a piece worker in a sweatshop sells her labour to her employer, she does so freely and thus whatever wages she receives are fair, since they are the result of free bargaining. This is despite the fact that her poverty and need lead her to have little choice in what she accepts for her work. However, if this is freedom then it is not clear that freedom is the kind of value that we should endorse unequivocally or in favour of other values. Other critics have focused on his account of just acquisition.

But even if one accepts this account of justice, and accepts that the unpatterned outcomes of the market are principled, the arguments for characterising the market as a distinct mechanism remain. For what is still true is that, principled or not, in a market there is no authority overseeing that the pattern of distribution that emerges for any particular set of goods or across society as a whole. It is then a different kind of distributive mechanism from those more traditionally associated with theories of justice that tend to aim at achieving specific overall patterns.

As a distributive mechanism we can also pick out both positive and negative aspects of the market. We should begin with the positive aspects for it is important to make the point that the market is not, as some leftists would have, entirely without virtue. It is not, as the socialist Charles Fourier once noted, a 'cesspool of moral filth' and devoid of any redeeming features, for at the very least it generates to some considerable social benefits.[10] Moreover, the incentives, in terms of financial rewards that underpin markets, are capable – in the right circumstances – of generating an unparalleled abundance and variety of goods.

In addition to these practical advantages, the market is, in a certain constrained sense, non-discriminatory. Rank, social status, race and gender are all (ideally at least) irrelevant to the allocation of goods in a market. All that matters is that one has access to money. Indeed, in the early modern period it was the tendency of the market to undermine respect for social distinctions between the traditional aristocracy and the lower orders (some of whom had become very wealthy) that led many to urge the authorities to introduce and maintain sumptuary laws for the regulation of consumption, especially in the area of dress.[11] Markets in clothes and the like allowed anyone with money to buy the fanciest of clothes, even if one was not noble by birth. In this regard, under ideal conditions, the market is distributively virtuous.

But here we should be careful not to overstate the case. Markets also have many negative distributive consequences. It is precisely because of the distributive effects of markets that some of the most vocal opposition to commercial society has arisen. The first here has its origins in the work of Michael Walzer. If most social goods are commodified, then the wealthy will be able to gain access to most goods in greater proportion to less well off members of society. This means that they will come to dominate civic life in a way that we, like Walzer, believe is pernicious. If universities, health care systems, recreational facilities, secondary education, entertainment and natural resources are all commodified and sold to the highest bidders, then the goods to be obtained from such resources will be enjoyed to a far greater extent by the wealthy than by poorer members of society. This we take to be undesirable. Commodification is pathological when it allows the wealthy to dominate the great majority of spheres of human flourishing in a community.

The point here is about the general distribution of goods across society and whether any single group should be able to dominate in all spheres of social life. The relevance of this to sport should be obvious. When the wealthy, who already enjoy privilege, are able to have greater access to sporting goods, then this simply compounds the injustices of society more generally. Think of the allocation of seating at the major Olympic events including the opening ceremonies and 100 metre sprints which are dominated by the international elite.[12] Here we have social goods which would be enjoyed by people from all classes which are in fact dominated by the wealthy. One would think given the general interest in the world in such events that a far fairer way of allocating tickets would be randomly by lot. So the commodification of sport is pathological when it allows the wealthy to dominate the social benefits that sport brings.

The distributive concern with commodification thus far has been with the domination of civic life by the wealthy. There are also important considerations concerning the distributive patterns applied to *particular* goods. There are some goods for which distribution by the market is entirely inappropriate, regardless of pattern of distribution across society as a whole. First, there are those goods which by their very nature should be distributed meritocratically. To distribute *desert goods* via the market, such as academic achievement awards, is a form of distributive injustice. Second, there are those goods which when commodified may well no longer be available to everyone. For instance, if access to a beach which had previously been free was commodified and entry fees are then charged, this might well deny access to some who previously had access. In such cases restriction of access where access had previously been unimpeded is a form of distributive injustice. Third, there are those goods, such as various health services, which satisfy basic needs. To distribute *need goods* by the market is to risk excluding some from access and where people are excluded then this is again a form of distributive injustice. In all of these cases commodification is pathological. The idea is that therein the market is at odds with basic tenets of distributive justice and is accordingly morally pernicious.

In the following sections we will explore in some considerable detail the implications for sport of each of these pathologies. However, before doing so there are two questions we should consider, the first of which is a meta-ethical question concerning the justification for admixing a number of distributive principles in a single theoretical framework. The reason for doing so is that human goods are pluralistic. Therefore some human goods are best realised within a meritocratic framework and for others human flourishing requires that everyone should have access to them. Our pluralism does not derive from the meaning of the goods themselves, as is the case with Walzer's pluralism, but from the structure of human interests. Human interests are so constructed that there will be a variety of ways of distributing the goods that realise those interests.

The second question is a methodological one and concerns our earlier point regarding the scarcity of distributive goods and thus the necessary sacrifices to which any principle of distributive justice or distributive mechanism must give rise. If we are to demonstrate that the price mechanism is not the appropriate means of distributing some of the goods of sport, then it needs to be clear that there is some better alternative. Our criticisms of market allocation cannot simply be criticisms that are open to any and all distributive systems. In what follows we aim to show that there are in fact preferable ways of distributing many of the goods of sport to that which are found in the market system.

The meritocratic allocation of prizes

Most of our contemporary sporting activity is oriented towards the winning of prizes, medals, trophies, and premiership flags. This is at the heart of competition – this is what sportspeople strive for. Such benefits are in fact *desert goods*, that is, they are goods which should be allocated meritocratically. If they were not to be allocated to the athlete who most deserved them, then we would say that an injustice had occurred. It would, for instance, be unfair for a best and fairest trophy to be awarded to an inferior player simply because his uncle was President of the club.

As desert goods there are relevant *desert bases*, that is the grounds upon which we determine that one potential recipient is either more, equally or less deserving than another. The basis of a person's desert must in the first place be a fact about that person such as their relative skills or achievement. So the fact that Uralla is in New South Wales or that 8 is smaller than 9 is not a reason for you to be awarded the best and fairest medal in your local hockey competition.[13] Second, it is usually thought (although this is not uncontroversial) that the desert base should be something for which the subject of desert is responsible.[14] Thus, to employ a sporting example, I should only be awarded a gold medal for the Olympic marathon if indeed it was me who ran it and I did not employ substitutes during various points of the race. To be sure, there are questions that could be raised here concerning whether winning athletes are in every case responsible for the individual properties which allowed them to succeed in their chosen sports. While there are strong grounds for the claim that the cricketer who spends hours hitting a golf ball against a corrugated iron tank to hone his batting is responsible for the skills which allow him to succeed, we might well wonder whether a 7 foot basket-baller is really responsible for the height which allows him to succeed. One might take this line of reasoning to its ultimate conclusion to arrive at the thesis that no one is responsible for anything. But, this must be wrong for there are cases, such as the athlete who trains assiduously, where we would want to say that the athlete in question is relevantly responsible for the powers and abilities which allow them to satisfy the basis of desert in their sport.

In competitive sports a great deal of effort is expended in analysing and measuring player's and teams' performances against the standards that are determined by the relevant desert base. These desert bases will differ from sport to sport. In the javelin the salient desert base is one's ability to throw a metal pole of a specified weight and length further than any other competitor, in hockey it is the ability to score more goals than one's opposition and in swimming it is the ability to move from one end of the pool through the water using a specific stroke faster than anyone else. Sports officials, including referees and officials, are there to determine who best satisfies the criteria for excellence in the sport; that is, they are adjudicators of desert bases. It is their duty to ensure that sporting honours are in fact distributed meritocratically. Ensuring that rules are adhered to, preventing violations of codes and interpreting the laws of the games are all ultimately oriented towards ensuring that the honours are given to the most worthy recipient. When a sporting prize is awarded to a competitor that we feel did not in fact best satisfy the standards of the sport, then we feel that an injustice has been done to other competitors. Typically it is the sports officials who are held responsible for any such injustice.

Take the Argentinian Soccer player Diego Maradona's famous 'Hand of God' goal in the 1986 World Cup game versus England. In this case Maradona scored a goal using his hand rather than his head. Since the laws of soccer prohibit touching the ball with one's hand, the goal was not scored fairly. Many English soccer fans still see that game as an injustice, for they do not believe the better team won the match, although it was not only that goal which separated the two teams. What implicitly underpins such complaints is a deep-felt belief that sporting honours are the kinds of goods that should be allocated meritocratically.

This brings us to commodification and the role of money in sport. To allow the distribution of prizes to be commodified would also be an injustice. To allow the Wimbledon Men's Singles Championship to be won by the person most willing to pay for it would be unjust to the other competitors precisely because this is a prize that should be distributed according to the principle of desert. Just as we would say it was unfair for the best and fairest to be awarded on nepotistic grounds, it would also be unjust to do so on the basis of one's financial standing.

At this point it might be objected that this way of putting our concern with the commodification of prizes involves some misdescription or misclassification. Any prize or trophy allocated by the price system would no longer be the prize that it is. Imagine that in 2014 the Wimbledon trophy is awarded to the person most willing to pay for it. In giving the trophy to the highest bidder, it would immediately lose the status it currently bears. In describing what is wrong with commodification then it might seem odd to speak of injustice. Would we say that it was unfair? It is unlikely we would do so for long, since the good would have changed its meaning and character the very moment the decision to auction it was made. The problem now looks more like one of destroying or corroding a social good, rather than one of unfair allocation. Commodification would be wrong, but not for reasons of justice.

How should we respond? Can we truly speak of money causing an injustice in this context? In response we agree that if we are talking about *explicit markets* then concerns about injustice are not really central to the moral harm of such commodification. But there are ways in which money can influence the distribution of sporting goods without destroying their meanings. If it were the case that dirty or illegal money could influence officials and referees to favour certain competitors, and that the public at large were not alerted to this fact, then money could allow a wealthy competitor to obtain a trophy without its status being affected. Let us call this *dirty commodification*. In such a case we would quite naturally say that an injustice had occurred. We would say that such an outcome was unfair to the other competitors who did not pay bribes because the prize was awarded on an inappropriate non-meritocratic basis. In *The New Lords of the Rings* Andrew Jennings claims that at the Seoul Olympics various boxing judges were bribed and deserving competitors missed out on gold medals that were rightfully theirs. His claim is not that the judges destroyed the meaning of the gold medals – and hence undermined its status as a human good – but rather that what occurred was fundamentally unfair.

Boxing in general is a special case, since it has a particularly colourful history of corruption involving promoters, judges, trainers and the governing bodies.[15] But there have been many other examples of sporting events where money has had an undue effect on the outcome through the machinations of corrupt officials. In such cases it makes perfect sense to talk of the injustice of the outcome.

In addition to dirty commodification, there are also cases of *quasi-commodification* where money indirectly influences the outcome. Here it is not that we have fully fledged markets such that one can directly buy sporting honours. Instead in cases of quasi-commodification it becomes difficult for those without adequate financial resources to compete effectively. If this comes to pass, then it is no longer clear that the competition is fair. It is not clear that those who win really are the most deserving with respect to the excellences that the sport is intended to develop, test and reward. Such quasi-commodification arises regularly in sports that involve technology. Take sailing as an example. This, like motor racing, is a sport in which success is largely determined by the quality of the equipment one has and those with more money can obviously buy superior equipment. If this is true then the competition is no longer a test of the competitors' relative sailing skills, their seamanship, but simply a measure of their wealth. This we suggest is also antithetical to the idea of competition. As Robert Simon notes, when a team wins a contest because of access to technology, we should ask ourselves whether the best team has really triumphed.[16] In this context the Norwegian philosopher Gunnar Breivik has argued that if performance-enhancing technology is to be available at all, then it should be made available to all competitors.[17] But this could not be the end of the story. For even if this was distributively more appropriate, there would still be non-distributive moral reasons for wanting to reject the suggestion. As Sigmund Loland notes in *Fair Play*, the harms to athletes from the use of, for instance, drugs would be such that even if this is an equitable solution it will still not be morally desirable.[18]

When sporting success is a partial function of how wealthy one is, then the competition is unfair, for justice requires that outcomes are determined by the respective merits and money on its own is not a relevant marker of merit. Some now feel that success in the English Premier League is simply out of the question for the poorer smaller clubs and that only a handful of elite clubs, such as Arsenal, Chelsea and Manchester United will ever win it. While there is no doubt that the Premiership is being awarded to the club with the best players (and in this sense the most deserving competitors), when some clubs can afford to buy the best players in the world and others cannot, it is not clear that the competition itself is fair. The commodification of players, so that clubs can buy whomsoever they like, means that those with the most money win the Premiership and this is hardly an adequate desert base. As Simon asks: 'Isn't the entire ethic of competition under-mined when the richest teams can buy the best players and in effect field a vastly superior team before the game has even begun?'[19] When the wealthiest teams can simply outbid other teams for the best players then the meritocratic basis of competitive sport is violated and we might quite rightly say that the competition is unjust.

Universal access, commodification and exclusion

A second category of distributive goods relevant to the commercialisation of sport are what we might call *universal access goods*. These are goods that as a matter of fact are accessible to all without the intervention of any explicit distributive mechanism or rationing device. Such goods are thus universally distributed and, importantly for our purposes, are acquired free of charge. For instance, think of air which – other things being equal – is available to all human beings without the intervention of the market or any other distributive institution. Or alternatively, to take a case more relevant to the present context, think of free-to-air broadcasts. These broadcasts are accessible to anyone with a television set. No charge is applied for the actual broadcast.

What is central here is that no one is directly excluded or restricted from access to these goods. In the literature this is referred to as 'non-excludability'.[20] Econ-omists and public choice theorists draw a further distinction here between those non-excludable goods which are 'joint' and those which are 'non-joint'. A good is 'joint' when consumption of the good by one member of the group for whom it is a good does not make access to the good more difficult for other members of the group. TV broadcasts would be a case in point. My accessing the electromagnetic waves does not prevent anyone else from doing so. A good is 'non-joint' when one person's consumption does make access to other members of the group for whom it is a good. Potable water might be a case in point. My drinking of a glass of water from a very large water tank means that the amount available for others is obviously diminished, although not necessarily in a way that affects others' capacity to satisfy their needs and wants for water since it may well be that there is enough and as good left over for everyone who wants to use it.

With these definitions in place we can identify two categories of non-excludable goods; *public goods* and *common pool goods*.[21] Public goods are goods for which access is unrestricted and which are joint. Our TV broadcast is a good example of a public good, since as we noted above my consumption of it does not affect the pool available for any other prospective consumers. Common pool goods, on the other hand, are goods for which access is also unrestricted but which are non-joint. Here, although consumption by one person does diminish the amount available for others, the goods in question are sufficiently abundant for society not to impose restrictions on use and access. Again air and water would be cases in point. (And once upon a time the fish in the sea were also thus regarded.)

What is true of both public goods and common pool goods is that access is not restricted. Commodification, however, threatens universal access. By commodifying we make access conditional upon the possession of sufficient financial resources to buy the good on the market. If one is not sufficiently wealthy, then one will be excluded from access to any commodified good. The commodification of universal access goods makes it possible for some members of the community to be excluded from goods to which they previously had access.

At this point it is important to stress that the commodification of such goods does not necessarily lead to exclusion. One might commodify a good and find that the prices are such that every one in a particular community (presumably a community untouched by extreme poverty) will have the same access that they had previously. The *status quo ante* is unaffected. But equally there will be cases where commodification does have distributive consequences. Where some citizens are extremely poor or where the prices charged for a commodifed good are exorbitant then commodification will lead to exclusion.

Our claim then is that exclusion from what had been universal access goods will often involve injustice. The moral harm here is captured by the idea that without some legitimate countervailing reason it is unjust to exclude people from a good to which they previously had access. Without some over-riding and compelling justification for doing so, the moral presumption should be against restriction of access. Commodification brings into place a potential rationing device where previously none had existed and in the absence of good reasons, such a transformation is morally wrong. All other things being equal, there is a presumption that instituting rationing, where none previously existed, harms people, for those who are excluded no longer have access to distributive goods which they once had.

This is not to suggest that there will never be any justification for restricting access. Circumstances will sometimes arise where we have good reasons for introducing rationing for a certain good where none previously existed and one way of doing so is to create a market in it. There are numerous examples of this in environmental policy. Imagine that an aesthetically pleasing but sensitive ecosystem is being overused by eco-tourists and is in danger of being substantially degraded. Here we might think it necessary to restrict access, limiting the number of visitors. One way of doing so would be to commodify access to the area by charging entrance fees. Commodification might be said to be not only permissible but desirable in this case.

That said there remains a presumption that commodification of universal access goods is distributively unjust. In the absence of any good reasons it is unfair to restrict people from goods to which they previously had access via the process of commodification. In so far as commodification leads to exclusion from goods which had previously been universally accessible, then, on distributive grounds, it is pathological.

One area of sport where such injustice arises is in any move of sporting broadcasts from free to air to pay per view. This is a process which is sometimes known as 'siphoning' and involves the commodification of access to actual broadcasts. Access here becomes contingent on paying a fee to the broadcaster in question. Through such a process of commodification, access to sporting broadcasts becomes conditional on being able to pay the subscription fees. In response to such concerns, some countries have passed legislation to safeguard events of 'major importance' for free-to-air television.[22] What lies behind such anti-commodifying legislation is the thought that it would be unfair for people to be excluded from access to viewing events which they once viewed for free.

Perhaps the most morally significant exclusion of this kind in sport has been the disenfranchisement of traditional supporters in many sports as those sports have become more commercially oriented. This is particularly noticeable with respect to access to sports grounds. If we take British soccer as an example, the redevelopment of grounds to cater for more professional wealthy audiences, the prohibition of more rowdy types of crowd behaviour and increases in ticket prices have led to the exclusion of many traditional fans from what had once been one of their prime sources of recreation and identity. Ticket prices are often so high as to make regular attendance at Premier League matches extremely difficult for ordinary working class fans. Given that they once were able to attend on a weekly basis, such commercial forces mean that a benefit they once had is no longer available to them. This we take to be a form of distributive injustice. While tickets have always been commodities, in recent times, in the wake of what we earlier called 'hypercommodification', the pressures for commercial exploitation have led to an effective expulsion of many traditional supporters. Since the reasons given for pursuing such commercial advantage are not ones we take to be morally justified, but simply reflect venal greed, then such exclusion is pathological.

What should be clear from our discussion of this and of the siphoning of broadcasts to pay-TV is that we regard opportunities to view sport as a social good or social benefit. If we thought of it as a burden or a bad thing then failing to distribute it to people who had previously had access would hardly be morally undesirable. However, there are many critics of the commodification of sport who regard spectatorship as morally harmful. Here a connection is drawn between the commercialisation of sport and the glorification of the elite.[23] The thought is that in conjunction with global broadcasting, the glorification of elite sport is responsible for a radical increase in the number of spectators. And since being a spectator is seen as morally harmful, this is then a reason for repudiating the commodification of sport.

This kind of reasoning is common on the militant Left and it has a long heritage there. For instance, although this was not part of an attack upon the commodification of sport, the revolutionary Marxist Leon Trotsky was hostile to spectator sport since he thought that it distracted the working class from politics and dampened their revolutionary fervour. Such antagonism to spectator sport has carried over into many Leftist critiques of commodification. Adorno provides a withering, somewhat elitist, attack on the 'howling devotees of the stadium' whose alienation in labour is carried over, on their day off, into the 'wretched' environment of mass culture.[24] In the United Kingdom, Keir Hardie, a legendary figure in the Labour Party and the first socialist parliamentarian, viewed sports just as harshly. Hardie considered sport in general to be 'degrading' while the most popular game of soccer was an 'abomination'.[25] Again Brohm provides another virulent attack upon commercial sport in writing:

> As a form of mass entertainment, sport is a process whereby the population is reduced to an ideological mass. Sport is a means of regimentation and dehumanisation – see, for example, the role of soccer in Brazil, Britain or Spain, or of cycling in Italy and France, or of baseball in the USA etc. Spectator sports are a mass political safety valve, a system of social diversion and an element in pre-military conditioning.[26]

Paul Hoch makes similar claims about spectator sport in *Rip Off the Big Game* when he suggests that sport has taken over religion's role as the opiate of the masses.[27] Brohm goes on to suggest that the ceremonies at major sports competitions are just like big military parades or pre-fascist rallies, 'with their "traditional" or military music, the flag rituals, rhythmic marches, national anthems and medal ceremonies'. Brohm claims that the best examples of this kind of ceremonial event are provided by the Hitlerite Games of 1936 in Berlin. The connections between sport and the fascist cult of the body are given more graphic consideration by the Frankfurt School, notably through Horkheimer and Adorno's comparison of instrumental sports teams with the empty sex described by the Marquis de Sade.[28]

Equally on the aristocratic right, and particularly within the Amateurist movement we find disdain for being a spectator. As Dunning and Sheard note in their study of amateurism in rugby union, according to the amateur ethos participation is physically and morally beneficial but spectatorship has no such desirable effects.[29] It was thought that the shift from 'sport' to 'spectacle' was degrading for players and spectators alike. Here they cite the writings of a nineteenth-century commentator, one H.H. Almond, who argues that: 'no idle spectators should be allowed to stand looking on at school side, The very sight of loungers takes the spirit out of the players, and the loungers should be doing something else if they are too feeble for football. "Spectating" is ... the greatest of all football dangers.'[30]

Watching sport could only lead to harm. There was obviously some class bias involved in such antipathy. As Dunning and Sheard note, there was concern amongst many aristocrats at the congregation of large working class crowds who behaved in 'openly excited manner'.[31] It ran not only counter to the aristocratic sports ethos which stressed the importance of controlling one's emotions, but was viewed as a threat to public order.

In more recent times some critics of spectator sport have suggested that it has negative effects upon participation in sport. The idea is that the commercial emphasis upon elite sport leads to lower levels of participation. Commodification is thus (perhaps indirectly) responsible for diminishing people's engagement in what is a fundamental human activity. In response, there are two points worth making. First, it is not at all clear that being a spectator at elite sports discourages participation at other levels. One imagines that the global televising of soccer during the World Cup, for instance, is a great boon to the popularity of the game at all levels. Second, and this is relevant to the previous criticisms, we should be sceptical of claims that being a spectator is morally harmful in itself. Perhaps if one becomes involved in certain anti-social forms of hooliganism, then some forms of moral damage might occur, but merely being a spectator at a sport one loves seems entirely harmless. Such critical claims are rarely made of audiences at the ballet or the opera and we see no reason for thinking that being a spectator at sporting fixtures is in any way relevantly different from viewing the arts. Indeed any attempt to draw distinctions here appear entirely *ad hoc*. For just as audiences at the ballet engage in acts of discrimination so too do sporting audiences in acknowledging a fine piece of team play or individual skill. In short all sports contain noteworthy aesthetic codes that are enjoyed and interpreted by spectators and players.[32] Spectating is, in our view, a social good and this is why processes of commodification which restrict access and exclude fans from goods which they previously enjoyed involve forms of injustice.[33]

Equality and basic needs

There is a third category of distributive goods for which the allocative mechanism of the market will often give rise to injustice and this concerns those goods which should be distributed on the basis of need because they are necessary conditions of human flourishing. Let us calls these *basic need goods*. The paradigmatic examples of such goods (outside of the context of sport) would be such things as food, health care, shelter and clothing. They are items that everyone should have access to because they are the basic pre-conditions for living a decent human life. Everyone thus has an equal right to access to such goods. To distribute a basic need good according to any principle other than need, when all needs with respect to the good can be met, would violate norms of justice.

Distributing according to basic needs is best understood as an egalitarian principle. What underpins this is the moral claim that all persons have basic needs that should be met and that everyone has an equal right to have such needs met. This should not be confused with the claim that all goods need to be allocated equally, which would involve a much more extensive egalitarian principle. It is simply the claim that we should all be treated equally in terms of our access to the basic goods required for living a decent human life.[34] The argument here is similar to that made by Bernard Williams in 'The Idea of Equality' where he concludes that rather than allocating all resources equally, our social policy should be oriented towards distributing what he calls 'vital goods' on the basis of need.[35]

The reasons for thinking that the market will give rise to injustice with respect to the allocation of these goods are quite simple. Even if one does not believe that there are in fact any such goods, the reasons for thinking that the class of such goods would be at odds with market distribution should be clear. As we noted, markets distribute to those with the financial resources to pay. However, if one lacks such resources then clearly one will miss out on use. The market discriminates between those with resources and those without and between those with more of such resources and those with less. Whilst we might not be overly concerned about this when dealing with luxuries and objects of conspicuous consumption, such as yachts and rare bottles of wine, when we are dealing with goods that satisfy basic needs then there is reason for concern. If people are excluded from access to basic need goods because they do not have sufficient money, then this is a fundamental form of injustice.

This is not to suggest that the market will always have such distributive consequences. If these basic goods are in good supply and there is a reasonable spread of wealth across a society such that no one lives in extreme poverty then a market in basic need goods will not have unjust consequences. Commodification is only distributively unjust here when, as a matter of fact, some members of society do not have access to basic need goods in a situation of abundance. Often this will not be the case; but in those cases where such distributive outcomes do arise, we may say that commodification is pathological.

At this point some might argue (perhaps rather implausibly), that the market does in fact distribute on the basis of need. The thought is that the amount someone is willing to pay for a commodity simply reflects their level of desire and this in turn reflects their relative need. Whether or not someone chooses to buy a good then is nothing more than a function of his or her level of need. Through millions of similar exchanges across a market society we will arrive at a pattern of social distribution that reflects the relative needs of the members of that community. The problem with this line of reasoning is, of course, that the citizens making decisions about what they are willing to pay for a resource have vastly different levels of wealth. That a billionaire is willing and able to pay more than a beggar for a block of cheese does not in any way reflect the relative levels of need. We would not conclude that the billionaire is more needy because of the higher sum he is willing to pay.

To be sure, if we were all equally endowed then the prices we are willing to pay would typically reflect our relative levels of desire (if not need). Indeed, the philosopher of law Ronald Dworkin formulates a theory of equality that is based on what follows in a market situation from equal initial endowments. But, as it stands, modern market societies are marked by radical inequalities in wealth and income, and accordingly market prices are not a reflection of our relative desires and needs. Moreover, in such societies, the poorer members of society are often excluded from basic need goods, such as adequate shelter, because of the prices that these goods bring in the market.

Our argument then involves a more radical claim than was the case in our discussion in the previous section, where we only made reference to the *status quo ante* and did not talk about needs regardless of history. In the case of basic need goods the claim is that even if one has no history with respect to a particular good, that is, even if one has not previously had access to it, one can still have an entitlement based on the fact that it satisfies a basic need. This should be clear in relation to goods such as shelter and food. Even where one has not had prior access to adequate food and shelter, a person has an entitlement to these goods because they are necessary preconditions for flourishing. In order to have an entitlement here we do not need to show that a person has previously had access. All that is required for entitlement is the fact that the potential recipient is human and that the good is required for his or her flourishing. The harm of missing out on such a good is not to be explicated with respect to some prior set of circumstances from which they are made worse, rather it is that all persons need these goods regardless of their history.

Our general claim then is that the market, left to its own devices, is an inappropriate mechanism for distributing basic need goods; to do so will lead to injustice in cases where not everyone has sufficient financial resources to purchase them. This does not imply that such basic goods should be placed outside the sphere of commodities. Indeed with respect to basic need goods, such as food and shelter, there will often be good reasons for not treating them as 'blocked exchanges' since markets in these goods can generate a highly desirable abundance. Instead we might employ what Radin calls 'incomplete commodification'. This involves the use of the State to avoid the possibility of the market failing to meet basic needs. If we take housing as an example, the State might build cheap and affordable housing, as a supplement to the commercial housing market, to ensure that all have access to adequate shelter. Or the State might impose limits on the prices that can be charged for rental properties.[36] Or again the State might provide rental assistance for those unable to meet the prices charged on the commercial housing market. The general point is that where markets fail, the State should intervene to ensure all have access to basic need goods.

The import of this claim of justice for sport is perhaps less clear at first than in our discussion of meritocratic goods and universal access goods. Are there any such goods in the sporting realm? We believe that there are but in order to see this we need to place access to sporting events within an appropriate historical context. Sport and leisure activities have acquired great cultural importance in Western post-industrial societies, not only for their health benefits but (at an elite level) for their centrality to everyday public experience. In recognition of this, in the period since 1945, many social democratic Western governments have introduced policies of sport for all with the aim of enabling all social groups to encounter a wide range of physical pastimes. In general, access to cultural goods like sport, has acquired such importance that for many social scientists they provide a useful tool for measuring levels of relative inequality, poverty and deprivations in

Western societies. Christopher Berry, for instance, suggests that access to tele-vision is one important index of citizenship within the contemporary world.[37] The opportunity to access certain sporting facilities, such as a swimming pool or an equipped gymnasium may be considered in equivalent terms; a similar point might be made about having the opportunity to access elite sporting events.[38] They are all increasingly important public goods and to be excluded from access to them is to be excluded from goods which are basic elements of modern citizenship.

It thus follows that the commodification of sport is pathological when it excludes persons from access to these goods, either at the actual level (for example through grass roots participation, match attendance) or what we might call the 'virtual' level (by watching on television or via other media). To provide a more concrete example, commodification is pathological, for instance, when it leads to pubic land used for sport being sold off to private developers, or when it culturally-significant sporting events are switched from free-to-air broadcasts to pay-TV with the result that some fans to be excluded from access. Given the important role that many sporting events like the Olympics, Superbowl, Wimbledon or the Premier League now play in the cultural lives of citizens, to be excluded from access is to be excluded from a basic need good.

Commutative justice: exploitation and a just wage?

Thus far our interest has been solely with issues of distribution. But the advent of market relations, in particular with respect to the professionalisation of sport, brings with it questions from another of Aristotle's categories, namely commu-tative justice. Professionalisation involves the establishment of commercial con-tracts between players, sports associations and commercial groups such as the media and manufacturers. If we do commodify the activities of sportspeople in this way then clearly there are questions which arise concerning the justice of the contracts signed. What wages or fees should players receive? What counts as a just or fair wage? What kind of contractual obligations can employers reasonably impose on sportspeople? Should contracts agreed upon when a player is under duress be regarded as binding? We might well regard some contracts as exploita-tive, both with regard to their financial arrangements and the kinds of obligations they impose. Where this is the case then clearly this is a case of injustice.

In sport there is a long history of players and athletes being exploited in condi-tions that often more closely resemble Medieval vassalage than modern wage-labour.[39] First, there have been many cases where the sportspeople's bargaining rights have been severely curtailed. For instance, Ian Tyrell in 'Money and Morality: The Professionalisation of American Baseball' notes that in the nine-teenth century the so-called 'reserve rule' meant that American baseball players could not bargain with the clubs and associations for which they played.[40] He suggests that while the introduction of a business element into baseball had improved payments, it also gave promoters much more power over the players' lives.[41] Tyrell notes that once the concept of professionalism was accepted, it changed the relative balance of power. 'So long as people played for fun, it was difficult to enforce rules of behaviour and standards of play.'[42] Once players came to depend on sport as their sole means of livelihood, they could be disciplined through threats to their salaries. This is but one example of how professional contracts have lead to increased control over sportspeople's lives. Often clubs and associations have imposed obligations through the professional contracts that were demeaning, onerous or unconscionable. For instance, the training regimes imposed upon some athletes would not be tolerated in many armed forces. The pre-season training at American football clubs is highly intensive and can be particularly dangerous when undertaken in high temperatures. Between 1995 and 2002, 19 young players died from heatstroke in training at high school and college levels.[43] In sports such as rugby union and cycling, the team-bonding and character-building training programmes have included boot-camp practices such as doing military drills while stripped naked and deprived of sleep.[44] While they may not be explicitly listed on the athlete's contract, participation in demeaning and spurious exercises is an apparent professional necessity. Any athlete who refused to participate or failed to complete these exercises to the coach's satisfaction, is liable to lose status and membership within the sports team, and this to have his or her sporting career placed in serious jeopardy.

Second, there has also been straight financial exploitation. There have been many occasions on which a sport has flourished commercially and yet which the players have languished in relative poverty. For instance, in the late 1940s this was true of North American baseball and the reluctance of clubs to pay good salaries persuaded some players to cross the Rio Grande into Mexico and vastly increase their income.[45] At around the same time soccer players from all across South America joined a breakaway league in Columbia. Players based in, for example, Buenos Aires, were able to escape what amounted to forms of servitude by moving north and increasing their salaries several–fold while playing a shorter season.[46] More recently, the 1970s saw leading international cricketers join up with World Series Cricket in a bid to increase their earnings. Prior to WSC, international cricket revenues had risen dramatically but the elite players were given, as one commentator put it, 'a somewhat mean share of quite a rich cake'. For example, the Australian test players were paid less than A$1000 per test while the Australian Cricket Board raked in nearly A$2 million in the annual revenues.[47] In circumstances where sporting associations, media and merchandising outlets are making millions of dollars, it is obviously unfair for the players not to reap a greater amount of the reward than was the case at that time.

There are special reasons why elite sportspeople are particularly vulnerable to what we might call 'desperate exchanges', that is, exchanges undertaken from unequal bargaining positions. There are two reasons why the bargaining circumstances are often unequal; namely the psychological vulnerability of 'sports tragics'; and the economic insecurity of many sportsmen and women. Let us begin with the former point. Elite sportsmen and women achieve the levels of skill they do through not only their inherent natural abilities but also through years of dedication and training. Often this is motivated by an extremely romantic love of their sport. Consider the young netballer who is selected to play for New Zealand.

Typically, through her years of training she will have dreamt many times of representing her country – indeed realising that dream is one of her primary motives. It would be rare to find netballers at this level who have not lived and dreamed of national representation since they were young girls. Their level of desire to realise this goal has involved sacrifice in the past and it means they are more likely to accept exploitative conditions than if they were not so driven by this goal. In general because they often have such romantic attachment to their sport, there is often little that sportspersons will not do in order to reach the highest level and this leaves them vulnerable to exploitation.

Another factor is that many elite sportswomen and men come from underprivileged backgrounds, be it from the lower classes in the West or from the underdeveloped Third World. Sport often represents one route via which they might escape from poverty and deprivation. Thus, in order to ensure that they do not miss this opportunity they are again open to exploitation. The fact that the poor are willing to engage in desperate exchanges has been a point made by many philosophers since the time of the ancient Greeks. Boxing is a good example of this. Although boxing has its share of ardent followers who venerate its grace, the sport is underpinned by a culture of desperate exchange. Boxing is a dangerous sport and boxers risk both their mental faculties and long-term physical health. Little wonder that the world's top fighters typically hail from the poorest communities, notably the black and Hispanic ghettoes of North America. In recent years there has been some considerable concern about European soccer clubs taking advantage of soccer players from African and other developing nations.[48] Similar criticisms have been directed at American and Japanese baseball clubs for setting up bases in Latin America and ruthlessly exploiting young Latino talent.[49]

Recently, in Western Europe there have been some moves which have strengthened the bargaining positions of sports players. The Bosman ruling decreed that to prevent players moving to clubs of their choice is an unfair restraint of trade. Although this makes explicit the commodified nature of the players' relationship to a club or association, it has benefits since it allows players to move freely and to have more control over the kinds of bargains into which they enter. Given the fact that players have often been treated like chattel by clubs, and that elite sports people treat their game as a profession regardless of rulings like the Bosman one, then we suggest that these kinds of moves are for the good. Forced to choose between potential exploitation and a small increase in the professionalisation of players, then we believe that it is better to support moves which reduce the opportunities for exploitation.

One concern then is that the contracts that sportspeople sign are not exploitative. Of course, there are libertarian philosophers, such as Robert Nozick, who would argue that so long as one is not forcibly coerced into any commercial arrangement, then whatever two contracting parties agree to is fair or just. For Nozick freedom is the most important value and thus commercial arrangements which are freely chosen should be respected. It is the process by which a contract is formed that determines its justice rather than its content. Nozick argues that it is morally inappropriate for the State or any other agency to interfere in the freely chosen capitalist acts entered into by consenting adults. The sexual metaphor here is quite deliberate, for Nozick believes that just as it is inappropriate for the State to interfere in what consenting adults do in their bedrooms, it is equally wrong for them to interfere in commercial transactions between such agents.

There are two consequences for sport. First, any contract to which an athlete freely consents is just or fair. So long as the contractual process does not involve any physical coercion or blackmail, then the contract is fair. Second, given that the player and her sporting club have engaged in a mutually consenting commercial bargain, then any interference by third parties, be they sporting associations or state bodies is unjust. It is unjust because it involves a violation of the freedom of agents to contract without external interference. So regulation of the contracts that players sign with their clubs would be unjust.

There are good reasons for rejecting this libertarian approach to the issue of justice. Underpinning Nozick's theory is the view that material circumstances are never coercive. But this is clearly false. Extreme poverty forces people to do many things that they would not otherwise do, just as surely as having a gun pointed at one's head. The Medieval philosopher Gerald Odonis once remarked that taking a loan from a money-lender when one is in severe financial trouble is not an act of freedom, but is rather like paying money not to be hanged.[50] Nozick is not unaware of this line of criticism. Indeed in an article entitled 'Coercion' he argues that coercion only concerns physical and psychological threat occasioned by another agent.[51] On this very narrow definition of coercion, a person floating in the sea who agrees to pay an enormous amount of money to his rescuer is not coerced. Here we have what most people would take as a *reductio* of the position. If this is not coercive then surely the definition of coercion is too narrow. Further, if his theory describes contracts agreed upon in such circumstances as just, then this gives us good reason for rejecting it. All too often sportspersons have found themselves in circumstances analogous to that of the drowning man and have accepted arrangements that have been exploitative.

As well as the issue of the kinds of contractual obligations, there are also questions of what kinds of rewards are appropriate for athletes. What counts as a just wage or a just profit for the activities of a sportsperson? On one end of the spectrum there are those who would see all such contracts as *necessarily exploitative* of the employee. If we begin with the Marxist nostrum that the wage-labour contract involves a fundamental form of injustice, then we can see how such an argument might be made. Recall that according to Marx, the labourer is exploited because he is not paid the full value of his work. The profit of the wage-employing capitalist – which represents the difference between what he pays his workers and what he receives in exchange from the goods that his workers produce – is only realised via the failure to pay the worker what the products of his labour will bring on the market. One might argue, following this Marxist line of reasoning, that sportsmen and women are exploited financially because their activity realises profits for the capitalists of sport (e.g. the private sporting clubs, commercial media and sporting goods franchises). Such profits can only be gained through a failure on the part of such capitalists to pay sportspeople the true value of their labour. We see this reasoning implicitly at work in Paul Hoch's *Rip off the Big Game* when he writes:

> The present owners [of sportsteams in the United States] perform no worthwhile or necessary function whatever. (And the only injuries they get from the game are the arm strains accumulated raking in the profits.) Instead of the vulture's share of the take, these owners should be paid what they deserve, for the amount of work they do – absolutely nothing.[52]

Whilst we have some sympathy with the sentiments expressed, such reasoning overstates the case since it rejects any possibility that capitalists ever create or do anything of value. But as Aquinas long ago acknowledged, there is work – and often a great deal of work – undertaken by the merchant or commercial agent when organising a commercial enterprise. Aquinas focused on the risk undertaken by the capitalist and the effort in bringing goods to the market and these lessons are also applicable *mutatis mutandis* to the modern context. Whether such activity that warrants the level of remuneration that capitalists typically reap is another question, but we should not deny that some reward is appropriate.

At the other end of the spectrum are those right wing theorists who think that so long as the reward of a sportsperson is gained through free bargaining in an open market then that bargain is morally legitimate. There is no unjust price. Such thinkers might well even be tempted to endorse R.G. Collingwood's provocative suggestion that such talk is irrational for a just price is a contradiction in terms. Collingwood claims that '[t]he question of what a person ought to get in return for his goods and labour is a question absolutely devoid of meaning'.[53] According to Collingwood the only rational questions are what market agents can get in return for their goods or labour and whether they ought to sell them at all. But, as we noted above, this ignores the extreme disadvantage in which many market agents often find themselves. Prices often are unjust when through ignorance or material deprivation sportspersons sell themselves too cheaply.

Our view, then, sits somewhere in the middle. The rewards for sporting activity arrived at through market bargaining are often unjust although they are not necessarily so. Whilst we make no attempt to provide a precise account of what would count as a just reward, it is nonetheless clear that players should receive a reasonable reward for their efforts. In particular, in cases where the sport makes millions of dollars for clubs, media, merchandising outlets and other commercial groups, it seems unfair for players not to be reasonably rewarded. Moreover, it would also be unfair for there to be a large discrepancy between the rewards enjoyed by players and that enjoyed by Chief Executive Officers or the owners of a club.

Summary

In this chapter we have explored the distributive implications of the commodification of sporting goods. Our line of argument here is that commodification will often have undesirable distributive consequences. When it does so it is 'distributively' pathological. In demonstrating how this might be so we have outlined three important and distinct distributive spheres, each with their own principle of allocation.[54] Indeed it is the appropriate principle that defines the sphere. It is against these principles that commodification will be assessed for being distributively pathological. To be distributively pathological is to be unjust. Commodification is distributively pathological when it leads to the displacement of the principle of allocation appropriate to a sphere.

The first sphere is that of the merit goods. These are goods which should be distributed according to principles of desert or merit. Here, in the sporting context, we have in mind the prizes, trophies and honours that are at the heart of competitive sport. It is unjust for such goods to be commodified since to do so would mean that these goods would not be allocated to the most meritorious candidate. (Notice also here that in this sphere commodification is necessarily unjust, whereas in the following two spheres it is only contingently so.)

The second sphere is that of the universal access goods. These are goods to which everyone currently has access. Free-to-air broadcasts of sporting events would be a case in point. To be excluded from goods to which one previously had access, simply in order for another to make a profit, is morally unjustifiable. When commodification leads to exclusion from these goods, all other things being equal this is unjust.[55]

The third sphere we considered is that of the basic need goods. These are goods that satisfy basic human needs and which all have a right to on the basis of their very humanity. To be excluded from these goods is unjust regardless of whether one has ever had access to them. We might consider television access to major sporting events as an example. When commodification leads to exclusion from basic needs goods of sport it is unjust.

Finally, in addition to questions of distributive justice, we also briefly considered the issue of commutative justice in sport. While we have not attempted to provide details of what would count as a just wage or just fee, nonetheless we have considered some general guidelines for contracts to be fair. First, contracting agents need to be mindful of the bargaining circumstances of many aspiring sportspersons. Often such sportspersons, through their financial circumstances or their desire to represent club and country, leave themselves open to what we might call 'desperate exchanges'. Where players are vulnerable in this way, sporting clubs and associations should not take advantage of players and athletes to draw up exploitative contracts, either in regards to the financial rewards nor in terms of their conditions. Second, where there is an enormous amount of money in a sport then it seems reasonable that sportspeople receive a reasonable share of that income. They should be appropriately rewarded. Obviously what counts as appropriate here is necessarily open to an enormous amount of interpretation, but it will involve certain constraints on both sides of the bargaining table.

If the goods of sport are to be allocated fairly, these then are the rules of distribution by which they should be distributed.

6 Scoring an own goal
When markets undermine what they sell

Introduction

Our fourth and final pathology concerns cases where the market diminishes or destroys the value of the very things that commercial agents wish to sell. Our claim is that the commodification of sport is pathological amongst other things when it destroys or diminishes the good-making features upon which commercial profits are based. This we shall call the 'pragmatic pathology'.

To provide an illustration of this pathology consider the following. In this case the drive for profits might lead commercially oriented administrators to alter practices and structures in a way that undermines the appeal to traditional fans. For example, Australian rugby league has not recovered its supporter base since the so-called 'Super-League War' in the 1990s, when two rival pay-television networks fought bitter legal and commercial battles to dominate televised coverage of the sport.[1] The feud was sparked when Optus (owned by Kerry Packer) won the television contract for the ARL competition in 1995, only for Foxtel (owned by Rupert Murdoch) to reinvest AS$350 in founding a rival tournament (the Super League) with its own team and players. Many traditional fans were outraged by the way that players, clubs and media analysts allowed themselves to be bought by billionaires who were struggling to monopolise televised rugby. Amidst a cascading slide in attendances at fixtures, a compromise was reached in 1997 to found one league (the NRL). Nevertheless, in the aftermath, other football codes – soccer, Australian Rules football and rugby union – enjoyed considerable surges in popularity at the expense of rugby league.[2]

For another example, consider how a sport might become so obviously and gratuitously oriented towards quick profits that fans are turned off and less of them support it. For instance, many in Australia find the crass commercialism of sporting telecasts objectionable and, accordingly, choose to listen to the commercial-free radio broadcasts on the Australian Broadcasting Commission. It does not take much imagination to see that some of these fans, if they have no non-commercial options, might eventually turn off forever. Here, we see the potential for commodification to damage goods that predate the advent of the market (or the hypermarket) and in so doing it (somewhat ironically) it might diminish their value as commodities.

One might well wonder how this could be possible. If commercial agents were motivated by self-interest in the form of the profit motive, then why would they do anything that is detrimental to their economic interests? Why would they damage or destroy the value of the commodities upon which their pursuit of wealth is based?

The answer to this is to be found in the short-term orientation of many market enterprises. Commercial agents often operate with only a view to short-term profits and not to the long-term interests of the game. So while markets can be the occasion of genuine innovation and productivity, they can also give rise to what economists call 'market failure'. This refers to the failure of a market to bring about the allocation of resources that best satisfies the wants of society.[3]

One way in which markets sometimes fail is in the continuing production of the non-commercial goods that provide the necessary basis for social activity including market life. Think, for instance, of the depletion of fishing stocks by many fishing companies. Although it is in every fisherman's long-term interests to safeguard fishing stocks, in the short term it is in each fisherman's economic interests to catch as many fish as possible. Without effective regulation to control the free-market practice, fishing stocks will dwindle, endangering the employment and livelihoods of most fishermen. This is but part of a more general problem of markets failing to provide 'public goods'.[4] As we shall argue below, there are many cases in sport where markets fail to provide the public goods necessary for the reproduction of the game in question. Often, for instance, the elite class of a sport will siphon off such a great deal of the revenue raised, and put so little back into its grassroots, that the sport itself suffers in the long run. But if the grassroots is necessary for the continuing success of the sport, and to assist in achieving broader objectives such as improving public health and community life, then requisite money should be reinvested there, even though there is no short-term economic advantage in doing so. A healthy grassroots is in this sense a public good.

These failings of the market occur not only at the level of the reproduction of the material conditions necessary for the continuation of the sport, but also occur at the level of the ideas and attitudes generated towards sport by some market activity. (It is a failing at the level of what was once called 'ideology'.) If a sport comes to be regarded fundamentally as a mere commodity – and ultimately is so regarded by the general public – it may well be that this undermines public interest in that sport. The point is once again that markets contain internal contradictions, specifically the undermining of their own profit by failing to respect the goods which they allocate.

In one sense the concern here is not so much moral as prudential or pragmatic. If we define the 'moral' as involving an interest in something over and above immediate self-interest, then we might say that the concern with how markets fail on their own terms is not moral but prudential. Let us assume, in the spirit of Kant, that prudential reasoning is essentially concerned with the realisation of one's own welfare.[5] To act prudently is to take care of one's own interests. On this model any person who undermines the realisation of his or her own conception of welfare is prudentially irrational. Similarly any activity which systematically undermines its own goal(s) is prudentially irrational.

The latter is precisely what is involved in some forms of market failure in sport. In so far as the vendors of sporting commodities damage the goods on which they rely for their profits, then they undermine the conditions of their own welfare and hence act irrationally in a prudential sense. In such circumstances, we might say that the market itself acts imprudently. It is not that market agents fail others, but that they fail themselves.

In another sense, however, our concerns here are more than simply prudential – it is not just that commercial agents threaten their own profits by some forms of commodification, but that they damage something that is valuable in itself. For instance, when the Super League fiasco occurred in Australia, the competing entrepreneurs threatened to destroy a social institution that many people in the Eastern States of Australia valued dearly.

In the following sections we explore some concrete ways in which certain forms of commodification threaten to undermine the very practices that make sport valuable both in itself and as a means to profit.

The manifest image, markets and crises of legitimation

In the first chapter we discussed the 'Manifest Image of Sport', by which we meant the image of sport as it typically appears to those in the general public who enjoy it as spectators, either through attendance at live sporting contests or through various media, such as television broadcasts and the print media. The manifest image involves a vision of a world of sport that is, in one sense, entirely distinct from our own everyday lives. It is world in which many of ordinary concerns are suspended. Moreover, we can be more specific about the content of that world. Therein sporting ideals, such as the mutual pursuit of excellence and pride in one's club, are pursued unequivocally by champion athletes. This is a central element of what draws many people to sport; the enjoyment is in watching *genuine competitions* between elite athletes and it is this which they enjoy.

There are a number of ways in which the intrusion of the market and market values into sport can shatter this image so as ultimately to undermine public interest. If the ideals and values contained within the manifest image come to be seen as illusory, then in the long run this will diminish its value as a commodity. When the manifest image of sport is undermined in this way, we may expect, in the phrase of the German social theorist, Jurgen Habermas, a legitimation crisis to occur.[6] Habermas employed this concept to describe a very particular set of social and political circumstances. He argued that post-war capitalist societies, despite their welfare states, struggle to secure popular legitimacy for a social order that is prone to economic crises and is arranged systematically to advantage elites. Our usage of the term is somewhat different; we employ it to describe how the process of commodification can rob social phenomena of their most important public qualities, the very facets that are most coveted in market terms.

The first important element of the manifest image, then, is the vision of a world which is distinct from the world we inhabit which, amongst other things, is one in which economic considerations loom large. Yet hyper-commodification can undermine this. In modern commodified sports we find many who administer sport, as well as those who play, engaging in what Radin calls 'market rhetoric' which is to use the language of business to understand their practices. (This is precisely what goes on when Michael Jordan calls his team a 'franchise'.) If the use of market rhetoric by those in charge of development comes into wider public consciousness, then this can affect the sense in which the ordinary is suspended, since the ordinary is also dominated by economic concerns.

Somewhat ironically, an important part of what marketing people do involves disguising the commodified nature of commodities, in order to foster the view amongst consumers that these products possess powers and properties that transcend their economic value. Thus a pair of Levi Strauss jeans is viewed as more than just a piece of tailored denim; instead it is a fashion item with properties and meanings that confer certain forms of social status and distinction upon the buyer. Of course, in fostering such public perceptions, marketers seek to add to the value of their products in a way that serves to increase, usually exponentially, the market price of these articles relative to their production costs. Marketers fail if consumers do not internalise these seductive messages that have been wrapped around the product in such a way that it is viewed as 'just another commodity'.

We see this feature of marketing in operation in sport where many sporting enterprises go to great lengths to demonstrate that they are more than just a profit-oriented business (and in this way ensure that their profits are maximised). For instance, leading sports clubs such as Manchester United make a great deal of their long histories and proud traditions in their product promotions. Thus, the market becomes a sphere in which these clubs cement their public standing, as more than 'just another enterprise', in a way that promotes the sale of their merchandise.[7]

There are other ways in which the sporting 'lifeworld' can be penetrated by commercial understandings. The idea that we enter a world unlike our own can also be shattered when market power is too obviously a principal determinant of sporting success. In everyday life, success is often determined by one's relative wealth. If it becomes apparent that success on the track and the field is simply a function of one's relative wealth then this too can jeopardise the perception that the world of sport is different.[8]

Of course, there is far more to the enjoyment of sport than just its playful contrast to the routines of life, particularly the commodified elements of work and leisure. Spectators and broadcast audiences enjoy watching genuine contests between athletes engaged in a mutual pursuit of excellence or playing for the honour of their teams. This is a central element of the Manifest Image of sport.

But again the hyper-commodification of sport can undermine such an image when it becomes too obvious that players and administrators are primarily motivated by money. When players, for instance, continually shift clubs for better financial deals or when they allow money to get in the way of national representation, then this may lead supporters to believe that commercial motives have evacuated the ideals of pride in the jersey or the pursuit of individual excellence.[9] Whilst it is true, as we noted in chapter 3, that the mere presence of commercial motives does not mean that other ideals that we associate with the Manifest Image are not also present, when it appears to supporters that players are predominantly motivated by money, then this (rightly or wrongly) can lead to a great deal of disaffection amongst fans.[10] Equally, administrators can undermine the Manifest Image of sport when they are seen to be acting predominantly from financial considerations. To give an example, if a club were to introduce a new away uniform (kit or strip), solely for the purposes of making more money from merchandising, and the general public recognises that this is the reason for its introduction, then again this might lead to disaffection.

Perhaps the biggest challenge to the manifest image of sport involves the venalisation of the sporting *ethos* as is most strikingly illustrated in cases of corruption. Evidence of such corruption will provoke public suspicion about the genuineness of sporting contests and this in turn must diminish interest in the specific sport. When athletes and sporting administrators view sport merely as a means to making money, then it is not such a large step to taking money for illegal purposes. If we take the case of cricketer Hansie Cronje, we see that his actions affected the view that the contests between national sides were in fact genuine contests.

To take another example, recall Andrew Jennings' claims about corruption in the Olympics.[11] Regardless of the truth of such allegations, the point that Jennings makes with respect to the consequences of corruption is entirely apposite, since corruption in sport of this kind is deadly to public interest. Sport only makes for good business when the contests are regarded as genuine and not somehow 'fixed'. Equally, widespread knowledge of doping in sport can seriously debilitate public interest due to a loss of confidence in the fairness of contexts.[12] The Olympic sports of weight-lifting and various track and field events have suffered severely through many doping scandals since the late 1980s, so that audiences and commentators often view results in these competitions with jocular scepticism. Similarly, the MLB has been criticised for not doing enough to eradicate steroid abuses in baseball. Consequently, many fans suspect that the home run records set in recent years are not drug-free.[13] The point is that public knowledge of corruption, be it through bribery or drug-abuse, is injurious to nurturing public interest.

Thus, in the long run, for sport to remain a profitable enterprise for those who invest in it, it cannot stray too far from the Manifest Image. Where the influence of money undermines this image, we can say that commodification is 'pragmatically pathological'.

Lop-sided competitions and uncertainty of outcome

Another important way in which markets can be pragmatically pathological is when they give rise to lop-sided or uneven competitions. Under capitalism, markets have a general tendency towards *oligopoly* and *monopoly* so that we no longer have many buyers and sellers engaged in competition. There is a natural reason for this. In many industries we find that only a handful of corporations control the distribution and production of social goods. Large-scale operations typically have natural competitive advantages over smaller ones in such things as economies of scale and thus tend to drive the smaller businesses out until only a few companies dominate the industry. Moreover, it is clearly in the interests of larger businesses to reduce the number of their competitors and so often they will engage in deliberate campaigns to send smaller rivals 'to the wall'. In some industries, where it is strongly felt that monopoly or oligopoly is harmful to the national interest, governments will enact anti-monopoly legislation to ensure greater competition. In such cases, the government clearly does not believe that markets left to their own devices, will foster a competitive environment that involves many buyers and sellers.

Similar kinds of commercial pressures towards monopoly operate in sport. Large and successful sporting clubs have commercial advantages that enable them to compete more successfully on the field, and their continued success on the field reinforces their commercial advantages. If we take the English Premier League as an example, we see that because of their past successes, larger clubs like Arsenal, Chelsea and Manchester United have much larger financial resources on which to draw. This means that they are able to obtain better players and coaches, which in turn ensures future success.

Such outcomes are symptomatic of lop-sided competitions wherein only a few of the major clubs can ever expect to win the championship. By itself, this inevitably has a negative impact upon the potential of that sport to generate and sustain public interest. It reduces the 'uncertainty of outcome' that is an essential feature of a good competition.[14] In a United Kingdom survey in late 2004 published in *The Guardian* it was shown that most fans have given up hope of their club winning the title. The poll, undertaken by a sports think-tank, the Sports Nexus, in conjunction with YouGov, said that 89 per cent of Premier League fans feel that only the very wealthiest have a realistic chance of winning the title.[15]

If many fans do not believe that their clubs have a genuinely realistic chance of winning, then they are less likely to be as interested in the competition than they might otherwise have been. One leader in *The Observer* made this very point in October 2004 when commenting on the predictable three-horse race for the English Premiership:

> The outcome of the Premiership is increasingly predictable. Arsenal's 'invincibles', chasing their 50th match unbeaten today, are beautiful to watch, but unhealthily dominant. If the first three in an Olympic marathon were known after six miles – or even before the start – with everyone else competing for fourth place, how compelling would we find that?[16]

Similarly, in baseball, clubs like the New York Yankees and Boston Red Sox have annual revenues that are more than twice that of some of MLB teams, meaning that their market value is up to five times greater than their small rivals.[17] These vast inequalities translate into an ever-increasing competitive disadvantage, as fans of small clubs like the Kansas City Royals lose interest in watching their team fail to compete with the big guns. Little wonder that, at a match in April 1999 against the Yankees, several thousand disgruntled Royal fans held up banners demanding that the MLB 'Share the Wealth' before leaving the stadium in protest.

We should not think that commercially-derived unevenness is a new phenomenon. In his researches on baseball in the nineteenth century, Ian Tyrell found that the advent in the 1860s of city teams funded by joint stock companies and groups of wealthy capitalists brought new problems. As a result the competition was often extremely lop-sided since some teams were fully professional while others were only semi-professional. Tyrell notes that partly as a consequence of this, season attendances fell dramatically between about 1868 and 1875.[18]

To be sure, inequality between clubs in terms of their financial resources is not the only route to lop-sided competitions. Anyone who has ever played in an amateur sporting league based on local regions will know that unevenness can occur for many other reasons, not the least of which might simply be the simple fact that some regions will produce many more gifted sportspeople at a particular point in time than their neighbours. Although it is not money that causes such lop-sidedness, in such cases interest in the competition is also diminished.

Additionally, there is the phenomenon of team loyalty or partisanship to consider here, wherein fans want their teams to win prestigious competitions on a regular basis. It might well be argued that these fan sentiments more than outweigh preferences for any pleasurable uncertainty of outcome. However, this argument fails to take into account a variety of important factors. First, if one team dominates over a lengthy period of time in a particular competition, the latter will lose its significance and prestige among fans. The top clubs and fans will then seek out alternative forms of competition, against more serious rivals, that confer greater status upon the winners.[19] Second, in competitions that are dominated by a small number of teams, while the crowds that follow these sides remain relatively high numerically, the decline in public interest may be gauged by other factors, such as the loss of atmosphere at fixtures. For example, in many European soccer leagues, the atmosphere at 'home' matches involving the top teams can be very poor in part because of the highly predictable and often boring ways in which victories are secured. Third, there are instances in which domination of a sport may coincide with a decline in public interest. This was the experience of Australian cricket during the late 1990s and early 2000s, when the all conquering national team could not stem diminished interest in the game.

Overall we suggest that in the world of commodified sport, having more money gives a sporting club advantages on the field over less well-off rivals. Such an advantage over time can make for a competition that is less interesting because it lacks genuine uncertainty of outcome. What all of this reflects is a unique feature of sport as a business or commodity. A large part of what sporting enterprises sell is competition. (Competition is their product if you like.) Unlike other commercial enterprises where it is financially advantageous to eliminate all of one's rivals, within sport this is not the case. Sporting clubs need to have genuinely competitive rivals for there to be public interest in their activities. Across rival sports there will, of course, be commercial advantages in eliminating the competitors, but not so *within* any sport. It is in the very nature of sport that there must be competition if it is to be commercially successful.

The market then is pragmatically pathological when it undermines competition

by enabling some clubs to have excessive advantages through their greater pur-
chasing power. In the face of such concerns, sporting associations have often
brought in measures to ameliorate the effects of the market. In the final chapter we
shall discuss a variety of such measures, such as for instance, salary caps that have
been introduced in some sports to place upper-limits on the amounts of money
that can be spent buying top-class players.

We might say then that sporting leagues, in response to the dangers of pure
market competition, often function as what Steve Overman calls 'sports cartels'.[20]
Sports cartels are groups of teams that agree to limit forms of commercial competition between themselves. The teams do so primarily out of self-interest. The
cartel system protects each team, not only from outside competition but also from
the dangers of lop-sidedness. They do so because they are aware that if commercial
competitions were left unchecked, it would undermine uncertainty of outcome
and ultimately would diminish their sport as an object of public interest. The
formation of such cartels can be seen as a tacit admission of the unique nature of
sport as a business.

In North America the major league sports are dominated by four sports cartels
– the NFL, MLB, NHL and NBA. The cartel has a number of advantages. For
instance, strong management within the cartel means that revenue sharing
between member clubs is possible and in this way some competitive imbalances
can be addressed. But, at the same time, the cartel system also has its problems.
Most notably, it prevents new teams from entering the major leagues. In this way
the model serves the particular competition controlling interests of established
teams within the sport, and not always in the interests of sport as a whole.

Killing the source

Another pragmatic pathology associated with the hyper-commodification of sport
arises when the market damages the source of future players and fans. Markets can
undermine the successful reproduction of a sport practice-community (to use
MacIntyre's phrase), especially when venal short-term interests take precedence
over the long-term ones. In so doing they can corrode their own long-term
profitability.

Let us begin by considering declines in fan support that might be attributed to
market forces. Sometimes the pursuit of short-term profit can have long-term
effects on the profitability of a sport. Administrators often fail to take a longer
view of the good of their sport. To take a recent example, in 2004 in Australia, the
broadcast of English Premier League soccer was 'siphoned off' the SBS network
onto pay-TV networks and as a result free-to-air broadcasts of the League were no
longer available. This meant that many current fans (as well as some potential
future players of the sport) had no access to these broadcasts. Indeed, Premiership
officials took the short-term view that it was better to take the pay-TV money for
immediate gain than to use network television to develop longer-term affiliations
and affections towards English clubs among Australian viewers. One would not be
surprised if this had consequences for the popularity of soccer in Australia.

Clearly there are questions of justice here concerning rights to access (of the kind that we discussed in chapter 5), but there are also *pragmatic* questions concerning the long-term interests of the game. While it might appear strange to make such a claim about a foreign broadcast, in Australia there are special circumstances. For many years the National Soccer League has been in disarray. Despite the fact that soccer (as it is called to distinguish it from the other football codes) is very popular with respect to participation levels amongst adults and juniors, the elite national league has failed to recover from its years of chronic indebtedness and maladministration.[21] In an era of intensified media and sporting globalisation, Australian interest in soccer is generated through watching the English Premiership, particularly in following the fortunes of fellow nationals, such as Harry Kewell (Leeds then Liverpool FC) and Mark Viduka (Leeds then Middlesborough FC). The practice of broadcasting the Premiership only to the minority who have pay-TV is not in the game's long-term interest in Australia. Indeed siphoning is likely to harm the continuation of interest in the game, since pay-TV effectively segregates the majority of the market from habitual encounters with the 'product'.[22] Wherever markets lead a substantial portion of the fan base to be excluded from access to the sport in question we can say that commodification is pragmatically pathological.

Other ways in which markets can undermine cultural reproduction in a sport is when they cater to new wealthy audiences at the expense of less-wealthy traditional supporters and in so doing price traditional fans out of sport.[23] In this context it is useful to differentiate fans in terms of the distinction between local traditional supporters and cosmopolitans. Cosmopolitan supporters, as one finds in European soccer generally, are often drawn to the game by its marketing, preferring to peruse the most fashionable aspects of the sport, with little sense of place or long-term grounded identification with a specific club. More traditional fans have a different quality of relationship to their clubs. Whilst the cosmopolitans might evince a detached critical relationship to sport there is, as Michael Walzer points out a 'sense in which the cosmopolitan is parasitic on people who are not cosmopolitans'.[24] For if the locals did not remain at home to reproduce the communal sports cultures, be it in soccer, cricket, or basketball, there would be little for the cosmopolitan to experience and much less of sporting value with which to engage. In this way, by pandering to a new class of cosmopolitans at the expense of traditional fans, sporting authorities run the danger of 'killing the source' of the sporting experience.[25]

Alternatively, a focus on attracting new fans from across the spectrum of society might lead those in charge of sport to develop the sensational elements of a sport at the expense of the *integrity* of the game and ultimately its longer term interests. Robert L. Simon, considers the possible consequences of what might happen to American Gridiron if the sport were to accede to a demand on the part of new audiences for more and more violence.[26] In this scenario, in order to sell more tickets, professional football eliminates rules that protect vulnerable players such as quarterbacks and punt returners. He notes that authorities might even move towards the Extreme Football League experiment of the late 1990s. One consequence of this, he suggests, is that there is likely to be more injuries to star players, less exciting contests and ultimately fewer sales. Thus Simon concludes, focusing only on what sells may not ultimately be in the best financial interests of team-owners and players.[27] An alternative possible consequence might be the sport being taken less seriously, somewhat akin to the way that professional wrestling is now regarded, ultimately at the cost of interest on the part of serious sports fans, such that it simply becomes a form of energetic vaudeville.

It is not only the interest of fans which can be threatened by market forces. Sometimes the 'production' of players can also be affected. For example, if those in charge of elite sports follow sharp business practices that involve maximising short-term profits at every opportunity, then this can mean that very little is reinvested in sport's grass-roots. Reinvestment in local sporting clubs and associations is a long-term strategy and not one guaranteed to optimise the bottom line. If the only obligation of business is to share-holders, as Milton Friedman once notoriously claimed, then obligations to the grass-roots will not figure in the reasoning processes of elite sports administrators.[28]

Failure to reinvest may well have negative effects on the long-term health of a sport. If many small, non-professional clubs fold through a lack of funds, then this can only harm the sport. Without healthy local clubs and associations, the elite clubs are likely to have less of a pool of talent to draw on for players (not to mention the fact that Saturday warriors are typically avid fans of the elite versions of their own sport).[29]

The world's most popular sports have not been immune from this problem. For instance, the English Premiership has been built since the early 1990s on a series of massive television deals with the pay-television station BSkyB.[30] Unlike earlier distributive systems which filtered money down through the English leagues and local soccer associations, the Premiership clubs have retained that television income for themselves. Meanwhile, Premiership clubs continue to pay minimal sums, if any, to recruit players from non-league or youth clubs. There are far fewer forms of guaranteed assistance from top level clubs to help pay for grassroots facilities, such as upkeep of public pitches, training areas or dressing-rooms. Overall, the resource gap between the Premiership and grassroots soccer has grown enormously, leaving the latter poorer in real terms. And as the Premiership has taken off, old 'football hotbeds' have suffered a massive decline in player numbers, particularly at youth and local league level.

Moreover, participation can be affected if some communities are *functionally* excluded from access. Undoubtedly, a significant element of the motivation to participate and to remain involved in a sport emanates from an early and continuing exposure to that sport at the elite level. Watching how the game may be played at its highest standard, and at the same time experiencing a social induction and education in the sport's history and popular culture, combine to build the participant base of any sport. Further, in an age that constantly inflates the public standing of celebrities, exposure to the performances of these star athletes assists in legitimising the everyday practice of that sport. Sports that fail to maintain a constant presence in the general public consciousness, notably through routine free-to-air television coverage, are liable to lose their popular standing and to experience a weakening in their grass-roots participant base.

We might wonder at this point what concrete sociological evidence might there be that hyper-commodification – and in particular the rise of pay-TV – has actually given rise to such 'labour shortages'. The evidence here remains sketchy for at least three reasons. First, there are numerous social factors that might be connected retrospectively to any discernible decline in the sports participation of one particular community. It may be, for example, that a major change in the political system or a public scandal leads to a decline in participant numbers. Second, we are dealing with counter-factual circumstances here, in attempting to hazard a guess as to what the standing of a sport might have been were it not for rampant market forces. Third, there may be other factors which lead athletes from one particular community to be squeezed out of elite sport rather than give up the sport. For example, the new international division of labour in sport means that elite professional sports clubs in the West are able to recruit athletes from a wider geographical pool, particularly from developing nations where the coaching and reimbursement of budding talents is far cheaper than at home. Twenty or thirty years ago, the recruitment of these cheap overseas talents in sport, like professional athletics, soccer, baseball, and basketball was nowhere near as extensive as it is today.[31] Alternatively, in the past, Western sports leagues were filled primarily with home-grown talents.

We should also acknowledge in discussing these issues that there is little chance that modern professional sports will die off completely through the erosion of player numbers. Nonetheless this does not mean that many sports have not experienced difficulties in this regard. Sports with one or several major rivals in terms of public appeal have an arguably harder time. Two sports that have been under significant financial and popular pressure since the late 1980s have been professional baseball in North America and cricket in England. During the 1990s, major league baseball experienced a drop in financial growth and public interest compared to other sports (notably basketball and American football). Although the MLB recruited more players from Latin America to offset these problems, the sport seems to have lost much of its potential source of exciting talent from African-American communities which now see far less of the professional game. Harry Edwards, an early American black sociologist of sport, had no doubt that, when it occurred, the shift of professional baseball from network to pay-television would have a deleterious impact. He argued, 'The black working class and underclass which produces most of the players aren't going to pay for cable ... fewer and fewer black kids are going to get to watch baseball. And that's going to mean the role models won't be there for them ... fewer and fewer of them will play baseball.'[32]

Similarly, English cricket has faced the twin problems of expanding its popular playing base beyond wealthy children and Indian and Pakistani communities while counteracting the growing global and all-year-round appeal of soccer as 'the national sport'. Writing in the mid-1990s, one analyst argued that if top cricket fixtures were restricted to pay-television stations, the consequences for the game's future 'could be catastrophic':

The casual viewer – the person who drops in and out of test matches, and probably watches only one-day games – will not have access to televised cricket. Without access through television, it may not be possible to draw new fans into the game. The effect will be to tighten the noose around the neck of cricket, choking off the supply of players from any source other than those, mostly public [large fee-paying], schools which force cricket upon their pupils.[33]

Nevertheless, in December 2004, the ECB (English cricket's governing body) signed a £220 million television deal for 2005–9 that guaranteed exclusive rights for major cricket fixtures to BSkyB, the leading UK satellite broadcaster. A small highlights package was awarded to a new network station, Channel 4, which consistently attracts low ratings. The deal provided the ECB with only a modest 10 per cent gain in revenues compared to earlier deals with network and pay-television broadcasters. Immediately, most analysts roundly condemned the ECB for failing to ensure that young and old fans would be able to watch top fixtures. Former England captain, Alec Stewart, declared, 'Young girls and boys should be able to see cricket without having to pay for it. The ECB have to look at the whole picture. They may be getting a big cheque but, long-term, English cricket will suffer.'[34] The former ECB chairman, Lord MacLaurin, made a similar criticism.[35]

One might seek to dismiss these suggestions on the grounds that they reflect little more than an intuitive unease about the sporting impact of commodified viewing. Yet that criticism is itself vitiated by the outlook of sport organisations themselves. When, in their infancy, television stations started to show a strong interest in sports coverage in the early post-war period, most sport officials were fearful that the new medium would reduce audiences and participants, particularly if fixtures were broadcast live or regularly. However, distrust subsequently turned to partnership when television networks brought new revenues into sport, notably in the form of contractual rights, fees and spin-off monies from trackside advertising.[36] Moreover, and crucially in this context, economists have come to report that television coverage assists sports in building and maintaining audiences, enabling new league systems to survive and prosper.[37] Invariably, if an elite sport is faced with serious sporting rivals and still makes itself accessible only to a minority audience through commodified television stations, then one would expect it to remain a backwater pastime or endure only shallow growth.

Summary

These then are but some illustrations of ways in which market forces might 'score an own goal' and undermine the basis of their own profitability. We are not suggesting that these outcomes will occur as a matter of necessity nor that these are the only ways in which market forces might be pragmatically pathological. The point is simply to demonstrate how sometimes – despite the apparent paradoxical nature of the claim – the pursuit of profits can ultimately be self-defeating. When market forces do lead to such outcomes we suggest that they are pragmatically pathological.

It is also important to notice the overlap here with some of the other pathologies we have discussed in earlier chapters. For instance, when sporting broadcasts are siphoned onto pay-TV and some former viewers are no longer able to enjoy their chosen sports, this not only raises relatively practical issues about the long-term financial interests of the sport; it also brings forth questions on the matter of injustice. We do not need to choose between the alternative accounts of the bad-making features of such cases, for it is not exclusively a problem of injustice or against the long-term interests of the game. It might well be both. In moral theory, as in other areas of human inquiry, there can often be more than one reason for rejecting a course of action.

We turn now in our final chapter to some illustrative examples of public policy responses to these pathologies. The aim will not be so much to provide a blue-print for the transformation of sport, but to provide some examples of how one might translate these concerns into action.

7 Moral philosophy out on the track
What might be done?

Introduction

Our initial puzzle concerned how we might make sense of the general public disquiet about the influence of money and markets in sport. Do our intuitions that there is something wrong with hyper-commodification have any rational basis to them? Is it possible to explain what is wrong with 'this sporting Mammon' without invoking either the ideals of amateurism or Marxian socialism?

We believe that sports fans are right to be worried about the hyper-commodification of sport, for there is a real danger of many important values in sport being lost. Accordingly, in the preceding chapters we identified four distinct ways in which the commodification of sport might give rise to undesirable outcomes.

1   *The Motivational Pathology*: the commodification of sport is pathological when it corrodes the attitudes of those who participate in sport so that they no longer pursue sport as a goal in itself.
2   *The Instrumentalist Pathology*: the commodification of sport is pathological when it leads others to regard athletes and sport itself as mere means and not as ends-in-themselves.
3   *The Distributive Pathology*: the commodification of sport is pathological when it gives rise to forms of distributive injustice.
4   *The Pragmatic Pathology*: the commodification of sport is pathological when it undermines the long-term profitability of any sporting activity.

On our account, commodification is morally undesirable when it gives rise to any of these pathologies. Further we suggest that it is the occurrence of these very pathologies that explains much of the unease that the general public have with respect to hyper-commodified sport. In seeking to make sense of the widespread disenchantment of many sports-fans with modern sport, we need to understand the ways in which markets can go wrong. Significantly, our pathologies show how it is possible to object to the undue influence of money, as is the wont of the Amateurist project or the Marxist, without entirely abolishing markets in sport.

The question to which we turn now concerns how, in very general terms, we might prevent such outcomes occurring in sport. What kinds of *sports policies* might we pursue if we wish to avoid these market pathologies arising? As we noted in earlier chapters, our general approach to the problem of commodification is non-abolitionist, in that we support a mixed market economy. Thus we endorse the maintenance of markets as the means of producing and distributing a *great many* social goods so long as such activity is subject to State regulation. At the same time we also maintain that some things should not be bought and sold (for instance, marriage or voting rights) and hence should be placed outside the range of the market.

Applied to sport this means that our policies will fall under one of three general headings. First, there will be some initiatives that will involve *blocked exchange*, that is, the prohibition of market exchanges in a particular good. Just as one might wish to outlaw the selling of children, there will also be some sporting events and objects that should not be bought and sold. Second, some of our suggestions will involve the *regulation* by the State or relevant sporting associations of market exchanges in sporting goods. In such cases, it is not that markets should be prohibited, but rather that the activities of market agents and the outcomes delivered by market processes should be constrained by the State with the aim of realising specific moral and pragmatic ideals. Finally, some of our policy suggestions will involve *moral exhortation*, rather than formal institutional policy. Here the idea is to encourage individuals and groups that operate within the market to take ethical considerations into account when making their decisions. So, to give an example, one might well produce educational material designed to foster a concern amongst elite sports-stars with industrial conditions in which the sports gear they promote is produced and to avoid buying goods from companies that exploit their workers. The aim here would be for clubs, players and associations to buy goods from the least exploitative companies. In this instance, one relies on some form of moral conscience on the part of players, administrators and fans in order to realise the desired social outcomes.

Our strategy then will be to provide a series of suggestions – some of which involve blocked exchange, some of which involve regulation and some of which involve moral exhortation – oriented towards the prevention of the pathologies we have outlined thus far. We begin with the ownership of elite sports teams, and then move to questions of the regulation of market practices, reinvestment in the grass roots and forms of moral edification.

Before exploring these policy suggestions, a few caveats are in order. First, we make no pretence that what we present is a fully developed and thorough blueprint for the ethical reorganisation of sport. Our aim is simply to provide some indication, in broad outline, of the kinds of policies that might be implemented with the aim of preventing commodification being pathological. A genuine blueprint for the avoidance of market pathologies would be a large volume in itself.

Second, we do not wish to give the impression that the moral problems associated with commodification exhaust the ethical concerns to be found in sport. There are many other issues, such as cheating and the use of drugs in sport, which cannot be subsumed solely under the heading of commodification. While it might well be true – and there are good reasons for thinking it so – that money is often causally responsible for such undesirable phenomena, nonetheless they still arise in non-commercial environments. For instance, drug usage to improve sporting performances reached epidemic proportions in many of the Eastern Bloc countries at the height of the Cold War. If we were to provide a blueprint for the 'ethical reorganisation of sport' it would need to deal with many topics over and above those associated with money. Commodification is not the end of the ethical issue.

The organisation, ownership and re-mutualisation of elite sport

Let us begin with the organisation and, in particular, the property arrangements of modern elite sport. We begin with elite sport because it is here that the pathologies of commodification are most evident, since it is top-level sport which is of most value to commercial interests.

Ideally the communities out of which they originally emerged should own sporting associations and sporting clubs. Instead of being run by cliques of investors or multi-national corporations, it would be best if they were owned by and administered through the relevant community groups. We stress this at the outset because many of the pathologies we have discussed are in no small part due to the activities of large commercial organisations. For instance, if we take the tendency to treat sport merely as a commodity, this is certainly more likely to arise when clubs are listed on the stock exchange than when they are not able to be bought and sold. Equally, ownership by such commercial groups will often lead to maximising commercial strategies that take little heed of moral considerations such as justice. All other things being equal, access for less wealthy fans is more likely to be a relevant consideration for a community-based club than it will be for a club owned by a billionaire investor or an investment fund. One way of avoiding such outcomes would be for clubs and associations to be placed on the list of blocked exchanges.

This might appear excessively utopian when one is dealing with elite sport, but we can point to some striking examples of highly successful, community-owned sporting institutions. For example, in the NFL, the Green Bay Packers have a longstanding public tradition founded upon an extremely wide community shareholding, with ceilings placed on the volumes of shares held by any one individual. The club's issue of additional shares in late 1997, to remain competitive in a highly commercial league, was also directed at maintaining this wide community ownership. In soccer, the Barcelona team is effectively a mutual society that is owned by its members – who number over 100,000 – and which is run along democratic lines. Major decision-making powers are held by the General Assembly that represents members. Attempts to commercialise the club by reducing the legislative power of the Assembly have been resisted by supporters' movements, most notably *L'Elefant Blau*.[1]

One possible strategy for preventing the occurrence of our pathologies would be for the private ownership of clubs and leagues to be abolished. This would not mean that markets in elite sport would be entirely abolished or that elite players would not be paid handsomely for their efforts. Indeed, as the example of the Green Bay Packers demonstrates, community ownership does not preclude extensive commercial activity on the part of the clubs and associations. Community owned clubs can licence sporting goods, pay high salaries to athletes, allow their players to engage in commercial endorsements and so on. In making the clubs and associations 'blocked exchanges' we would simply be limiting the range of the market in a way that is intended to prevent the kinds of extreme commercial behaviour that ignores important values and ideals associated with sport. (Here, of course, we assume that such community organisations are, all other things being equal, less likely to be corruptive than large scale capitalist ones.)

Unsurprisingly, we are not the first to make such suggestions. For example, in his book *They Call it a Game* Bernie Parrish offered a similar alternative to the private monopolistic ownership of teams, leagues and players in the United States. Therein he wrote:

> The franchises should be owned by municipal corporations legally tied to the stadium authorities, having public common-stock ownership, with stock being offered to season-ticket holders on the basis of first refusal ... a formula could be worked out to pay the players a percentage of the total income. Then the profits after expenses could be earmarked for the revitalisation of the inner cities – improved wages for police, firemen, teachers and other civil servants; upgrading of city and country hospitals, and care for the aged; to name a few recipients.[2]

Parrish's point here that if municipalities owned clubs, then the revenues could be employed to provide local amenities and facilities is an important one. We see no reason that revenues raised in sport should not be injected back into communities.

Given the current level of private ownership of elite sports teams and events in places like the United States and Europe, any project to foster public ownership would require a massive social change. It would require the remutualisation of sports clubs, a transferring ownership from private to community groups and as such would meet tremendous opposition from those private interests who currently own and profit from private sports. While it is not unrealistic to believe that those sports teams currently publicly owned can maintain their non-private status, plans for remutualisation are unlikely to succeed in the near future.

If this is true, then any policy prescriptions would need to rely predominantly upon intervention into the activities of the market by both the State and sport's governing authorities. One minimal strategy would be for the State to appoint independent regulators to oversee specific sports at a national level. There are *analogous precedents* for such appointments. For instance, in the United Kingdom official regulators oversee important public utilities such as gas, electricity and telecommunications, to protect consumer interests in services that are viewed as fundamental needs. The appointment of official regulators for sport would reflect the latter's importance within society.

Sport regulators might also be empowered to investigate and eradicate corrupt practices on and off the fields of play. More broadly, these regulators should safe-guard the interests of specific sporting communities that are harmed if abandoned to market forces. For example, sporting regulators might challenge the prices of 'official' merchandise that are often charged by sporting organisations. A prime target here might be the mark-ups on trademarked replica shirts for sports teams. Sales of replica soccer shirts are worth more than £200 million per annum in the United Kingdom. Alternatively, these sporting regulators might be empowered to monitor the systems employed by governing bodies to distribute tickets for key fixtures.

The role fulfilled by the officials of sport's governing bodies might also be redefined, with greater emphasis placed on public service rather than business interest. In other words, sports officials would ultimately be responsible to their fellow citizens rather than to institutional powerbrokers.

Another possible strategy would be to curtail the role of other private organi-sations, such as subscription-based media networks, corporate sponsors, and merchandise corporations in the development of sports. While sports clubs may establish partnerships with local businesses at a community level, we should be wary of commercial relationships that would undermine the participatory ethics or symbolism of the sporting institution. Similarly, merchandising and broadcasting organisations should not drive all changes to the organisation and structure of sport. Such changes should come from within the practice of sport itself.

A final institutional strategy would involve both supporters groups and local authorities having a right to be involved in decision-making and administration within privately owned elite sporting clubs. In the United Kingdom, the voice of fans can be heard through the 'Supporter Trusts' that have been established at almost every major soccer club. The Trusts provide each member with a share in the club that it represents, thereby allowing supporters to attend annual general meetings. Trusts also provide a forum for expressing supporter opinions on issues relating to the club and, in the ideal circumstances, they are able to gain a representative seat on the board of directors. Some Trusts have taken over the control of clubs that have suffered very badly in financial terms. Through the participation of fans, the ideals and values of those who regard sport as an end-in-itself are more likely to be part of the decision-making process and in this way pathologies of the market are less likely to arise. Similar points can be made with respect to local authorities. Even if the teams are privately owned, a better system would allow representatives of the local authorities to at least hold a public stake in sports teams.[3]

Interestingly, public input into the development of elite sport is not an entirely novel idea. There are some noteworthy cases in which civic participation has extended into the formation of pressure groups, social movements and providen-tial societies. In the United States, numerous local pressure groups have grown up to challenge extremely expensive stadium-building projects that would be funded by public money. For example, the 'Stadium out of Chinatown' movement in

Philadelphia succeeded in blocking construction plans that would have adversely affected residents and the community fabric in one area of the city.[4]

The point is that either through (i) changes to the ownership of elite sporting leagues, clubs and teams or (ii) limiting the prerogatives of ownership, many of the pathologies discussed earlier might be avoided. Ideally clubs would be communally owned. But in the absence of the political will required to bring about such changes, as a second-best option the prerogatives of ownership should be severely curtailed. If the activities of private owners were regulated by the State and relevant sporting authorities, then this might ensure that ideals specific to sport, such as the mutual pursuit of excellence, as well as more general values, such as those pertaining to distributive justice, continue to be part of the landscape of elite sport. Finally, fans and local authorities could be given a role in the decision-making processes of elite clubs. Through these mechanisms private owners would not, as is currently the case, have *carte blanche* to pursue venal strategies.

The regulation of unjust and counterproductive market practices

Having established the necessity of regulating the commercial activities of private sporting teams, let us now give some attention to the details of such regulation. How might the State and sporting authorities regulate in order to avoid the occurrence of our market pathologies?

To be sure, it must be acknowledged that there are already regulatory practices in place oriented towards limiting the influence of money in sport. For instance, there are a number of measures which were introduced to prevent various forms of corruption in sport, such as the bribing of judges and vote buying by cities competing for the elite events such as the Olympics. For instance, the IOC has introduced some anti-corruption measures to combat vote fixing by cities bidding to host Olympic events.

There are good reasons, however, for going beyond this rather minimal level of regulation. Over and above the prevention of corruption we believe that policies oriented towards both the alleviation of injustice and fostering the long-term health of sport are required. The first of these more extensive policies concerns the method employed to allocate elite players. What we wish to avoid here is the phenomenon of clubs 'buying success' that we suggested in chapter 6 is injurious to the health of sport. Buying success is 'pragmatically pathological' because it both severely diminishes 'uncertainty of outcome' and often generates forms of distributive injustice, since it is unfair for sporting success to be simply a function of the size of one's bank account. Interestingly, some economists have already speculated that uncertainty of outcome will become increasingly important as the commodification of sport intensifies, for example through vast rises in income from television.[5] This is but an acknowledgement of how a commercial orientation in one area might undermine the commercial viability in another.

In order to prevent the buying of success, associations in team sports might institute salary caps, redistributions of league incomes and a draft system (as indeed the English Rugby Premiership did in recent years). 'Salary caps' involve sports governing bodies introducing financial controls on club rosters. These salary caps would limit the total wage budget at each club, ensuring that there would be no clustering of 'big money' players at any one team. Alternatively one might introduce 'player value caps'. These are more complicated and would function like the 'fantasy league' game that is popular among soccer fans. This system would require a panel of independent arbiters to establish a value for each player in the league; each club would then be required to hold a squad whose total player value did not exceed an agreed universal figure. Another measure to prevent success being bought would involve the pooling of league revenues (such as television monies and income from spectator attendances), and an equitable distribution of these sums among all member clubs.

Draft systems could also be introduced to maintain uncertainty of outcome between clubs. National sporting federations might seek to establish and oversee strong nursery systems for the development of elite players. Such national coaching frameworks would allow the institution of a 'draft system' of player recruitment in team sport. Teams that have been failing to perform might be given first pick of new players. In fact, such a policy is operational in many US sports, notably American football, where a strong college sport system feeds the professional leagues with an annual crop of 'rookies'. Clearly, it would also be more easily implemented in sport systems where the State and sport authorities take an active role in player development. Such a system would require the relevant authorities to exercise substantially greater power than any individual clubs within the sport.

'Buying success' also involves clubs recruiting the best available players, with the aim not only of improving their teams' competitive skills on the pitch, but also to weaken their rivals. The most destructive instance is the stock-piling of excellence which involves recruiting top players who are then simply listed as 'squad members' but have little chance of actually competing in matches. One method of preventing this stock-piling of excellence, would be for associations to restrict the roster sizes of teams to ensure that all players have active roles to play. Each club would be required to field an individual player for a minimum number of competitive games during each season.

A second area where regulation might be required is with respect to the access of fans to sporting events and sporting broadcasts. Let us begin with major sporting events. The hyper-commodification of such events can directly undermine the interests of some of the most dedicated supporters and audiences. In the United Kingdom, for instance, the cost of entry to some sports events has risen by over 800 per cent in the past two decades. Priority access to leading events – such as soccer cup finals, rugby and cricket test matches, and Wimbledon's Centre Court – is increasingly restricted to corporate sponsors. Equally, the most dedicated sports supporters are forced to pay heavily. Sports fans must either pay large amounts of money to maintain their allegiances, reconfigure their identification towards high-profile teams, or give up their support on the grounds of cost.

One response to this problem of access would be for sports governing bodies to set prices for these events at far lower levels than those that currently obtain. Queuing might then be employed to deal with the problems associated with scarcity. It would be a matter of 'first in, first served'. To be sure, this would not solve the problem of scarcity, but would ensure that the allocation of these scarce resources is not solely determined by the relative wealth of those who want them. Another response would be for sporting authorities to ensure also that tickets to the largest events are distributed according to fair criteria. Currently, gaining entry to the world championships or leading finals in most professional sports is best achieved by paying extortionate sums to 'scalper' organisations that have previously acquired large bundles of tickets prior to their sale to the public. Tickets could also be distributed as a priority among the most committed, long-standing supporters of athletes or teams that are involved in these fixtures. For example, if Scotland and Australia were to play each other in rugby's World Cup final, the fans who have attended most fixtures involving either team through to that stage could be given first refusal on tickets. A small minority of tickets (say 10–20 per cent) might be reserved for individuals who have worked in a voluntary or semi-voluntary role within the host nation, either in regard to the specific tournament or in serving the sport in general. The rationale for such a policy would be that these supporters and dedicated workers within the sport constitute the most deserving recipients of tickets to sporting events. Sport's governing bodies and national governments might also criminalise ticket scalping for profit, as is sometimes currently done, whether this occurs outside the ground or through internet sites.

Another related area of distributive concern involves the siphoning of broadcasts of major events onto pay-TV. In order to safeguard the public provision of elite sport, the State might expand the list of 'crown jewel' sporting events that must be shown on free-to-air television. We noted in chapter 5 that European national policies varied on the listing of specific events for free-to-air television, and that in some instances, major political conflicts justifiably arises when pay-TV intrudes upon viewing rights.[6] Of course, there will be crown jewel events in each different country.[7] In Australia, for instance, the list of crown jewel events would include the Melbourne Cup, the Australian Football grand final, the Australian Open tennis competition and the National Rugby League final. Equally, in the United States there are many events, such as the NBA final and the World Series baseball finals that would in all likelihood be included on such a list. The point is that for any particular constituency, there will be a series of important events for which everyone should ideally have access via free-to-air broadcasts.

Some major sports clubs or leagues might well argue in response that they are under intense commercial pressure to sign deals with subscription television stations. However, if sports clubs and leagues introduced some of the measures set out earlier – such as salary caps, and greater equity in the distribution of revenues across clubs – then these pressures would be largely deflated.

A third area where regulation might be enacted is with respect to the activities of sporting agents. In many quarters sport agents have gained some unenviable reputations for their inflation of athlete salaries in some sports. In the short-term, sport authorities should tightly regulate the activities of agents. In the longer-term, it might be preferable for athletes' unions to represent the interests of professional athletes.

Reinvestment in the grass-roots

Our policy suggestions thus far have focused solely on elite sport. But if sport is to remain healthy in all of the relevant respects, the grass roots must also be healthy and, accordingly, they should also be an important part of any policy initiatives. The grass roots are not only the breeding grounds for future elite athletes, but of value in their own right for the opportunities they provide for the general public to pursue excellence and enjoy the pleasures of competition. Grass roots sporting organisations also provide ordinary people with opportunities for participation in decision-making processes in events and social structures that affect them directly.

The first policy suggestion here concerns the reinvestment of resources generated in elite sports into local grass roots sporting associations. We suggest that a great deal more revenue from elite sporting competitions should be filtered down to grass-roots levels. Currently, the vast majority of revenues from major competitions such as the NFL, the NRL and the English Premiership are distributed among member clubs with little regard to the grass-roots institutions that nurtured and developed the talents of the participating athletes. Equally, the facilities of elite clubs and associations might be opened out of season to local communities at low or no cost to the user. For example, elite sport clubs possess important capital and human resources, such as gymnasia, swimming pools, and often teams of scientists, that would be of major benefit to local communities and which are in any case used only for restricted periods by professional athletes. The move towards the mutualisation of sports clubs would promote the principle that members, supporters and the surrounding community be granted access to elite sporting facilities.

The justification for pursuing such policy initiatives is in one sense pragmatic. If a sport does not reinvest in its grass roots, and grass roots participation declines, then in the long run this will be harmful to the elite sport. Indeed it is from the grass roots that talented new players emerge and it is through participation in grass roots sport that many people gain their interest in sport at an elite level. Of course, it is not unknown for an elite sport to flourish and for club level participation to be in decline. Here interest is generated primarily through broadcasts of the elite level competition. But one would have to be concerned about the long-term prospects of any sport in this situation.

But equally there are specifically moral reasons for reinvestment in the grass roots. Since any sport relies on non-elite competitions for the production of future elite sportsmen and women, it owes the grass roots a debt. For elite clubs, competitions and sporting corporations not to reinvest in its grass roots is, in effect, for them to 'free-ride'; to simply take the benefits without contributing to the system that creates those benefits in the first place. Further, playing sport is a good in itself for those who play it. Grass roots competitions are not only valuable for the future champions they produce, but also for the opportunities they provide for people to enjoy the autotelic goods of which we spoke in earlier chapters. Therefore it would be a good thing for money to be reinvested in the grass roots to ensure the continuation of a valuable sphere in which people develop and maintain their fitness, cooperate with team-mates and strive to improve their athletic performances.

A second policy suggestion that might help here involves fostering the participatory element that is a distinctive feature of much grass roots sport at an organisational level. Through involvement as linesmen, timekeepers, committee members and so on, club supporters engage in an important and immediate form of citizenship. In this there is a marked difference with the depleted social relationships that generally arise within privately owned, profit seeking sports institutions.

Further, it is important to remember that sport is a major cultural activity through which individual people and groups come into contact with one another and develop important social relationships. In team sports part of the frisson of sporting contests – both at an elite and a club level – derives from the social differentiation of players and supporters from those of other teams and the interplay arising from these distinct identities. Such exchanges are notably not founded upon monetary or commodity principles. Of course, such rivalries can sometimes descend into hatred and violence, but such pathologies are the exception rather than the rule. The vast majority involve healthy interactions. In this way, when things go well, sport is capable of facilitating friendly symbolic exchanges between different communities.

Moral education and individual action

So far we have focused on formal institutional responses. But we should not think that this is the only policy route. There are some pernicious elements of commodification of sport that are probably best dealt with outside of state or institutional frameworks through individual action. To bring about change here would require 'moral education' of individuals, rather than State interventions. Indeed this is particularly true of the two pathologies that concern the loss of important participant ideals in sport and the treatment of sport as a *mere* commodity. Actions by the State and sporting institutions can provide a framework in which sport is less likely to be treated as a mere commodity. But so long as money is involved, such institutional action cannot prevent venal attitudes towards sport. If important values, such as for instance the mutual pursuit of excellence, are to survive as operative ideals of those involved in playing elite sport, we will also require individuals to resist the pressures the market places on their value system. To be sure, there are dangers here of 'moralism'. Too often eminent sportspeople and administrators invoke such values only to ignore them in practice, and without accompanying institutional action, moral education is likely to be nothing more than ethical window-dressing. Nonetheless, as part of a broader strategy to avoid the pathologies of hyper-commodification, moral education has an important role to play.

Let us begin here with those responsible for the organisation and administration of sport. Over the past twenty years they have come to be highly influenced by management models that regard sport as a mere commodity. Such managers make decisions solely based on the bottom line. Under this 'market rhetoric' (to use Margaret Jane Radin's evocative phrase), every human interaction is understood as a market exchange. What might be helpful here are educational discussions that emphasise the importance of non-monetary values in sport and the vulnerability of such values to corrosion by commodification. Administrators need to be reminded constantly that sport is not just a *mere* commodity.

Equally athletes themselves would ideally resist the emergence of venal attitudes. Sport goes best when athletes do not to regard sport as a *mere* means to individual wealth. They should maintain their focus on the various non-monetary values – such as the mutual pursuit of excellence – that sport is capable of realising. They should be made aware of the importance of such values and the potential corrosion of them by the commercial world.

Athletes should also be reminded that while self-interest is a legitimate motive in sporting life, it should be leavened by accompanying moral side-constraints. Sportspeople should not act venally and, accordingly, some financial offers they should refuse. For instance, the sportspersons who toured South Africa in the 1980s, in contravention of the Gleneagles Agreement, undermined important movements for social change in the pursuit of quick wealth.[8]

Finally, we should not forget the potential power of sports fans to influence the ways in which sport develops. As both consumers and citizens sports fans make choices which can affect the direction of the development of sport. For instance, sports fans might avoid events, teams or institutions that are driven particularly by corporate greed, financial expansionism or the simple pursuit of large margins. Somewhat ironically, this would be to use market power to prevent particular forms of hyper-commodification.

Summary

What might well strike some readers about these policy suggestions is that a great many of them have been implemented to varying degrees in many sports over the past fifty years. Although some of the suggestions, such as those concerning remutualisation, are rarely enacted, others, such as those relating to the draft system, are quite common. On reflection this should not be all that surprising since community concerns about hyper-commodification, if not expressed using that terminology, run deep. Accordingly, some policies have been enacted to limit the influence of money in sport. But no *systematic* attempt has been made to ensure that money does not undermine the values of sport. Through our identification of the four pathologies we provide the theoretical grounds for a wide-ranging and systematic policy response to hyper-commodification.

It is important here to reiterate the non-abolitionist nature of our policy proposals. In keeping with the general thrust of the book, we have focused on alleviating the particular noxious aspects of commodification within sport, rather than on advocating either the sweeping abolition of all social exchanges that generate surplus value or the immediate termination of all capitalist relations of production.

We do not pretend that our list of possible policies is exhaustive of the measures that are required to deal adequately with the harms associated with the hyper-commodification of sport. Clearly, there will be further measures one might introduce which we have not covered. What we have presented are some important policy ideas that would aid in preventing sport degenerating into a realm of fantastic venality. Nor do we pretend that bringing about such changes would be an easy matter. In order for the kinds of policies we propose to be enacted, it would require considerable resolve on the part of those in charge of sport. Here the power of large commercial interests is not be underestimated. But equally, we do not believe that such changes to sport are impossible. If sport is to survive as a valuable practice that realises important human goods, then these are in fact an urgent necessity and such impediments must be overcome.

Finally, it is important that we note the limits of this inquiry: commodification is not the end of matters of ethics in sport. We should not give the impression that if policies such as ours were enacted then the battle for a more ethically appropriate sport would be won. There are many practices other than those associated with commercialisation that are ethically unsavoury. Here we need think only of issues such as the use of performance-enhancing drugs, cheating and other forms of unsporting behaviour. These are not directly related to the influence of money, since any sporting competition with highly desired trophies, medals and flags will provide athletes and others with sufficient motivation to act corruptly. Nonetheless, despite all of that, financial incentives undoubtedly increase the temptations for corruption. By diminishing the influence of money in sport, and reawakening in its practitioners a love for goals other than money, then the temptations for corruption will be less appealing. In this way, our policy suggestions are part of a more general project to ensure that sport remains a sphere of life in which the mutual pursuit of excellence, the autotelic goods of participation and the ideals of fair play are realised.

Notes

1 This sporting Mammon?

1 See: www.ipsos-asi.com/news/SuperBowl03Scores.pdf
2 J. Walvin, *The Only Game: Football in Our Times*, London: Pearson, 2001.
3 W. LaFeber, *Michael Jordan and the New Global Capitalism*, New York: W.W. Norton, 2002, p. 137.
4 'Beckham heads rich player list', BBC Sport, Wednesday 1 December, 2004, http:// news.bbc.co.uk/sport1/hi/football/4057485.stm
5 Karl Marx, *The Communist Manifesto*, Peking: Foreign Languages Press, 1970, p. 35.
6 For example, one boy born in the 1970s into a lower working-class housing estate in north-east Scotland was named after a great Hungarian player, Zoltan Varga, who played briefly for Aberdeen.
7 See Margaret Jane Radin, *Contested Commodities: The Trouble with Trade in Sex, Children, Body Parts and other Things*, Cambridge, MA: Harvard University Press, 1996, pp. 6–8.
8 Simon Rae, *It's not Cricket: A History of Skulduggery, Sharp Practice and Downright Cheating in the Noble Game*, London: Faber and Faber, 2001, p. 268.
9 See: www.breadnotcircuses.org/bread_alert_x_000914.html
10 H.J. Lenskyj, 'The Olympic Industry and Civil Liberties: The Threat to Free Speech and Freedom of Assembly', in R. Giulianotti and D. McArdle (eds), *Sport, Civil Liberties and Human Rights*, London: Taylor & Francis, 2005.
11 D.C. Coates, and B.R. Humphreys, 'The Stadium Gambit and Local Economic Development', *Regulation*, 23(2), 2000, pp. 15–20.
12 Andrew Jennings, *The New Lords of the Rings: Olympic Corruption and How to Buy Gold Medals*, Pocket Books: London, 1996, p. 47.
13 See K. Schmitz, 'Sport and Play: Suspension of the Ordinary', in W. Morgan and K. Meier (eds), *Philosophical Inquiry into Sport*, Champion, IL: Human Kinetics, 1988, pp. 29–38.
14 In making this statement, Parks still appreciates that, on the subject of professional soccer, 'one must never forget that for the organizers it is merely business'. Nevertheless, several anthropologists have noted the strong continuities that exist between the rituals of sport and religious ceremonies (see, especially, C. Bromberger, 'Football as World-View and as Ritual', *French Cultural Studies*, vi, 1995, pp. 293–311).
15 Christopher Lasch argues that the attempt to develop a separate realm of pure play distinct from work in fact gives rise to its very opposite, namely a business that can be analysed like any other business. It is the degradation of work that leads to this degradation of play. See Christopher Lasch, *The Culture of Narcissism*, New York: Warner Books, 1979, pp. 100–124, 248–50.
16 Lincoln Allison suggests that for the fan, sport is a refuge from and reaction to modernity. *Amateurism in Sport: An Analysis and Defence*, London: Frank Cass, 2001, p. 36. To borrow the language of critical social theory, sport may be understood in its purest sense

as non-productive play, in balancing our utilitarian focus on the work-driven 'useful' with our creative exploration of the playful 'useless' (Cf. W.J. Morgan, 'Adorno on Sport: The Case of the Fractured Dialectic', *Theory and Society*, 17, 1988, p. 831).

17 In the language of economics, investment in sport by club owners has inclined more towards 'utility maximisation' (to win games and tournaments) rather than 'profit maximisation' (Cf. P.J. Sloane, 'The Economics of Professional Football: The Football Club as a Utility Maximiser', *Scottish Journal of Political Economy*, 18(2), 1971, pp. 121–146 and G.W. Scully, *The Market Structure of Sports*, Chicago, IL: University of Chicago Press, 1995).

18 Mike Marqusee, *Anyone but England: Cricket and the National Malaise*, London: Verso, 1994, p. 119.

19 R. Sandy, P.J. Sloane and M.S. Rosentraub, *The Economics of Sport: An International Perspective*, Basingstoke: Palgrave, 2004, pp. 68–69.

20 The Hillsborough disaster occurred in Sheffield at the 1989 FA Cup semi-final between Liverpool and Nottingham Forest. Several thousand Liverpool fans were allowed to pour into a central 'pen' in the ground, leading to fatal levels of crowd crushing. Despite watching the disaster unfold on CCTV, the police commander refused to take the step of allowing the perimeter gates inside the ground to be opened.

21 For example, Test match cricket, which is played over five days, now tends to feature a far greater degree of positive, attacking play than twenty or thirty years ago.

22 Polley then proceeds to acknowledge that the range of anger and persistence of opposition to the heavily commercialised sporting scene are real and 'crucial to our appreciation of post-war British sport'. *Moving the Goalposts: A History of Sport and Society since 1945*, London: Routledge, 1998, pp. 81–82.

23 Certainly, Bannister received no direct commercial benefit, but his record-breaking run did require pacemaker runners and meticulous planning of a kind more commonly associated with today's professional athletics.

24 We discuss amateurism in chapter 3, but there the concern is with its relationship to the idea of sport-for-sport's sake, rather than the pre-commodity history of sport.

25 N. Tranter, *Sport, Economy and Society in Britain 1750–1914*, Cambridge: Cambridge University Press, 1998, pp. 67–68.

26 See Elliott J. Gorn and Warren Goldstein, *A Brief History of American Sports*, New York: Hill and Wang, 1993, pp. 189–190.

27 See W.E. Sweet, *Sport and Recreation in Ancient Greece*, Oxford: Oxford University Press, 1987, p. 4 and W.J. Baker, *Sports in the Western World*, Revised Edition, Urbana, IL: University of Illinois Press, 1988, pp. 21–22.

28 Tim Park writes:

> After the pomp and ideals of opening ceremonies, then, what could be less educational than the spectacle itself and the suspicions that surround it? Or more exciting, more likely to inflame the passions? Infallibly, it seems the overall frame of the brotherhood of man contains a festival of bad behaviour on the part of the players, and paranoia, resentment, and Schadenfreude on the part of the fans. Far from diminishing people's interest in the sport, ironically it is precisely the unpleasant incidents and negative sentiments that fuel its vigorous growth.
>
> (*New York Review of Books*, July 18, 2002)

29 George Orwell, 'The Sporting Spirit', in *The Penguin Essays of George Orwell*, Harmondsworth, Middlesex: Penguin, 1994, pp. 321–323.

2 Moral philosophy, sport and commodification critique

1 Standard neo-classical economic definitions of the commodity simply define a commodity as a tangible economic product that contributes directly or indirectly to the satisfaction of human wants. This does not provide us with much insight into what

occurs when a good is commodified. For this reason the Aristotelian account is more useful. See, for instance, the definition in *Collins Dictionary of Economics*, 2nd edition, Christopher Pass and Bryan Lowes (eds), London: Harper Collins, 1993.

2 Aristotle, *The Politics*, trans. John Warrington, London: Heron Books, 1948, [1257a].

3 It is important not to confuse such processes of change with what we might call *juridification*; that is, the process of more and more areas of social life coming under the aegis of legal jurisdiction.

4 Radin, *Contested Commodities*, pp. 6–8.

5 Elizabeth Anderson, *Value in Ethics and Economics*, Cambridge, MA: Harvard University Press, 1993, pp. 143–145.

6 Mike McNamee also makes this point when exploring MacIntyre's critique of the role of institutions in corrupting practices. See Mike McNamee, 'Sporting Practices, Institutions and Virtues: A Critique and a Restatement', *Journal of the Philosophy of Sport*, 22, 1995, p. 65.

7 For a critical discussion of Murdoch's bid see A. Brown and A. Walsh, *Not for Sale: Manchester United, Murdoch and the Defeat of BskyB*, Edinburgh: Mainstream, 1999.

8 Ian Tyrell distinguishes between professionalisation that involves playing sport as an occupation or being paid for playing and 'commercialisation' which involves running sport like a business. See Ian Tyrell, 'The Professionalisation of American Baseball', in Richard Cashman and Michael McKernan (eds), *Sport: Money, Morality and the Media*, Kensington, NSW: University of New South Wales Press, 1981, p. 88.

9 Eric Dunning and Kenneth Sheards discuss 'broken time' payment in their book *Barbarians, Gentlemen and Players: A Sociological Study of the Development of Rugby Football*, Canberra: Australian National University Press, 1979, pp. 149–150.

10 See A. Mason, 'Our Stephen and Our Harald: Edwardian Footballers as Local Heroes', *International Journal of the History of Sport*, 13(1), 1996, pp. 71–85 and Chas Critcher, 'Football Since the War', in John Clarke, Chas Critcher and Richard Johnson (eds), *Working Class Culture: Studies in History and Theory*, London: Hutchinson, 1979.

11 Marqusee, *Anyone but England*, p. 120.

12 Robert L. Simon, *Fair Play in Sport: The Ethics of Sport*, 2nd edition, Boulder, CO: Westview Press, 2004, p. 173.

13 Steven J. Overman, *The Influence of the Protestant Ethic on Sport and Recreation*, Aldershot: Avebury, 1997, p. 335.

14 Radin, op cit., pp. 6–8.

15 The argument for decommodification has been revived, albeit cautiously, by Wallerstein in his neo-Marxist analysis of the contemporary global system. See Immanuel Wallerstein, *The Decline of American Power*, New York: New Press, 2002.

16 Karl Marx, *Capital*, vol.1, Moscow: Progress, 1954, pp. 132–133.

17 Some might question whether it is really a theory of injustice since Marx at various places condemned justice talk as just 'bourgeoisie moralism'. But we must never forget that this is the man who talks with extreme distaste about the way capitalism denigrates and exploits people before the 'juggernaut of capital'. For useful discussions of Marx as a moral philosopher see Richard Norman, *The Moral Philosophers*, 1st edition, Oxford: Clarendon Press, 1983, pp. 173–201 and Stephen Lukes, *Marxism and Morality*, Oxford: Oxford University Press, 1985.

18 See Marx, *Capital*, vol.1, pp. 476–478. See also Tom Bottomore (ed.), *A Dictionary of Marxist Thought*, Oxford: Basil Blackwell, 1983, pp. 472–475.

19 Karl Marx, *Early Writings [1], Economic and Philosophical Manuscripts*, trans. T.B. Bottomore, London: Watts, 1963, p. 191.

20 Marx, *Capital*, vol.1, pp. 76–77.

21 Jean-Marie Brohm, *Sport: A Prison of Measured Time*, translated by Ian Fraser, Worcester: Pluto Press, 1978, p. 34.

22 Brohm, ibid., pp. 13–14, 23, 27, 179–180.

23 Brohm, ibid., p. 105.

24 For a useful (and fuller) discussion of these issues see David Miller, 'Why Markets?', in *Market Socialism*, Julian Le Grand and Saul Eslin (eds), Oxford: Clarendon Press, 1989, pp. 25–49.

25 For a critical (and we would suggest overly unsympathetic) account of the zero-sum element in Marxism see James W. Child, 'Profit: The Concept and its Moral Features', *Social Philosophy and Policy*, 15(2), Summer 1998, pp. 243–282.

26 Bernard Mandeville, *The Fable of the Bees*, vol. 1, Oxford: Clarendon, 1957 [1705], pp. 36–37, 369.

27 George Simmel, *The Philosophy of Money*, 2nd enlarged edition, David Frisby (ed.), London: Routledge, 1990, p. 286. Simmel also notes (p. 323) that in Medieval England it was a mark of bondage if an adult male was not allowed to give away his daughter or sell an ox without the lord's permission.

28 George Simmel, 'The Metropolis and Mental Life', in *The Sociology of George Simmel*, trans and ed. Kurt H. Wolff, Glencoe, IL: Free Press, 1990.

29 H.J. Paton, *The Moral Law or Kant's Groundwork of the Metaphysics of Morals*, London: Hutchison, 1946, p. 102.

30 Immanuel Kant, *The Metaphysics of Morals*, trans. Mary Gregor, Cambridge: Cambridge University Press, 1991, p. 177.

31 Ibid.

32 For a discussion of these uses see Adrian Walsh, 'Are Market Norms and Intrinsic Valuation Mutually Exclusive?', *Australasian Journal of Philosophy*, 79(4), December 2001, pp. 525–543.

33 For a more detailed discussion of the limits of a Kantian commodity critique see Adrian Walsh, 'Teaching, Preaching and Queaching about Commodities', *The Southern Journal of Philosophy*, 36(3), 1998, pp. 433–452.

34 However, it was widely reported in May 2005 that Barcelona were set to reverse this tradition by accepting sponsorship from the 2008 Beijing Olympics organisers.

35 Anderson, *Value in Ethics and Economics*, p. 10.

36 Notably, she also goes beyond the two-fold classificatory system we find in Kant of modes of valuing. For Anderson there are a wide variety of proper modes of regard.

37 Anderson, op cit., pp. 144–146.

38 Radin, op cit., pp. 103–104. We should note that Radin uses the term 'incomplete commodification' equivocally to cover both on the one hand what we would ordinarily call regulation and on the other the capacity of commodified and non-commodified meanings to co-exist.

39 Alasdair MacIntyre, *After Virtue*, London: Duckworth, 1985, p. 194.

40 William J. Morgan, *Leftist Theories of Sport: A Critique and Reconstruction*, Urbana, IL: University of Illinois Press, 1993, p. 144.

41 Ibid.

42 Robert Nozick, *The Examined Life*, New York: Simon and Schuster, 1989, p. 177.

43 Morgan, op. cit., p. 148.

44 Cf. Mike McNamee, 'Sporting Practices, Institutions and Virtues: A Critique and Restatement', *Journal of the Philosophy of Sport*, 22, 1995, p. 68.

45 We are reminded here of Neil Postman's comment that 'despite sport's close association with the entertainment business, it is still possible to attach virtues such as clarity, honesty and excellent to its practice'. Neil Postman, *Amusing Ourselves to Death*, New York: Penguin, 1985, pp. 125–126.

46 Simon, *Fair Play in Sport*, p. 175.

47 Ibid., p. 178.

3 Financial motives, venality and the ideals of sport

1 William Doyle, *Venality: The Sale of Offices in Eighteenth-Century France*, Oxford: Oxford University Press, 1996.

2 Allen Guttmann makes a very similar point when he clams that it is useful to define spots as autotelic physical contests, that is, 'nonutilitarian competitions carried out for their own sake'. Guttmann notes that his definition is an 'ideal type' that is never realised perfectly in practice. See Allen Guttmann, *Sports Spectators*, New York: Columbia University Press, 1986, p. 4.

3 MacIntyre, *After Virtue*, p. 188. MacIntyre uses the example to illustrate the distinction between intrinsic and extrinsic goods. MacIntyre suggests that if the child comes to value the goods specific to chess, the child will no longer have any desire to cheat, for cheating would deny him or her the opportunity to excel at those internal goods.

4 McNamee suggests that the employment of too strict a delineation between intrinsic and extrinsic goods does not enable us to capture an important range of goods in which 'the personal satisfactions and their attendant motivations' mean that a given a valued and valuable means to securing external goods. For such cases he suggests we use the term 'relational valuing'. See McNamee, 'Sporting Practices, Institutions and Virtues', p. 75.

5 Overman, *The Influence of the Protestant Ethic on Sport and Recreation*, p. 197.

6 Ibid., p. 193. See Michael Novak, *The Joy of Sports*, New York: Basic Books, 1976.

7 Morgan, *Leftist Theories of Sport*, pp. 130–131.

8 Johan Steenbergen and Jan Tamboer, 'Ethics and the Double Character of Sport: An Attempt to Systematise Discussions of the Ethics of Sport', in M.J. McNamee and S.J. Parry (eds), *Ethics and Sport*, Routledge, London, 1998, p. 45.

9 Ibid.

10 We should emphasise that we are not ignoring the possibility of external cultural differences in interpreting the rules of sport – e.g. in rugby there are different interpretations of the laws in the northern and southern hemispheres.

11 For useful discussions of these ideas see Sigmund Loland, *Fair Play in Sport: A Moral Norms System*, London: Routledge, 2002 and Robert L. Simon, *Fair Play: Sports, Values and Society*, Boulder, CO: Westview Press, 1991.

12 John O'Neill, 'The Varieties of Intrinsic Value', *The Monist*, 75(2), April 1992, pp. 119–137.

13 Mike McNamee distinguishes this sense of intrinsic value using the term 'inherent'. See M.J. McNamee, 'Valuing Leisure Practices: Towards a Theoretical Framework', *Leisure Studies*, 13, 1994, pp. 288–309.

14 At the same time this does not rule out the possible explanatory value of such accounts *tout court*.

15 Barry Schwartz in *The Battle for Human Nature: Sense, Morality and Modern Life*, New York: Norton and Co., 1986, writes:

> Organisations buy teams to make money, or even to lose money as long as the losses bring tax advantages. They don't work to promote the pursuit of excellence in the sport; they work to promote the pursuit of profit. Schedules are determined, game sites and times established, and playing conditions arranged not to ensure that athletes will always be able to perform at the limits of their capacity, but to ensure maximal television audience and the lucrative television contracts that they bring with them. Professional teams relocate at the first sign that there is additional profit to be made elsewhere, or threaten to do so as a way to blackmail their home cities into making concessions on stadium rental and the like.
>
> (p. 272)

16 For a detailed discussion of this point see Tony Lynch and Adrian Walsh, 'The Mandevillean Conceit and the Profit Motive', *Philosophy*, 78, 2003, pp. 43–62.

17 Antony Flew, 'The Profit Motive', *Ethics*, 86, 1976, p. 314.

18 Ibid.

19 Joseph Butler, *Fifteen Sermons Preached at the Rolls Chapel and a Dissertation Upon the Nature of Virtue* with an introduction, analyses, and notes by The Very Rev. W.R. Matthews, London: G. Bell and Sons, 1953, Sermon XI, p. 173, p. 166.

20 Ibid., p. 173.
21 See Gideon Haigh, *The Cricket War: The Inside Story of Kerry Packer's World Series Cricket*, Melbourne: Text, 1992, pp. 16–19.
22 Rae, *It's Not Cricket*, p. 247.
23 Simon also makes this very point. See Simon, *Fair Play: The Ethics of Sport*, 2004, p. 182.
24 In Lynch and Walsh (op. cit.) a distinction is drawn between the 'lucrepath' for whom money is the sole or dominant consideration in one's motivational set and the 'lucrephile' for whom the pursuit of money is constrained by various moral considerations.
25 Cf. McNamee, 'Sporting Practices, Institutions and Virtues', p. 75.
26 Plato, *The Laws*, trans. Trevor J. Saunders, Harmondsworth: Penguin, 1970, Bk. XI, 918d–918e.
27 Allison notes how the total amount of charitable giving in Britain fell by almost a third between 1993 and 1997, at the same time as charity had become a more commercial and state-dominated activity. Lincoln Allison, *Amateurism in Sport*, p. 65.
28 See Simon Wilde, *Caught: The Full Story of Corruption in International Cricket*, London: Aurum Press, 2001.
29 Ibid., pp. 22–23.
30 This should be clear from even the most cursory reading of Simon Wilde's book.
31 Allison, op. cit., p. 65.
32 Wilde, op. cit., pp. 60–61.
33 Rae, op. cit., p. 250.
34 For an overview of this literature see Bruno Frey and R. Jegen, 'Motivation Crowding Theory', *Journal of Economic Surveys*, 15, 2001, pp. 589–611.
35 Mark R. Lepper and David Greene, 'Overjustification Research and Beyond: Towards a Means–End Analysis of Intrinsic and Extrinsic Motivation', in Mark R. Lepper and David Greene (eds), *The Hidden Costs of Rewards: New Perspectives on the Psychology of Human Motivation*, Hillsdale, NJ: Lawrence Erlbaum, 1978, pp. 109–148. See also Bruno Frey, *Not Just for the Money: An Economic Theory of Personal Motivation*, Cheltenham: Edward Elgar, 1997.
36 Morgan, *Leftist Theories of Sport*, p. 142.
37 Ibid.
38 David C. Young, *The Olympic Myth of Greek Amateur Athletics*, Chicago, IL: Ares, 1984, p. 86.
39 Ibid., p. 73.
40 D. Stanley Eitzen, 'The Sociology of Amateur Sport: An Overview', *International Review of the Sociology of Sport*, 24(2), 1989, p. 95. Cited in Allison, op. cit., pp. 21–22.
41 Eric Dunning and Kenneth Sheard, *Barbarians, Gentlemen and Players*, 2nd Edition, London, Routledge, 2005, pp. 131–132.
42 Marqusee, *Anyone but England*, p. 77. Marqusee goes on to suggest that the specific virtues that the amateurs lauded are best understood as part of an attempt to 'redefine the manliness associated with the game (and the English) in ways that suited those who did not work with their bodies' (ibid.).
43 Marqusee, ibid., p. 74.
44 Allison, op. cit., p. 23.
45 Mike Marqusee ponders this question in *Anyone But England*. He writes: 'Maybe I wind up at one with the old amateur ideology, believing that what matters is playing the game, not winning or losing, not taking sides' (p. 256).
46 Ibid., pp. 76–77.
47 There is another telling story from Grace's visit to Australia in 1873–74 that illustrates the capacity for mercenary behaviour on the part of the good doctor. As Rae tells the story:

> There was to be one fixture in the colony of South Australia. This Grace auctioned off to the highest bidder, which turned out not to be Adelaide [the capital city] but

the Yorke's Peninsula Association. The price was a simply staggering £800, more than twice that paid anywhere else on the tour. However, having achieved their great aim of putting their Adelaide neighbours' noses out of joint, the men of the Peninsula looked forward to sitting back and enjoying their three days of Grace-given glory. They were to be disappointed. Behind their backs, their smiling guest had entered into a secret deal to play a final, unscheduled match at Adelaide. This was sufficiently well known – or at least rumoured – to deter the expected crowds making their way from Adelaide to the peninsula, and as a result the Yorke's Peninsula consortium was left heavily out of pocket.

(Rae, op. cit., pp. 74–75)

48 Rae, op. cit., p. 84
49 Marqusee, op. cit., p. 76. Indeed, the 'shamateur' was sufficiently common to be the subject of gentle satire by E.W. Hornung in his Raffles books where the central character is a clearly hypocritical amateur.
50 Young, op. cit., p. 19.
51 Wray Vamplew, 'Playing for Pay: The Earnings of Professional Sportsmen in England 1870–1914', in Cashman and McKernan, *Sport*.
52 Tyrell, 'The Professionalisation of American Baseball', pp. 91–92.
53 Ibid, p. 92.
54 Ellis Cashmore, *Making Sense of Sports*, 2nd edition, London: Routledge, 1996, pp. 176–177.
55 Allen Guttmann, *From Ritual to Record*, New York: Columbia University Press, 1978, p. 30.
56 Cashmore, op. cit., p. 177.
57 Young, op. cit., p. 63.
58 Cited in Young, op. cit., p. 21.
59 Guttmann, op. cit., p. 31.
60 Marqusee, *Anyone but England*, p. 78.
61 Young, op. cit., p. 21.
62 For a discussion of the split between amateurs and professionals in rugby see Eric Dunning and Kenneth Sheard, *Barbarians, Gentlemen and Players: A Sociological Study of the Development of Rugby Football*, Canberra: Australian National University Press, 1979. The book also contains (p. 177) an interesting sociological discussion of why professionalism was regarded neither as morally nor socially suspect in nineteenth century English society.
63 Rae, op. cit., p. 85.
64 Marqusee, op. cit., p. 74.
65 Allison, op. cit., p. 73.
66 Rowland Ryder, *Cricket Calling*, London: Faber & Faber, 1995, p. 182.
67 Richard Holt, *Sport and the British: A Modern History*, Oxford: Oxford University Press, 1989, p. 107.
68 Allison, op. cit., p. 20.
69 Allen Guttmann, op. cit., p. 31. Guttmann's reference here is H. Graves, 'A Philosophy of Sport *Contemporary Review*', 78, December 1960, reprinted in Ellen W. Gerber (ed.), *Sport and the Body*, Philadelphia, PA: Lewa and Febiger, 1972, p. 10.
70 Allison, op. cit., p. 18.
71 Young, op cit., p. 15.
72 Young, ibid., p. 15.
73 John Hargreaves, *Sport, Power and Culture*, Oxford: Oxford University Press, 1987, p. 46.
74 Young, op. cit., p. 21.
75 Ellis Cashmore writes:

There are few current examples of amateurism left in today's sport. Gentlemanly pastimes and the noble spirits that guided them have ceded place to an industry with products, producers, and buyers and this has transformed the structure and, in some cases, the content of modern sport. A corruption of a misty ideal it may be, but the trend is undeniable and quite unstoppable. Sport has changed in nature over the past century; it hasn't so much been infiltrated by business, but rather it *is* business.

(Op. cit., p. 179)

76 A similar argument is made regarding corruption in the developing world. Development agencies in particular stress that corrupt practices among civil servants would be undermined if wealth could be generated in order to pay fairer salaries to these officials.
77 See Eliot Asinof, *Eight Men Out: The Black Sox and the 1919 World Series*, New York: Henry Holt and Co., 1988.
78 Young, op. cit., p. 48.
79 Allison, op. cit., p. 13.
80 Marqusee, op. cit., p. 77.
81 See Allison, op. cit., p. 17.
82 Brohm, *Sport*, p. 45.
83 On sport and cultural adaptation see, in particular, Allen Guttmann, *Games and Empires: Modern Sports and Cultural Imperialism*, New York: Columbia University Press, 1994, pp. 184–188.
84 See Allison, op. cit., pp. 6–8 for a useful discussion of related ideas.
85 Overman, *The Influence of the Protestant Ethic on Sport and Recreation*, p. 348.
86 C.L.R. James, *Beyond a Boundary*, New York: Pantheon Books, 1983.
87 See C.L.R. James, 'The Proof of the Pudding', reprinted in H. McD. Beckles and B. Stoddart (eds), *Liberation Cricket*, Manchester, Manchester University Press, 1995.
88 Marqusee, op. cit., p. 255.
89 Allison, op. cit., pp. 136–141.
90 Young, op. cit., p. 7.
91 Allison, op. cit., pp. 163–164.

4 Commodification and objectification: treating athletes and sport itself as *mere* means

1   Paton, *The Moral Law*, p. 96.
2   See R.S. Downie and Elizabeth Telfer, *Respect for Persons*, London: George Allen and Unwin, 1969.
3   For an appraisal of these various positions, see Richard Giulianotti, *Sport: A Critical Sociology*, Cambridge: Polity, 2005.
4   See Theodor W. Adorno, *The Culture Industry*, London: Routledge, 1991, pp. 76–77.
5   Brohm, *Sport*, pp. 55–56.
6   Immanuel Kant, *Lectures on Ethics*, trans. Louis Infield, New York: Harper and Row, 1963, p. 165.
7   Ibid.
8   In the *Groundwork*, the Respect for Persons principle is located at 4:429 and the price-dignity dictum at 4:434.
9   See Walsh, 'Are Market Norms?', pp. 525–543.
10 R.S. Kretchmar, *Practical Philosophy of Sport*, Champaign, IL: Human Kinetics, 1994, pp. 95–98. For a discussion of Kretchmar's categories see Cei Tuxill and Sheila Wigmore, 'Merely Meat? Respect for Persons and Games', in Mike McNamee and Jim Parry (eds), *Ethics and Sport*, London: Routledge, 1998, pp. 104–115.
11 Kretchmar, op. cit., p. 99.
12 Brohm, op. cit., pp. 55–56.
13 See John Hoberman, *Mortal Engines: Human Engineering and the Transformation of Sport*, New York: The Free Press, 1992.

14 In Australian Rules, for instance, it is common in the first quarter of the Grand Final for opposing players to deliberately target the stars of the other side with the aim of hurting them to such an extent that they will not be able to participate. In one infamous case in the 1989 grand final a Hawthorn player Dermot Brereton was crushed by an opposing player at the opening bounce and a testicle was ruptured. The attack had been planned prior to the game by the Geelong coaching panel since Brereton was a rough player himself and the idea was to 'get him' before he harmed any of the Geelong players. Brereton despite being extremely unwell came back on the field and played a major part in Hawthorn's ultimate victory.

15 Simon, *Fair Play in Sport*, p. 174.

16 Simon makes the point in the following way: 'Rather, they are too often seen as mere products or resources whose function is to provide wins; they quickly lose the support of fans and may even open themselves to abuse when they fail' (ibid., p. 181).

17 Indeed, there is a common suspicion that the enormous inflation of salaries in UK soccer has led many players to embrace their celebrity all too eagerly, thereby losing touch with modern realities experienced by the vast majority of supporters.

18 Marqusee, *Anyone but England*, p. 255.

19 Simon, op. cit., p. 173.

20 Ibid.

21 Tyrell, 'The Professionalisation of American Baseball', p. 96.

22 Tim Park, *The New York Review of Books*, 18 July 2002.

23 Simon, op. cit., pp. 172–173.

24 Ibid., p. 174.

25 Schwartz, *The Battle for Human Nature*, pp. 276–277.

5 Sport, commodification and distributive justice

1 See Aristotle, *Nicomachean Ethics*, trans. W.D. Ross, London: Oxford University Press, 1969, [1130b18–1131a6].

2 Michael Walzer, *Spheres of Justice*, Oxford: Basil Blackwell, 1983, pp. 98–99.

3 For a useful discussion see Fred Hirsch, *The Social Limits to Growth*, Cambridge, MA: Harvard University Press, 1976, pp. 27–31.

4 The 'Bread Not Circuses' Coalitions in Melbourne and Toronto have waged dedicated campaigns aimed at safeguarding local taxpayers money for welfare services rather than expenditure on marketing and sports facilities to win the hosting rights for the Olympic games. See Helen Lenskj, *Inside the Olympic Industry: Power, Politics and Activism*, New York: SUNY Press, 2000.

5 Bruno Frey, *Economics as a Science of Human Behaviour*, extended 2nd edition, Dordrecht: Kluwer, 1999, p. 166.

6 Walzer, op. cit., p. xiii.

7 For a discussion of the market as one distributive mechanism amongst a number see Frey, op. cit., pp. 167–168.

8 Eric Roll, *History of Economic Thought*, London: Faber & Faber, 1973, p. 453.

9 Robert Nozick, *Anarchy, State and Utopia*, Oxford: Basil Blackwell, 1974, p. 160.

10 Charles Fourier, *Harmonium Man: Selected Writings of Charles Fourier*, Mark Poster (ed.), New York: Anchor Books, 1971, p. 150.

11 While Erasmus had advocated sumptuary laws so as to prevent luxury undermining the civic morals, Adam Smith thought it the 'highest impertinence and presumption' of kinds and ministers 'to watch over the economy of private people' by measures such as sumptuary laws. See Christopher Berry, *The Idea of Luxury: A Conceptual and Historical Investigation*, Edinburgh: Edinburgh University Press, 1994, pp. 160, 164.

12 See Jennings, *The New Lords of the Rings*.

13 See Joel Feinberg 'Justice and Personal Desert' in *Doing and Deserving*, Princeton, NJ: Princeton University Press, 1970, pp. 55–94.

14 See George Sher, *Desert*, Princeton: Princeton University Press, 1987 and Geoffrey Cupit, 'Desert and Responsibility', *Canadian Journal of Philosophy*, 26, 1996, pp. 83–100, for useful discussions examining the place of responsibility in desert.

15 For instance, see Jack Newfield, *The Life and Crimes of Don King*, London: Virgin, 1996. More generally see Thomas Hauser, *Chaos, Corruption, Courage and Glory: A Year in Boxing*, New York: Sports Classic Books, 2005.

16 Simon, *Fair Play: The Ethics of Sport*, p. 190.

17 Cited in ibid.

18 Loland, *Fair Play in Sport*, pp. 78–83.

19 Simon, op. cit., p. 173.

20 See Jan-Erik Lane, *The Public Sector*, London: Sage, 1993, p. 22.

21 See Mancur Olsen, *The Logic of Collective Action*, Cambridge, MA: Harvard University Press, 1965, pp. 14–15.

22 The European Commission established an Audiovisual Policy to that end for its members to pursue. Austria, Germany, Ireland, Italy and the United Kingdom have been most active in itemising sports events to be safeguarded. For a critical discussion of this legislation, see Harry Arne Solberg, 'Cultural Prescriptions: The European Commission's Listed Events Regulation – Over-Reaction?', *Culture Sport Society*, 5(2), pp. 1–28.

23 Cf. T. Tannsjo, 'Is our Admiration for Sports Heroes Fascistoid?', *Journal of the Philosophy of Sport*, 25, 1998, pp. 23–34.

24 Adorno, op. cit., p. 78.

25 See Dai Smith and Gareth Williams, *Fields of Praise*, Cardiff: Cardiff University Press, 1980, p. 121.

26 Brohm, *Sport*, p. 51.

27 Paul Hoch, *Rip Off the Big Game: The Exploitation of Sport by the Power Elite*, New York: Anchor Books, 1972, p. 19.

28 See Max Horkheimer and Theodor W. Adorno, *The Dialectic of Enlightenment*, London: Allen Lane, 1973. For a discussion of these issues, see John M. Hoberman, *Sport and Political Ideology*, Austin, TX: Texas University Press, 1984.

29 Eric Dunning and Kenneth Sheard, *Barbarians, Gentlemen and Players: A Sociological Study of the Development of Rugby Football*, Canberra: Australian National University Press, 1979, p. 162.

30 Cited in ibid., p. 162.

31 Ibid., p. 163.

32 As Robert L. Simon says:

> Sporting audiences, no less than other audiences, are called upon to appreciate excellence and to apply critical standards of judgment. Emotional bonds to favorite teams and players, when constrained by the norms of respect for persons and appreciation of excellence, can enrich our existence and motivate us to do our best.
>
> (Op. cit., p. 178)

33 Anthony King, *The End of the Terraces: The Transformation of English Football in the 1990s*, London: Leicester University Press, 1998.

34 For useful overviews of recent philosophical debates on equality see Will Kymlicka, *Contemporary Political Philosophy: An Introduction*, 2nd edition, Oxford: Oxford University Press, 2002 and S.L. Hurley, *Justice, Luck and Knowledge*, Cambridge, MA: Harvard University Press, 2003.

35 Bernard Williams, 'The Idea of Equality', in *Problems of the Self*, Cambridge: Cambridge University Press, 1973, p. 240.

36 See Radin, *Contested Commodities*, pp. 107–110.

37 Berry, *The Idea of Luxury*, p. 221.

38 In Finland, the right to sport has received formal legislative endorsement. See Bruce Kidd and Peter Donnelly, 'Human Rights and Sport', *International Review for the Sociology of Sport*, 35(2), pp. 131–148.

39 R. Giulianotti, *Football: A Sociology of the Global Game*, Cambridge: Polity, 1999, pp. 106–109. For the biography of one exploited player, see Gary Imlach, *My Father and Other Working Class Football Heroes*, London: Yellow Jersey, 2005.

40 Ian Tyrell, 'Money and Morality: The Professionalisation of American Baseball', in Cashman and McKernan (eds), *Sport*, p. 91.

41 Ibid., p. 95.

42 Ibid., p. 94.

43 See *USA Today*, 18 July 2002.

44 *The Guardian*, 9 July 2005.

45 Paul D. Staudohar, 'Baseball's Changing Salary Structure', in Paul D. Staudohar (ed.), *Diamond Mines: Baseball and Labor*, New York: Syracuse University Press, 2000.

46 See Tony Mason, *Passion of the People? Football in South America*, London: Verso, 1995.

47 See Christopher Martin-Jenkins, *Cricket – A Way of Life*, London: Century, 1984, p. 174.

48 Following various critical investigations by soccer analysts and journalists, FIFA's President, Sepp Blatter, lambasted European clubs for this 'despicable' practice of 'social and economic rape' in developing societies. See Blatter's criticisms in the *Financial Times*, 17 December 2003.

49 See Arturo J. Marcano Guevara and David P. Fidler, *Stealing Lives: The Globalization of Baseball and the Tragic Story of Alexis Quiroz*, Bloomington, IN: Indiana University Press, 2002.

50 Odd Langholm, *The Legacy of Scholasticism: Antecedents of Choice and Power*, Cambridge: Cambridge University Press, 1998, p. 65.

51 Robert Nozick, 'Coercion', in S. Morgenbesser *et al.* (eds), *Philosophy, Science and Method*, New York: St Martin's Press, 1969, pp. 440–472.

52 Hoch, *Rip Off the Big Game*, p. 69.

53 R. G. Collingwood, 'Economics as a Philosophical Science', *Ethics*, 1926, p. 174.

54 There is no suggestion that these are the only categories of goods. For a start, there are a whole range of goods that can, and perhaps even should, be allocated on the market.

55 Note that here the pathological content is *contingent* rather than being *necessary*, as was the case for the merit goods.

6   Scoring an own goal: when markets undermine what they sell

1 On the Super League episode, see David Rowe, 'Rugby League in Australia: The Super League Saga', *Journal of Sport and Social Issues*, 21(2), 1997, pp. 221–226. See also Douglas Booth and Colin Tatz, *One-Eyed: A View of Australian Sport*, Sydney: Allen & Unwin, 2000, pp. 188–190.

2 See Murray G. Phillips and Brett Hutchins, 'Losing Control of the Ball: The Political Economy of Football and the Media in Australia', *Journal of Sport and Social Issues*, 23(3), 2003, pp. 215–232; and Mike Coleman, *Super League: The Inside Story*, Sydney: Pan Macmillan, 1996.

3 John Jackson *et al.*, *Economics*, 5th edition, Sydney: McGraw-Hill, 1998, GL.16.

4 For the canonical discussion of public goods, see Olsen, *The Logic of Collective Action*.

5 For a discussion of prudential reasoning, as Kant conceives of it, see Roger J. Sullivan, *Immanuel Kant's Moral Theory*, Cambridge: Cambridge University Press, 1989, pp. 31–43.

6 See Jurgen Habermas, *Legitimation Crisis*, Boston, MA: Beacon Press, 1975.

7 For a discussion of individual sports stars and league systems as commodities, see David L. Andrews (ed.), *Michael Jordan Inc.: Corporate Sport, Media Culture, and Late Modern America*, New York: SUNY Press, 2001.

8 For example, in American baseball and European soccer leagues, some clubs earn more than ten times their rivals' takings from television revenues. In an open labour market, the wealthiest clubs are soon able to identify and recruit the best players, thus maximising

their chances of competitive success while systematically damaging the prospects of their rivals.

9 As the man who designed the famous national soccer strip of Brazil recently remarked, 'The shirt has been hijacked by the CBF [Brazilian Football Confederation] who sold it to Nike. The shirt is not a symbol of Brazilian citizenship. It is a symbol of corruption and the status quo.' Cited in Alex Bellos, *Futebol: The Brazilian Way of Life*, London: Bloomsbury, 2003, p. 73.

10 For an early critical analysis of the impacts of professionalisation among athletes, see Ian Taylor, 'Soccer Consciousness and Soccer Hooliganism', in Stanley Cohen (ed.), *Images of Deviance*, Harmondsworth: Penguin, 1971, pp. 134–164.

11 Jennings, *The New Lords of the Rings*, p. 299.

12 Ibid., p. 7. Jennings notes that any taint of drug-use in the Olympics would undermine their commercial potential. He argues that in the Seoul Olympics the number of people who tested positive to doping was much higher than the public were led to believe, but that this was hidden for financial reasons. For an earlier historical example, see Tyrell, 'The Professionalisation of American Baseball', pp. 88–89.

13 One recent survey suggested most baseball players believe that steroids have contributed significantly to record-breaking performances (*USA Today*, 15 March 2005).

14 On the economics of uncertainty of outcome in sport, see Glenn Knowles, Keith Sherony and Mike Haupert, 'The Demand for Major League Baseball: A Test of the Uncertainty of Outcome Hypothesis', *The American Economist*, 36(2), 1992, pp. 72–80. This research and others cited suggests that uncertainty of outcome for baseball games has a significant impact upon attendance, with the strongest crowds being drawn to fixtures in which the home team was slightly favoured to win.

15 *The Guardian*, Jeremy Alexander, Monday 8 November 2004, http://football.guardian.co.uk/News_Story/0,1563,1345863,00.html

16 *The Observer*, Sunday, 24 October 2004. See also Denis Campbell, 'The game that ate itself', *Observer*, Sunday 24 October 2004, http://football.guardian.co.uk/print/0,3858,5046518-103,00.html

17 See: www.forbes.com/2005/04/06/05mlbland.html

18 Tyrell, op. cit., pp. 88–89.

19 In economics, this issue connects to the 'Louis-Schmelling Paradox' of professional sport. To maximise their prestige and income, top athletes and teams need serious challengers who will generate large audience interest in the competitive spectacle. Monopoly in sport is disastrous. Thus, every Joe Louis needs a Max Schmelling – with the strong possibility that brutal defeat might ensue. See Walter C. Neale, 'The Peculiar Economics of Professional Sport', *Quarterly Journal of Economics*, 78, pp. 1–14.

20 Overman, *The Influence of the Protestant Ethic on Sport and Recreation*, pp. 325–326.

21 One report estimates that roughly one million adults aged 16–65 play soccer regularly in Australia, with a similar figure attending fixtures, while over three times that figure watch on television (*The Age*, 30 May 2005). See also a government report from 2003 that notes soccer's general growth: www.ausport.gov.au/scorsresearch/ERASS2003.pdf

22 The *Sydney Morning Herald* (11 August 2004) reported that viewers would have to pay around AU$600 annually to watch the games on Foxtel. According to Australian government figures, less than one quarter of households in Australia subscribed to *any* pay-television station at that time (see: www.afc.gov.au/gtp/wptvanalysis.html); SBS is available free-to-air nationally.

23 See Denis Campbell, *The Observer*, Sunday 24 October 2004.

24 M. Carleheden and R. Gabriels, 'An Interview with Michael Walzer', *Theory, Culture and Society*, 14(1), 1997, pp. 113–130.

25 See Richard Giulianotti, 'Supporters, Fans, Followers and *Flaneurs*: A Taxonomy of Spectator Identities in World Football', *Journal of Sport and Social Issues*, 26(1), 2002.

26 Simon, *Fair Play: The Ethics of Sport*, pp. 187–188.

27 Ibid., p. 187.

28 Milton Friedman, 'The Social Responsibility of Business is to Increase its Profits', *The New York Times Magazine*, 13 September 1970, pp. 122–126.
29 For a discussion of the failure to invest in grass-roots development, see David Conn, *The Football Business: Fair Game in the '90s?*, Edinburgh: Mainstream, 1999, pp. 244–271.
30 In 1992, the combined BSkyB/BBC bid for exclusive television coverage of English soccer amounted to £214 million over four years; the 2001 deal (with BBC/BSkyB) was worth £1,129 million over three years. For a discussion of the various deals since 1992, see Simon Banks, *Going Down: Football in Crisis*, Edinburgh: Mainstream, 2002.
31 See Tony Miller, David Rowe, Jim McKay and Geoffrey Lawrence, 'The Over-Production of US Sports and the New International Division of Cultural Labor', *International Review for the Sociology of Sport*, 38(4), 2003, pp. 427–440.
32 Quoted in Richard Lapchick, *Five Minutes to Midnight: race and sport in the 1990s*, Lanham, MD: Madison Books, 1991, p. 290.
33 Jim Melly, 'Cricket 2000: How the Media Reinvented the Game', in Alistair McLellan (ed.), *Nothing Sacred: The New Cricket Culture*, London: Two Heads, 1996, p. 153.
34 See: http://news.bbc.co.uk/sport1/hi/cricket/4097137.stm
35 *The Observer*, 12 December 2004.
36 On the Australian situation, see Brian Stoddart, *Saturday Afternoon Fever: Sport in the Australian Culture*, Sydney: Angus & Robertson, 1986, pp. 99–110.
37 Scully, *The Market Structure of Sports*.

7   Moral philosophy out on the track: what might be done?

1 See: www.football-research.org/gof2h/Gof2H-chap12.htm
2 Bernie Parrish, *They Call it a Game*, New York: Dial Press, 1971, p. 290.
3 See Dennis Coates and Brad R. Humphreys, 'The Stadium Gambit and Local Economic Development', *Regulation*, 23(2), 2000, pp. 15–20. In North America, it was estimated that in 2001 the leading 99 clubs in the NFL, MLB, NBA and NHL received public subsidies of US$17.5 billion towards their sporting facilities. See Judith Grant Long, 'Full Count: The Real Cost of Public Funding for Major League Sports Facilities', *Journal of Sports Economics*, 6(2), 2005, pp. 119–143.
4 See: www.fieldofschemes and www.leagueoffans.com
5 Paul M. Downward and Alistair Dawson, *The Economics of Professional Team Sport*, London: Routledge, 2000, pp. 172–173.
6 In the UK, highly valued 'Category A' events currently include Wimbledon, the Scottish and English soccer cup finals, and the European Championships soccer tournament. English cricket's Test matches were demoted to Category B, allowing the subscription channel BSkyB to buy the rights to home fixtures for four years in a highly controversial move.
7 For a discussion of these issues, see David Rowe, 'Watching Brief: Cultural Citizenship and Viewing Rights', *Sport in Society*, 7(3), 2004, pp. 385–402.
8 The 1977 Gleneagles Declaration, signed by all Commonwealth nations, contained a commitment to withholding support for sport-related contact with the apartheid regime in South Africa.

Bibliography

Adorno, Theodor W., *The Culture Industry*, London: Routledge, 1991.

Allison, Lincoln, *Amateurism in Sport: An Analysis and Defence*, London: Frank Cass, 2001.

Anderson, Elizabeth, *Value in Ethics and Economics*, Cambridge, MA: Harvard University Press, 1993.

Andrews, David L. (ed.), *Michael Jordan Inc.: Corporate Sport, Media Culture, and Late Modern America*, New York: SUNY Press, 2001.

Aristotle, *Nicomachean Ethics*, trans. W.D. Ross, London: Oxford University Press, 1969.

——, *The Politics*, trans. John Warrington, London: Heron Books, 1948.

Asinof, Eliot, *Eight Men Out: The Black Sox and the 1919 World Series*, New York: Henry Holt and Co., 1988.

Baker, W.J., *Sports in the Western World*, revised edition, Urbana, IL: University of Illinois Press, 1988.

Banks, Simon, *Going Down: Football in Crisis*, Edinburgh: Mainstream, 2002.

Bellos, Alex, *Futebol: The Brazilian Way of Life*, London: Bloomsbury, 2003.

Berry, Christopher J., *The Idea of Luxury: A Conceptual and Historical Investigation*, Edinburgh: Edinburgh University Press, 1994.

Booth, Douglas and Colin Tatz, *One-Eyed: A View of Australian Sport*, Sydney: Allen & Unwin, 2000.

Bottomore, Tom (ed.), *A Dictionary of Marxist Thought*, Oxford: Basil Blackwell, 1983.

Brohm, J.M., *Sport: A Prison of Measured Time*, trans. I. Fraser, London: Ink Links, 1978.

Bromberger, C., 'Football as World-View and as Ritual', *French Cultural Studies*, vi, 1995, pp. 293–311.

Brown, A. and A. Walsh, *Not for Sale: Manchester United, Murdoch and the Defeat of BskyB*, Edinburgh: Mainstream, 1999.

Butler, Joseph, *Fifteen Sermons Preached at the Rolls Chapel and a Dissertation Upon the Nature of Virtue* with an introduction, analyses, and notes by The Very Rev. W.R. Matthews, London: G. Bell and Sons, 1953.

Campbell, Denis, *The Observer*, Sunday, October 24, 2004.

Carleheden, M. and R. Gabriels, 'An Interview with Michael Walzer', *Theory Culture and Society*, 14(1), 1997, pp. 113–130.

Cashman, Richard and Michael McKernan, *Sport: Money, Morality and the Media*, Kensington: New South Wales University Press, 1981.

Cashmore, Ellis, *Making Sense of Sports*, 2nd edition, London: Routledge, 1996.

Child, James W., 'Profit: The Concept and its Moral Features', *Social Philosophy and Policy*, 15(2), Summer 1998, pp. 243–282.

Clarke, John, Chas Critcher and Richard Johnson (eds), *Working Class Culture: Studies in History and Theory*, London: Hutchinson, 1979.

Coates, D.C. and B.R. Humphreys, 'The Stadium Gambit and Local Economic Development', *Regulation*, 23(2), 2000, pp. 15–20.

Coleman, Mike, *Super League: The Inside Story*, Sydney: Pan Macmillan, 1996.

Collingwood, R.G., 'Economics as a Philosophical Science', *Ethics*, 1926, pp. 162–185.

Conn, David, *The Football Business: Fair Game in the '90s?*, Edinburgh: Mainstream, 1997.

Cupit, Geoffrey, 'Desert and Responsibility', *Canadian Journal of Philosophy*, 26, 1996, pp. 83–100.

Downie, R.S. and Elizabeth Telfer, *Respect for Persons*, London: Allen and Unwin, 1969.

Downward, Paul M. and Alistair Dawson, *The Economics of Professional Team Sport*, London: Routledge, 2000.

Doyle, William, *Venality: The Sale of Offices in Eighteenth-Century France*, Oxford: Oxford University Press, 1996.

Dunning, Eric and Kenneth Sheard, *Barbarians, Gentlemen and Players: A Sociological Study of the Development of Rugby Football*, Canberra: Australian National University Press, 1979.

Eitzen, D. Stanley, 'The Sociology of Amateur Sport: An Overview', *International Review of the Sociology of Sport*, 24(2), 1989.

Elias, Norbert and Eric Dunning, *Quest for Excitement: Sport and Leisure in the Civilizing Process*, Oxford: Blackwell, 1986.

Feinberg, Joel, 'Justice and Personal Desert', in *Doing and Deserving*, Princeton, NJ: Princeton University Press, 1970, pp. 55–94.

Flew, Antony, 'The Profit Motive', *Ethics*, 86, 1976, pp. 312–322.

Fourier, Charles, *Harmonium Man: Selected Writings of Charles Fourier*, edited with an introduction by Mark Poster, New York: Anchor Books, 1971.

Frey, Bruno, *Not Just for the Money: An Economic Theory of Personal Motivation*, Cheltenham: Edward Elgar, 1997.

——, *Economics as a Science of Human Behaviour*, extended 2nd edition, Dordrecht: Kluwer, 1999.

Frey, Bruno and R. Jegen, 'Motivation Crowding Theory', *Journal of Economic Surveys*, 15, 2001, pp. 589–611.

Friedman, Milton, 'The Social Responsibility of Business is to Increase its Profits', *The New York Times Magazine*, 13 September 1970, pp. 122–126.

Giulianotti, Richard, *Football: A Sociology of the Global Game*, Cambridge: Polity, 1999.

——, 'Supporters, Fans, Followers and *Flaneurs*: A Taxonomy of Spectator Identities in World Football', *Journal of Sport and Social Issues*, 26(1), 2002.

——, *Sport: A Critical Sociology*, Cambridge: Polity, 2005.

Guevara, Arturo J. Marcano and David P. Fidler, *Stealing Lives: The Globalization of Baseball and the Tragic Story of Alexis Quiroz*, Bloomington, IN: Indiana University Press, 2002.

Guttmann, Allen, *From Ritual to Record*, New York: Columbia University Press, 1978.

——, *Sports Spectators*, New York: Columbia University Press, 1986.

——, *Games and Empires: Modern Sports and Cultural Imperialism*, New York: Columbia University Press, 1994.

Habermas, J., *Legitimation Crisis*, Cambridge: Polity, 1976.

Haigh, Gideon, *The Cricket War: The Inside Story of Kerry Packer's World Series Cricket*, Melbourne: Text, 1992.

Hargreaves, John, *Sport, Power and Culture*, Polity Press: Oxford, 1987.

Hauser, Thomas, *Chaos, Corruption, Courage and Glory: A Year in Boxing*, New York: Sports Classic Books, 2005.

Hirsch, Fred, *The Social Limits to Growth*, Cambridge, MA: Harvard University Press, 1976.

Hoberman, John, *Sport and Political Ideology*, Austin: Texas University Press, 1984.

——, *The Olympic Crisis*, New York: Caratzas, 1986.

——, *Mortal Engines: Human Engineering and the Transformation of Sport*, New York: The Free Press, 1992.

Hoch, P., *Rip Off the Big Game: The Exploitation of Sport by the Power Elite*, New York: Anchor Books, 1973.

Holt, Richard, *Sport and the British: A Modern History*, Oxford: Oxford University Press, 1989.

Horkheimer, Max, and Theodor W. Adorno, *The Dialectic of Enlightenment*, London: Allen Lane, 1973.

Huizinga, Johan, *Homo Ludens*, London: Routledge and Kegan Paul, 1949.

Hurley, S.L., *Justice, Luck and Knowledge*, Cambridge, MA: Harvard University Press, 2003.

Imlach, Gary, *My Father and other Working Class Football Heroes*, London: Yellow Jersey, 2005.

Jackson, John, *et al.*, *Economics*, 5th edition, Sydney: McGraw-Hill, 1998.

James, C.L.R., *Beyond and Boundary*, New York: Pantheon Books, 1983.

——, 'The Proof of the Pudding', reprinted in H. McD. Beckles and B. Stoddart (eds), *Liberation Cricket*, Manchester: Manchester University Press, 1995.

Jarvie, Grant and Joseph Maguire, *Sport and Leisure in Social Thought*, London: Routledge, 1994.

Jennings, Andrew, *The New Lords of the Rings: Olympic Corruption and How to Buy Gold Medals*, London: Pocket Books, 1996.

Kant, Immanuel, *Lectures on Ethics*, trans. Louis Infield, New York: Harper & Row, 1963.

——, *The Metaphysics of Morals*, trans. Mary Gregor, Cambridge: Cambridge University Press, 1991.

Kidd, Bruce, 'The Myth of the Ancient Games', in A. Tomlinson and G. Whannel (eds), *Five Ring Circus: Money, Power and Politics at the Olympic Games*, London: Pluto, 1984.

—— and Peter Donnelly, 'Human Rights and Sport', *International Review for the Sociology of Sport*, 35(2), 2000, pp. 131–148.

King, Anthony, *The End of the Terraces: The Transformation of English Football in the 1990s*, London: Leicester University Press, 1998.

Knowles, Glen, Keith Sherony and Mike Haupert, 'The Demand for Major League Baseball: A Test of the Uncertainty of Outcome Hypothesis', *The American Economist*, 36(2), 1992, pp. 72–80.

Kretchmar, R.S., *Practical Philosophy of Sport*, Champaign, IL: Human Kinetics, 1994.

Kymlicka, Will, *Contemporary Political Philosophy: An Introduction*, 2nd edition, Oxford: Oxford University Press, 2002.

LaFeber, W., *Michael Jordan and the New Global Capitalism*, New York: W.W. Norton, 2002.

Lane, Jan-Erik, *The Public Sector*, London: Sage, 1993.

Langholm, Odd, *The Legacy of Scholasticism: Antecedents of Choice and Power*, Cambridge: Cambridge University Press, 1998.

Lapchick, Richard, *Five Minutes to Midnight: Race and Sport in the 1990s*, Lanham, MD: Madison Books, 1991.

Lasch, Christopher, *The Culture of Narcissism*, New York: Warner Books, 1979.

Lenskyj, Helen, *Inside the Olympic Industry: Power, Politics and Activism*, New York: SUNY Press, 2000.

——, 'The Olympic Industry and Civil Liberties: The Threat to Free Speech and Freedom of Assembly', in R. Giulianotti and D. McArdle (eds), *Sport, Civil Liberties and Human Rights*, London: Taylor & Francis, 2005.

Lepper, Mark R. and David Greene, 'Overjustification Research and Beyond: Towards a Means-End Analysis of Intrinsic and Extrinsic Motivation', in Mark R. Lepper and David Greene (eds), *The Hidden Costs of Rewards: New Perspectives on the Psychology of Human Motivation*, Hillsdale, NJ: Lawrence Erlbaum, 1978, pp. 109–148.

Loland, Sigmund, *Fair Play in Sport: A Moral Norm System*, London: Routledge 2001.

Long, Judith Grant, 'Full Count: The Real Cost of Public Funding for Major League Sports Facilities', *Journal of Sports Economics*, 6(2), 2005, pp. 119–143.

Lukes, Stephen, *Marxism and Morality*, Oxford: Oxford University Press, 1985.

Lynch, Tony and Adrian Walsh, 'The Mandevillean Conceit and the Profit Motive', *Philosophy*, 78, 2003, pp. 43–62.

MacIntyre, Alasdair, *After Virtue*, London: Duckworth, 1985.

McNamee, M.J., 'Valuing Leisure Practices: Towards a Theoretical Framework', *Leisure Studies*, 13, 1994, pp. 288–309.

——, 'Sporting Practices, Institutions and Virtues: A Critique and Restatement', *Journal of the Philosophy of Sport*, 22, 1995, pp. 61–82.

—— and S.J. Parry (eds), *Ethics and Sport*, London: E & FN Spon, 1998.

Mandeville, Bernard, *The Fable of the Bees*, vol. 1, Oxford: Clarendon, 1957.

Marqusee, Mike, *Anyone but England: Cricket and the National Malaise*, London: Verso, 1994.

Martin-Jenkins, Christopher, *Cricket – A Way of Life*, London: Century, 1984.

Marx, Karl, *Capital*, vol.1, Moscow: Progress, 1954.

——, *Early Writings [1], Economic and Philosophical Manuscripts*, trans. T.B. Bottomore, London: Watts, 1963.

Marx, Karl and Frederick Engels, *The Communist Manifesto*, Peking: Foreign Languages Press, [1848] 1970.

Mason, A., *Association Football and English Society 1863–1915*, Brighton: Harvester, 1980.

——, 'Our Stephen and our Harold: Edwardian Footballers as Local Heroes', *International Journal of the History of Sport*, 13(1), 1996, pp. 71–85.

——, *Passion of the People? Football in South America*, London: Verso, 1995.

Melly, Jim, 'Cricket 2000: How the Media Reinvented the Game', in Alistair McLellan (ed.), *Nothing Sacred: The New Cricket Culture*, London: Two Heads, 1996.

Miller, David, 'Why Markets?', in *Market Socialism*, Julian Le Grand and Saul Eslin (eds), Oxford: Clarendon Press, 1989, pp. 25–49.

Miller, Tony, David Rowe, Jim Mckay and Geoffrey Lawrence, 'The Over-Production of US Sports and the New International Division of Cultural Labor', *International Review for the Sociology of Sport*, 38(4), 2003, pp. 427–440.

Morgan, W.J., 'Adorno on Sport: The Case of the Fractured Dialectic', *Theory and Society*, 17, 1983, pp. 813–833.

——, *Leftist Theories of Sport: A Critique and Reconstruction*, Urbana, IL: University of Illinois Press, 1993.

Morgan, William J., Klaus V. Meier and Angela J. Schnieder (eds), *Ethics in Sport*, Champaign, IL: Human Kinetics, 2001.

Newfield, Jack, *The Life and Crimes of Don King*, London: Virgin, 1996.

Nixon, H.L., 'The Commercialisation and Organisational Development of Modern Sport', *International Review of Sport Sociology*, 9, 1974, pp. 107 135.

Norman, Richard, *The Moral Philosophers*, 1st edition, Oxford: Clarendon Press, 1983.

Novak, Michael, *The Joy of Sports*, New York: Basic Books, 1976.

Nozick, Robert, 'Coercion', in S. Morgenbesser *et al.* (eds), *Philosophy, Science and Method*, New York: St Martin's Press, 1969, pp. 440–472.

——, *Anarchy, State and Utopia*, Oxford: Basil Blackwell, 1974.

——, *The Examined Life*, New York: Simon and Schuster, 1989.

Olsen, Mancur, *The Logic of Collective Action*, Cambridge, MA: Harvard University Press, 1965.

O'Neill, John, 'The Varieties of Intrinsic Value', *The Monist*, 75(2), April 1992, pp. 119–137.

Orwell, George, 'The Sporting Spirit', in *The Penguin Essays of George Orwell*, Harmondsworth: Penguin, 1994, pp. 321–323.

Overman, Steven J., *The Influence of the Protestant Ethic on Sport and Recreation*, Aldershot: Avebury, 1997.

Park, Tim, 'Soccer: A Matter of Love and Hate', *The New York Review of Books*, 18 July 2002.

Parrish, Bernie, *They Call it a Game*, New York: Dial Press, 1971.

Pass, Christopher and Bryan Lowes (eds), *Collins Dictionary of Economics*, 2nd edition, London: HarperCollins, 1993.

Paton, H.J., *The Moral Law or Kant's Groundwork of the Metaphysics of Morals*, London: Hutchison, 1946.

Phillips, Murray G. and Brett Hutchins, 'Losing Control of the Ball: The Political Economy of Football and the Media in Australia', *Journal of Sport and Social Issues*, 23(3), 2003, pp. 215–232.

Plato, *The Laws*, trans. Trevor J. Saunders, Harmondsworth: Penguin, 1970.

Polley, Martin, *Moving the Goalposts: A History of Sport and Society since 1945*, London: Routledge, 1998.

Postman, Neil, *Amusing Ourselves to Death*, New York: Penguin, 1985.

Radin, Margaret Jane, *Contested Commodities: The Trouble with Trade in Sex, Children, Body Parts and other Things*, Cambridge, MA: Harvard University Press, 1996.

Rae, Simon, *It's not Cricket: A History of Skulduggery, Sharp Practice and Downright Cheating in the Noble Game*, London: Faber and Faber, 2001.

Rawls, John, *A Theory of Justice*, Cambridge, MA: Harvard University Press, 1971.

Roll, Eric, *History of Economic Thought*, London: Faber, 1973.

Rowe, David, 'Rugby League in Australia: The Super League Saga', *Journal of Sport and Social Issues*, 21(2), 1997, pp. 221–226.

——, 'Watching Brief: Cultural Citizenship and Viewing Rights', *Sport in Society*, 7(3), 2004, pp. 385–402.

Ryder, Rowland, *Cricket Calling*, London: Faber & Faber, 1995.

Sandy, R., P.J. Sloane and M.S. Rosentraub, *The Economics of Sport: An International Perspective*, Basingstoke: Palgrave, 2004.

Schmitz, K., 'Sport and Play: Suspension of the Ordinary', in W. Morgan and K. Meier (eds), *Philosophical Inquiry into Sport*, Champion, IL: Human Kinetics, 1988, pp. 29–38.

Schwartz, Barry, *The Battle for Human Nature: Sense, Morality and Modern Life*, New York: Norton and Co., 1986.

Scully, Gerald W., 'Economic Discrimination in Professional Sports', *Law and Contemporary Problems*, 38, 1973–74, pp. 67–84.

——, *The Market Structure of Sport*, Chicago, IL: University of Chicago Press, 1997.

Sher, George, *Desert*, Princeton, NJ: Princeton University Press, 1987.

Simmel, George, 'The Metropolis and Mental Life', in *The Sociology of George Simmel*, trans. and ed. Kurt H. Wolff, Glencoe, IL: Free Press, 1990.

——, *The Philosophy of Money*, 2nd enlarged edition, David Frisby (ed.), London: Routledge, 1990.

Simon, Robert L., *Fair Play: Sports, Values and Society*, Boulder, CO: Westview Press, 1991.

——, *Fair Play: The Ethics of Sport*, 2nd edition, Boulder, CO: Westview Press, 2004.

Simson, Vyv and Andrew Jennings, *The Lords of the Rings*, New York: Simon and Schuster, 1992.

Sloane, P.J., 'The Economics of Professional Football: The Football Club as a Utility Maximiser', *Scottish Journal of Political Economy*, 18(2), 1971, pp. 121–146.

Smith, Dai and Gareth Williams, *Fields of Praise*, Cardiff: Cardiff University Press, 1980.

Solberg, Harry Arne, 'Cultural Prescriptions: The European Commission's Listed Events Regulation – Over-Reaction?', *Culture Sport Society*, 5(2), 2002, pp. 1–28.

Staudohar, Paul D., 'Baseball's Changing Salary Structure', in Paul D Staudohar (ed.), *Diamond Mines: Baseball and Labor*, New York: Syracuse University Press, 2000.

Steenbergen, Johan and Jan Tamboer, 'Ethics and the Double Character of Sport: An Attempt to Systematise Discussions of the Ethics of Sport', in M.J. McNamee and S.J. Parry (eds), *Ethics and Sport*, Routledge, London, 1998.

Stoddart, Brian, *Saturday Afternoon Fever: Sport in the Australian Culture*, Sydney: Angus & Robertson, 1986.

Sullivan, Roger J., *Immanuel Kant's Moral Theory*, Cambridge: Cambridge University Press, 1989.

Sweet, W.E., *Sport and Recreation in Ancient Greece*, Oxford: Oxford University Press, 1987.

Tamburrini, C. 'Sports, Fascism and the Market', in T. Tannsjo and C. Tamburrini (eds), *Values in Sport*, London: E & FN Spon, 2000.

Taylor, I., 'Soccer Consciousness and Soccer Hooliganism', in S. Cohen (ed.), *Images of Deviance*, Harmondsworth: Penguin, 1971, pp. 134–164.

Tranter, N., *Sport, Economy and Society in Britain 1750–1914*, Cambridge: Cambridge University Press, 1998.

Tuxill, Cei and Sheila Wigmore, 'Merely Meat? Respect for Persons and Games', in Mike McNamee and Jim Parry (eds), *Ethics and Sport*, London: Routledge, 1998.

Tyrell, Ian, 'The Professionalisation of American Baseball', in Richard Cashman and Michael McKernan (eds), *Sport: Money, Morality and the Media*, Kensington, NSW: University of New South Wales Press, 1981, pp. 86–103.

Vamplew, Wray, 'Playing for Pay: The Earnings of Professional Sportsmen in England 1870–1914', in Richard Cashman and Michael McKernan (eds), *Sport: Money, Morality and the Media*, Kensington: University of New South Wales Press, 1981, pp. 104–135.

——, *Pay up and play the Game*, Cambridge: Cambridge University Press, 1988.

Wallerstein, Immanuel *The Decline of American Power*, New York: New Press, 2002.

Walsh, Adrian, 'Are Market Norms and Intrinsic Valuation Mutually Exclusive?', *Australasian Journal of Philosophy*, 79(4), December 2001, pp. 525–543.

——'Market Pathology and the Range of Commodity Exchange: A Preliminary Sketch', *Public Affairs Quarterly*, 12(2), 1998, pp. 203–219.

——'Teaching, Preaching and Queaching about Commodities', *The Southern Journal of Philosophy*, 36(3), 1998, pp. 433–452.

Walsh, Adrian and Richard Giulianotti, 'This Sporting Mammon: A Normative Critique of the Commodification of Sport', *Journal of the Philosophy of Sport*, 28(1), 2001.

Walvin, J., *The Only Game: Football in our Times*, London: Pearson, 2001.

Walzer, M., *Spheres of Justice*, Oxford: Blackwell, 1983.

Wilde, Simon, *Caught: The Full Story of Corruption in International Cricket*, London: Aurum Press, 2001.

Williams, Bernard, 'The Idea of Equality', in *Problems of the Self*, Cambridge: Cambridge University Press, 1973.

Young, David C., *The Olympic Myth of Greek Amateur Athletics*, Chicago, IL: Ares, 1984.

Index

AC Milan 16, 17
access: to elite sporting events 101,
126–7; to sporting facilities 101, 128
administrators 130
Adorno, Theodor 67, 97
advertising 17
agents: sporting 127–8
Ali, Muhammad 72
Allison, Lincoln 54–5, 56, 60, 62
Almond, H.H. 97
Amateur Athletic Association (Britain)
50
amateurism 8–10; aristocratic prejudice
50–2; defining characteristics 47;
ethical definition 47; ethical hazards
53–4; historical inaccuracy 48–50;
material necessity 52–3; objections to
48; and rejection of payment 60
Amateurist movement 46
American Civil War 83
American football 9; college feeder
system 126; revenues 1; training
regimes 102; violence in 115–16
Anderson, Elizabeth 26
Aquinas, Thomas 60, 105
Aristotle 12, 22–3, 41, 58, 82
Arnold, Thomas 46
association football see soccer
athletes: as mere means 70–5
Athletic Bilbao 26
athletics: amateurism 50; move towards
professionalism 52, 53
Australian Broadcasting Commission
107
Australian rugby league competition
107

Australian Rules football: reorganisation
3; violence in 71, 140
automaton: sports person as 67, 70
autotelic goods 33–4; undermining by
venality 43–6

Bannister, Roger 8
Barcelona soccer club 26, 122
baseball: expansion in 1870s 49–50;
exploitation 103; lop-sidedness of
competition 112, 113; match-fixing
54; pitching 77; professionalisation
101; public interest pressure 117; rule
changes 77; steroid abuse 111; see also
Major League Baseball
basic need goods 98–101
basketball: internal development logic
79; loose officiating 77–8
Beckham, David 1–2
benevolence 39
Bergkamp, Dennis 1
Berlin Olympics 80, 97
Berlusconi, Silvio 16
Berry, Christopher 101
Berry, Scyld 17
betting: on cricket 3, 42
Black Sox Scandal 54
Blatter, Sepp 142
blocked exchange 25, 26, 121, 122–3
'Bodyline' series 48
Bosman ruling 17, 103
boxers: recompense 6
boxing: corruption 93; desperate
exchange culture 103
Brazil soccer strip 143
'Bread Not Circuses' Coalitions 140

Breivik, Gunnar 93
Brereton, Dermot 140
bribery 93
Brisbane Lions 15
broadcasts: free-to-air 94, 96, 116–17, 127; pay per view 96, 114–15, 118
Brohm, Jean-Marie 20, 21, 57, 67, 97
Brown, Jimmy 2
Brundage, Avery 46, 50
BSkyB 116, 118
Butler, Joseph 39

capital: organic composition 19
Categorical Imperative 66
'Category A' events 144
Chicago White Sox 54
chrematistic production 22–3
Cicotte, Eddie 54
citizenship 129
club loyalty 73
club ownership 122–4
coercion 104
Collingwood, R.G. 105
Columbia Pictures 26
Comiskey, Charles 54
commerce: Medieval philosophers on 60
commodification: classical definition 13; counterfactual 13; dirty 93; distributive justice and 87–91; and evacuation of autotelic ideals 44; exclusion and 95–6, 98; incomplete 27, 100, 135; quasi- 93; and venality 40–3; *see also* hyper-commodification
commodification critique: market abolitionism and 6–8; moral critique formulation 63; socio-historical challenge and 8–10, 56–9
commodity: conflation with mere commodity 69; definitions 12, 133–4
commodity fetishism 19
common pool goods 95
commutative justice 101–5
competition: and depersonalisation 70; ratcheting up of pressures 73; selling of 113
competitive monopoly 5
complex equality 86
consumption: regulation of 89

contracts: justice of 101–5
corporatisation of clubs 14
Corrosion Thesis 69, 75
corruption: effect on manifest image 111; measures to prevent 125; meta-normative 19; temptation to 3, 54, 131; through rule changes 78
corruption thesis 30
cosmopolitan supporters 115
cost–benefit analysis 13–14, 18
Coubertin, Baron de 46
cricket: amateurist ideology 47–8; Australian team success 40, 113; 'baggy green' cap 26; betting on 3, 42; 'Bodyline' series 48; class distinctions 51; as its own end 75–6; match-fixing 41–2; one-day 7, 77; public interest pressure 117–18; 'rebel' tour of South Africa 42–3; spread 57–8; televising 118; Test match 133; 20–20 format 76; in West Indies 59; World Series Cricket 2, 39–40, 102
cricketers: earnings 102; extended playing schedule effect on 76
Cronje, Hansie 3, 41–2, 111
'crown jewel' sporting events 127
cycling: training programs 102

depersonalisation 70–1; competition and 70; violence as 71
desert bases 91–2
desert goods 90, 91
desperate exchanges 102, 103
dignity: price and 24–5, 65, 67–8
dirty commodification 93
distributive justice 82–7; commodification and 87–91; entitlement theory 88; pluralist theory 86–7, 91; theories 85–6
distributive pathology 120
disvalue: generated by sport 11
doping/drug usage 111, 121–2
draft system 126
Dunning, Eric 97
Dworkin, Ronald 99

ECB 118
egalitarianism 85, 86, 98; political 86
Eitzen, D. Stanley 47

England and Wales Cricket Board (ECB) 118
English Premiership: broadcasts in Australia 114; financial prize of entry 73; formation 3; money influence in winning 94, 112; television income 116
ethics: non-commercialisation related 131
excessive survivalism 70, 73
exchange: blocked 25, 26, 121, 122–3
exchange-value 12
exclusion: commodification and 95–6, 98
explicit markets 93
exploitation 19, 21; vulnerability to 102–3
external goods 28, 34
Extreme Football League 115
extrinsic value 37

fair play 36, 47
fans: power of influence 130
FIFA 78–9
financial motives: predominance 40
Fischer, Bobby 70
Fitzroy Lions 15
Flew, Anthony 38–9
football *see* American football; Australian Rules football; soccer
Fourier, Charles 89
Foxtel 107
franchises 18, 110
Frankfurt School 97
free-to-air broadcasts 94, 96, 116–17, 127
freedom: in commercial arrangements 103–4
Frey, Bruno 85
Friedman, Milton 116
Fry, C.B. 47

game structure changes 76
genetic fallacy 57
gentleman amateur 50
Glanville, Brian 3
Gleneagles Agreement 43, 130, 144
golfers: competitive motivation 40
goods: expressive meanings 26; external

28, 34; internal 28, 33–4, 37, *see also* autotelic goods
Grace, W.G. 49, 137–8
grass-roots: investment in 108, 116, 128–9
greed 41
Green Bay Packers 122, 123

Habermas, Jurgen 67, 109
Hardie, Keir 97
Harding, Tonya 11
Henley Regatta 50, 52
heterodox thesis 50
Hillsborough disaster 6, 133
Hitler, Adolf 80
Hoch, Paul 20, 97, 105
Hocking, Gary 2
Holyfield, Evander 6
Horkheimer, Max 97
housing 100
human flourishing: optimisation 87
Hutton, Len 51
hyper-commodification 14, 96, 109–10; features 14

imperialism: and promotion of sport 57–8
incomplete commodification 27, 100, 135
injustice: theory of 19
innovation 20–1
institutions: practices vs 27–9, 44–5
instrumentalist pathology 120
internal development logic of sport/ games 34, 78–9
internal goods 28, 33–4, 37
International Amateur Athletics Federation 52, 53
International Congress of Amateurs 48
international division of labour 117
intrinsic value 33, 36–7; definition 37
IOC: vote buying 3, 125

Jackson, Shoeless Joe 54
James, C.L.R. 59
Jennings, Andrew 4, 93, 111
Jordan, Michael 1, 2, 110
juridification 134
just rewards 101–5

justice: categories 82; rectificatory 82; *see also* distributive justice

Kansas City Royals 112
Kant, Immanuel 23–5, 65, 66–7; on prostitution 69
Kelly, J.H.B. 52
Kewell, Harry 115
killing the source 114–18
King, Don 6
Kretchmar, Scott 70, 73–4

labour: international division of 117
Lancaster Rowing Club 50
league revenues: distribution 126
legitimation crisis 109
leisure democracies 15
L'Elefant Blau 122
Lewis, Lennox 6
libertarianism 85
Liston, Sonny 6
local authorities: involvement in elite clubs 124
Locke, John 57
Loland, Sigmund 94
Long, James 49
lop-sided competitions 112
Louis, Joe 6
Louis–Schmelling Paradox 143
lucrepath 137
lucrephile 137
ludic spirit 33

MacIntyre, Alasdair 27–9, 33, 34, 44–5
MacLaren, A.C. 49
MacLaurin, Lord Ian 118
Major League Baseball: Columbia Pictures deal 26; designated hitter introduction 77; financial inequalities 112; revenue 1; as sports cartel 114; steroid abuse eradication 111
Manchester United FC: Murdoch bid for 16; as transnational entity 14
Manifest Image 4–5, 109, 110–11
Manning, Peyton 1
Maradona, Diego 92
market abolitionism 6, 20; commodification critique and 6–8
market activity: benefits 20–1

market desert 88
market distributions 87–8; freedom in 88–9; negative aspects 89–90; positive aspects 89
market failure 108
market rhetoric 2, 13, 18, 110, 130
Marqusee, Mike: on cricket 5, 47, 51, 57, 75–6; on C.L.R. James 59; on soccer 5
Marx, Karl 12, 19–20, 58, 84, 85
Marxism 6–7, 18–20, 104
match-fixing: baseball 54; cricket 41–2, temptation to 54
merchandising 17; control of 124
merit goods *see* desert goods
meritocratic proportionalism 85
mixed motives 38, 60
MLB *see* Major League Baseball
modes of regard 26, 65
money: gravitational pull of 41
money economy: progressive aspects 21–2
monopoly 111–12, 143
Montreal Expos 15
moral education 129
moral essentialist approach 45–6
moral exhortation 121
Moral Law 67
moral pathologies 29–30, 120
moralism 129
Morgan, William 27, 28, 34, 44–6
motivational pathology 120
motivational structure: content 35
Murdoch, Rupert 16, 107

name changes 2
National Basketball Association (NBA) 1, 77–8, 114
national glorification 80
National Rugby League (Australia) 107
National Soccer League (Australia) 115
NBA 1, 77–8, 114
NCAA 54
need goods 90
New York Yankees 112
NFL 114, 122
NHL 114
non-excludability 94
Novak, Michael 33

Nozick, Robert 28, 88–9, 103–4
NRL 107

objectification 65, 67; of athletes 67; of
    spectators 67
Odonis, Gerald 104
oligopoly 111–12
Olympic games: Berlin 80, 97; bids 3,
    125; drug-use 111, 143; seating
    allocation 90; Seoul 93, 143
Olympic movement: amateurism 46, 50,
    51
Olympics: ancient Greek 50, 61
O'Neal, Shaquille, 1
oppressive rationalism 70, 74
Optus 107
Orwell, George 11
Overman, Steven J. 33, 58, 114
Owen, Michael 1
Owens, Jesse 80
ownership 122–4

Packer, Kerry 2, 39, 107
Pareto, Vilfredo 88
Park, Tim 4
Parrish, Bernie 123
participation: in organisation 129
pay per view broadcasts 96, 114–15, 118
persons: things vs 24
Philadelphia 125
Plato 41
player markets 73
player value caps 126
players: as means to profit 25
pluralism 86–7, 91
political egalitarianism 86
pornography 67
positional goods 84
Prabhakar, Manoj 42
practice-community: reproduction of
    114
practices: institutions vs 27–9, 44–5
pragmatic pathology 107, 120
Preston North End 73
price: and dignity 24–5, 65, 67–8
pride 36
principle of just acquisition 88
principle of rectification of injustice 88
principle of transfer 88

prizes: meritocratic allocation 91–4
production: for consumption 22; for
    exchange 22–3
professionalisation: team sports 16–17
prostitution 69
prudential reasoning 108
public goods 95, 108
Purely Belter 82
pursuit of excellence: mutual 74–5

quasi-commodification 93
queuing 127

Radin, Margaret Jane: 'incomplete
    commodification' 27, 100, 135;
    'market rhetoric' 2, 18, 110, 130
rectificatory justice 82
regulation 121, 123–4, 125–8; of
    consumption 89
replica shirts 124
representation: community 36
reserve rule 101
Respect for Persons principle 66, 69;
    violence and 71, 72
restraints on trade 5, 103
rewards: just 101–5
rituals of sport 132
roster sizes 126
rowing: amateurism 50
rugby league: Australian 3, 107
rugby union: historical sociology 47;
    move to professionalism 52; split
    between amateurs and professionals
    51, 138; spread 57–8; training
    programs 102; violence in 71
rule changes 34–5, 77; corrupting 78;
    external demands 79; internal
    demands 79
runaway individualism 70, 74

salary caps 114, 126
SBS network 114
scarcity 83–4, 91, 127; hard 84;
    moderate 83–4
Schumacher, Michael 1
Schwartz, Barry 79
seasons: extensions of 76
self-interest: selfishness vs 38–9
self-love 39

Seoul Olympics 93, 143
shamateurism 49, 53
Sheard, Kenneth 97
Sheffield Shield 2
Sheppard, David 51
Simmel, Georg 21–2
Simon, Robert L.: on American football
    violence 115–16; on
    commercialisation 30; on
    commodification of players 94; on
    'loose officiating' 77; on player
    markets 73; on rule changes 78; on
    sporting audiences 141; on
    technology access 93
siphoning 96, 114–15, 127
skills development 35
Slater, Michael 36
Smith, Adam 12
snooker: rule changes 77
soccer: in Australia 114–15; Brazil
    national strip 143; exploitation 103;
    'Hand of God' goal 92; Italian 16;
    loose officiating 77; move to
    professionalism 49; replica shirts 124;
    rule changes 78–9; salaries 140;
    South American 102; Supporter
    Trusts 124; turnover 1; violence in
    71; *see also* English Premiership
soccer clubs: as transnational entities 15
social burdens 83
social goods 83
social relationships: through sport 129
socialism 29
socio-historical challenge:
    commodification critique and 8–10,
    56–9
South Africa: Gleneagles Agreement
    43, 130, 143; 'rebel' cricket tour
    42–3
spectator sport: criticisms 96–8
spheres approach 26, 86
Spheres of Justice 26, 83, 86
sponsorship: corporate 17
sport: as commodity 1–6; as cultural
    activity 129; as end-in-itself 75; ends
    of 76; as mere means 75–80, 130; as
    non-productive play 132–3; as opiate
    of masses 97
sport for all 100

sport-for-sport's sake 33–5; emergent
    picture of ideal 63; material necessity
    objection 59–60; relation to
    amateurism 55–9; relation to sport
    itself 62
sports cartels 114
Sports Nexus 112
sports policies 120–1
sportsmanship 36
stadia conditions 6
'Stadium out of Chinatown' movement
    124–5
Stewart, Alec 118
sumptuary laws 89, 140
Super-League War 107
Superbowl: advertisements 1
Supporter Trusts 124
surplus: production of 21
swimming: Olympic 52

television: sport on subscription 7
tennis: move to professionalism 52
things: persons vs 24
ticket distribution 124, 127
ticket scalping 127
training: and production line work 67
Trotsky, Leon 97
TV time-outs 17, 76
Tyrell, Ian 49, 77, 101–2, 113
Tyson, Mike 6

uncertainty of outcome 112, 125, 143
universal access goods 94
use-value 12
utilitarianism 85
utility maximisation 133

value 25
Vamplew, Wray 49
venalisation of ethos 17–18
venality 40; commodification and 40–3;
    definition 17; undermining of
    autotelic goods by 43–6
vertical integration 15–16
Viduka, Mark 115
violence in sport 71–2; as
    depersonalisation 71; justification
    from consent 72; Respect for Persons
    principle and 71, 72

vital goods 99

Walzer, Michael 26, 83, 86, 90, 115
Washington Redskins 17
Washington Wizards 2
Waugh, Steve 40
weight-lifting 111
West Ham United 73
'Whiskas' 2
White, Jimmy 2
white line fever 71

William, Bernard 99
Woodful, Bill 48
Woods, Tiger 1
work: degradation of 132
World Series Cricket 2, 39–40, 102
Worrell, Frank 59
wrestling: professional 116

Young, David C. 50, 52, 53, 54, 61

zero-sum games 21